All Proud Americans! Take It! You Need It! "Your Reality Check"

Fraud, Deception and Pure Propaganda, Via "Uncle Scam", Mr. Hide Your Rights! Have "Duped Us", From Day One!

by

Eddie Duncan

Bloomington, IN  Milton Keynes, UK

authorHOUSE®

AuthorHouse™
1663 Liberty Drive, Suite 200
Bloomington, IN 47403
www.authorhouse.com
Phone: 1-800-839-8640

AuthorHouse™ UK Ltd.
500 Avebury Boulevard
Central Milton Keynes, MK9 2BE
www.authorhouse.co.uk
Phone: 08001974150

First published by AuthorHouse 5/10/2007

ISBN: 978-1-4259-6206-7 (sc)

Printed in the United States of America
Bloomington, Indiana

This book is printed on acid-free paper.

All Proud Americans!
Take It! You Need It!
"Your Reality Check"

Fraud, Deception and Pure Propaganda, Via "Uncle Scam",
Mr. Hide Your Rights! Have "Duped Us", From Day One!

Quey Quay @ Anno Domini 2003AD

Excuse Me! But, we will never
accomplish anything, this way.

Yea! That's True! But,
we don't have too!

Sovereign Rights Are Denied by Deception, Fraud And Continual Abuse, by "our" Government! The "Unknowing" Become Heir, To All Lies!

The People, are the true force, upholding justice, rights, and liberty!
Until, we neglect "our" role as "sovereign"!
Read the Declaration of Independence and the Federalists' Papers!

Or! "Be Unknowing, and Denied"!

Authors Preface

It is impossible for a man to learn, what he thinks he already knows! Most Americans believe that the U.S Government is protecting privacy rights and private property. The sad truth is, through the Act of 1871, and HJR 192, our government has abandoned its' duty to the supreme office holder, the sovereign Citizen.

The third Roosevelt administration, took advantage of its' pseudo authority and effectively duped the masses, by fraud, then, enacted the treasonous provisions of the "New Deal"! Yet, few Americans are actually aware of, that grand deception. We the People were dealt a foreign judicial system, which overturned the original "chain of command", and, unlawfully prosecutes all, for "Public Policy" violations.

The "Act of 1871" unlawfully claimed THE UNITED STATES as sovereign. In 1933, HJR 192 initiated "Public Policy", instead of Common Law, and, issued U.S. "debt instruments", Federal Reserve Notes, instead of silver certificates. Also, by design, the public education system, of the "U.S." government, deliberately, failed its' duty, to fully educate all Americans, of their lawful birthright, that of "sovereign" rights!

Article 1 Section 10 of the Texas Constitution states, quote; and no person shall be held to answer for a criminal offense, unless on an indictment of a grand jury, end quote! By law, no public servant is to act against your liberty, unless he has actually witnessed you, commit a felonious act, or exigent circumstances exit. Or, if there has been a sworn affidavit filed, naming you as the perpetrator of a felony.

His sworn duty is expressed in the preamble of Article 1 of the Bill of Rights, quote; That the general, great and essential principles of liberty and free government may be recognized and established, we declare: end quote!

Liberty is precious, second only to life itself! That is why "we the People" have authorized "public servants" to guard and protect "our sovereignty". They are authorized to act "only" against actual Common Law crimes. The essential duty of "public servants", was/is to serve and protect, the "liberty", property and sovereign rights of the People. Can "our" free society exist, abide, and flourish, if we do not honor our God given liberty as a precious part of life, not to be infringed upon without a binding cause? Liberty, precious, God given liberty, cannot be infringed upon, simply because "our" representatives, have chosen to allow their agents to misapply commercial codes, above the inherent rights of the sovereign People.

In this country, one is considered to be a criminal, if one is cited, not wearing a seat belt. And, if you fail to pay the agency, "claiming criminal behavior", they will arrest you! Even though, there is no victim, no verified complaint, no indictment, no felonious act, and no exigent circumstances existed, to condone your seizure.

The public servants within "our" government have sworn an oath, to protect the essential principal of liberty? Our God given, liberty! So, can a victimless crime, lawfully exist? Proverbs 3 – 30 & 31 says; Strive not with a man without cause, if he have done thee no harm. Envy thou not the oppressor, and choose none of his ways.

Thanks and Recognition;

Thank you God, for the shear magnificence of your creation, the unique way in which all choices and opportunities are presented, the fulfillment obtained, and the serenity of knowing an agape love, in an eternal dimension, soon to come!

Thank you Jesus, for choosing the path of love, enduring the agony, that was awaiting You in Jerusalem, and for loving all, even, beyond our understanding. Thank You for living a life of love, so devout, that through its' grace, all believers, are freed.

A Deeply Thankful,
Quey Quay

Many thanks to Joseph Milam for being where, he was, to be needed. Choosing a worthy destiny also rewards you with many wise and helpful friends.

Thanks again
Jemadar,

Thank you, Mr. Jay Stewart, for you're gifted insights, your diligence, and your purposeful generosity. The People need to "realize and claim" the documents defined within your book. "Land Patents, Memorandum of Law History, Force and Effect of the Land Patent" is, in a word, thoroughly dynamic!

Thank you Mr. Stewart

Many thanks for the grand contributions of Mr. Brent - Emory... Johnson and for the invaluable, heroic insights, presented in his masterful work! "The American Sovereign" reveals in no uncertain terms, your sovereign rights, and how our/this government has usurped them, and relinquished to you/us, "civil privileges"! To order this informative text, enlightening you of your true, and unalienable rights, call 1888 385-3733 or order on line at *www.freedomradio.us*

Thank You Mr. Johnson

My sincere thanks to those of awareness, (penitent believers), and thankfulness, those that honor, and are purposefully about a worthy desire! Those, that honor, love, and strive diligently, to help their fellowman, shall soon know, and find, divine companions, in eternity!

Those of unawareness, aboard a ship of fools, I would say, turn your hardened hearts around, and find the loving ground, "our" eternal garden! Then, honor the eternal life within, and before every soul!

A Brother in Christ,
Quey Quay

Table of Contents

Introduction

Dear Patriot,

Thank you for your interest in, and your willingness to proclaim the current issues of debate, within the judicial dockets across the breadth of this land calledAmerica. This is not, "America, land of the free"! This is now, the land of the "Freely Prosecuted", associated with all victimless crimes. Proverbs 3: 30 says, "Strive not with a man without cause, if he have done thee no harm". Proverbs 4: 2 says, For I give you good doctrine, forsake ye not my law. Yet, it is "self-evident" that our judicial system is no longer operating in accordance with the will of God, or the Constitution, "the Law of the Land". The "STATE" has made it emphatically clear, that "IT" has separated itself from the church, (from God)! To what end?

Note also that, our primary sources of "propaganda" aka-public information are television, radio, and newspapers. Yet, "their content", and the curriculum within all "STATE" public schools, is dictated by the legacy of a "treasonous resolution".

It could never be more clearly revealed "why" corporate U.S. sought, and gained control of the media, "more clearly", than by the horrendous events that transpired"DURING" the broadcast by Orsen Wells, and his portrayal of an invaded earth.

The horrendous aftermath of that broadcast was unquestionably, noted! And all, are now unquestionably controlled by, "an out of control" federal government. Why do Candidates pay exorbitantly, to slander each other on corporate airwaves, when they could campaign, (debate) on public channels, for pennies on the dollar?

In the Bulletin article, "How many more lies can America take"? Mr. Jim Wright expressed the many virtues of "our" Constitution, and the fact that it has been forgotten, ignored and defiantly abused by "our" public servants. The "New Deal", HJR-192, resolved to establish, a "Different Deal", a "socialist" U.S. government.

The God given rights of the sovereign People, wrested from the British, through the lives sacrificed, in defiant resistance to tyranny, were lost, by a "resolution"! Our right to "Common Law", substantive money, and Alluvial Land Titles has been abated by a "resolution"! The Socialists', "Public Policy" of HJR-192 is still "Policy"!

Public awareness must be brought to bear on <u>our</u> true "<u>Sovereign Citizenship</u>" as opposed to "<u>our</u>" current "nom de guerre", CORPORATE U.S. status. HJR-192, in practice, is a British parliamentary procedure! "<u>Practicing</u>" barristers are registered with the BAR, the "<u>B</u>ritish <u>A</u>ccrediting <u>R</u>egistry"! It is therefore, a foreign, treasonous judicial system, enforcing a "PUBLIC POLICY"! It is "<u>Not</u>" the judicial system mandated by "<u>our</u>" Constitution, guaranteeing "Common Law"!

Shortly after the roaring twenties, the Roosevelt administration ordered the new "national" banks to retain 10% more funds on deposit. That "fateful order" severely curtailed funds available to farmers, etc. and thus, "initiated" the depression of the thirties. And, after he and his constituents, had effectively caused the depression, and under the alleged authority of Executive Order, Franklin Delanoe Roosevelt, made the ownership of gold, (our constitutional standard for money) <u>ILLEGAL!!!</u>

He, and the foreign bankers <u>confiscated</u> "<u>all</u>" <u>gold</u>. They took "our" gold standard and replaced it with a <u>new species of money</u> and a <u>new judicial system</u>, that "<u>is not</u>" Common Law! Our current "<u>c</u>itizenship status", the lack of lawful process to obtain jurisdiction, all "misapplied" commercial codes, statutes, and ordinances, "our" species of money, tendered to "discharge" debt, and the lack of alluvial titles, are all part of the legacy, of a treasonous third term congressional <u>resolution</u>. On June 5th, 1933A.D., the Roosevelt administration initiated House Joint "RESOLUTION" 192 – Trading "With" The Enemies Act, aka "The New Deal", and, it was "JOINTLY RESOLVED" by an obedient constituency. IT WAS NEVER LAWFULLY ENACTED!

"<u>Yet</u>", it is <u>NOW</u>, "<u>our</u>" judicial system, (Admiralty/Equity), or, <u>socialism</u> under "public policy". Do you have a "socialist" security number? Whoever has joined, has also unknowingly relinquished their birthright of Sovereignty within a "free state", and, the <u>right</u> to "Common Law" under constitutional due process.

<u>We are being duped</u>! By lucre, our unawares, and our "thanklessness"! It is not a question of how many more lies can we endure. Rather, when shall we realize, "<u>All Americans Are Living A Lie</u>"? Our birthright, our lawful status, as sovereign Peoples of a free society, has been suppressed and withheld by a treasonous, usurping government, under their 1933 "New Deal"- "socialist public policy".

That treasonous, "new deal" resolution, continues today, to deny rights, and suppress the God given Liberty, of all Citizens within "our" great nation.

HJR-192 is somberly taught, as "history", by our STATE public schools. A similar system of governing was implemented and flourished, over sixty years ago, in a prominent Germany, but there, the children were referred to as "Hitler Youth".

We have been duped, into believing that we are U.S. citizens, when in fact, most are not! We are sovereign Americans, by our God given birthright. In order to be a U.S. citizen, one must have immigrated to this country, or, be one that was truly unfortunate to have been born in the business "District of Columbia", and would have no claim to the sovereign rights of American natives, born in a "free state". Under HJR-192 and its' socialist public policy, your sovereign birthright is ignored and suppressed. All "U.S. citizens" are considered to be, of a jurisdiction, foreign to that of a free state birthright, immigrants, and are thereby denied their birthright as sovereign, and thus, are entitled to only (litigated privileges)"civil rights".

The men who signed the Declaration of Independence were sovereign, and openly declared their right to rule their lives, own property free and clear, and to be free to seek their hearts desire, as long as they did not infringe on the rights of others. They expressed their moral beliefs, their hearts desires, and the tyrannies suffered, without cause or consideration, within that eloquent text.

Quote!

When in the Course of human Events, it becomes necessary for one People to dissolve the Political Bands which have connected them with another, and to assume among the Powers of the Earth, the separate and equal Station to which the Laws of Nature and of Nature's God entitled them, a decent Respect to the Opinions of Mankind requires that they should declare the causes which impel them to the Separation. We hold these truths to be self-evident, that all men are created equal, that they are endowed by their Creator with certain unalienable Rights, that among these are Life, Liberty and the Pursuit of Happiness – That to secure these Rights, Governments are instituted among Men, deriving their just Powers from the Consent of the Governed, that whenever any Form of Government becomes destructive to these Ends, it is the Right of the People to alter or abolish it, and to institute new Government, laying its' Foundation on such Principles, and organizing its' Powers in such Form, as to them shall seem most likely to effect their Safety and Happiness. Prudence, indeed, will dictate that Governments long established should not be changed for light and transient Causes; and accordingly all Experience has shewn, that Mankind are more disposed to suffer, while Evils are sufferable, than to right themselves by abolishing the Forms to which they are accustomed. But, when a long Train of Abuses and Usurpations, pursuing invariably the same Object, evinces a Design to reduce them under absolute Depotism, it is their Right, it is their Duty, to throw off such Government, and to provide new Guards for their future Security. End Quote!

HJR-192 Trading "WITH" The Enemies Act" was implemented by resolution, it was "NOT" Lawfully enacted! It "resolved" to change, ("changed!") the status of the entire native populous, through a new, matriculated system of "socialist" corporate identities, with new, litigated, "civil privileges"! All to the harm of, We the People! Such has been the patient Sufferance of the People, for three generations, under the "NEW DEAL" policies of this treasonous governing institution.

We, the People, must "realize and claim", our sovereignty, its' heritage and the rights duly accorded each Citizen. By birth, we are a nation of sovereign men and women! We the People, must rise in awareness of, the fundamentals of our nation, our Sovereign Nation"! Claim that, the dominion, which God all mighty has already given you, and share in the peace, honor, and tranquility of a "Universal Republic".

Our misguided, "legal fiction", socialist philosophy of numbered flesh, though now prevailing, will not prevail over Gods' will for His People. Sovereignty, of we the People, established, honored, and instructed of, is an ideal whose time has come. We must strive to establish and restore the virtues and true intent of our original Republic, until, the honor of man, within a "Universal Republic" prevails!

We, the native Peoples of a free society, the sovereigns, are the true force upholding justice, rights, and liberty, "our God given liberty"! Until! We neglect our role, as sovereign of/over "our" government! We must prioritize "our" course, contingent upon the God given sovereignty of each, under "Common Law"!

Please investigate The Federalist Papers, written by James Madison, Alexander Hamilton, and John Jay. It has been edited into modern language, and indexed for today's Political Issues, by Mary E. Webster. It dwells upon the intended, basic structure of "our" free self-governing American government, as apposed to being, a subject of a tyrannical king, or a government alleging, "OFFICIAL IMMUNITY"!

I have also written a thought provoking manuscript entitled;

Truth, and Relevance!
Are All Answers!

And, an intriguing, stranger than fiction, autobiography entitled;

Three Days; Destined...
"Within This Infinite Life"!

For more information about your rights as a sovereign American, please consider;

USCivilFlags.org
suijuris.net
tcleose.state.tx.us.
americansovereign.com
georgegordon.net
constitutionalguardian.com

truthsetsusfree.com/HJR192.htm
nossn.com
informationlinks.com
sovereignandfree.com/citizenship/
jurisdictionary. com
judicialaccountability.org

One should also consider;

Romans 6:16
1 Samuel 8: 5-7
Proverbs 3: 30
and Colossians 2:8 which states;

Luke 11:52
1 Samuel 10: 19
Proverbs 4: 2

See to it that no one takes you captive, through hollow and deceptive philosophy, and high sounding non sense, that comes from human thinking and from the evil powers of this world, and not from Christ.

"Truth or Temptation"

As the tides of the oceans,
So moves, the weary shark,

As do all creatures,
Possessed of hardened hearts,

They know not, what, they hunger for,
Yet, are sure and bound, to "only" hunger for more,

Keep therefore, to only the way of truth,
Or, surely Satan will know,

Weigh your choices, and be sure of,
A course of love and honor,

Nothing as that, to be found below.

Give unto each, and all things, unto its' turn,
That simple choice, will bring happiness, without yearn,

Open a sensitive diary, unto a precious day,
Note the blessings, choices and fulfillment, along "our" way,

Go thankfully, pray knowingly, and also be aware,
Gods' justice, is within all things, here, and there,

Wild horses could not now, drag me from my destiny,
Nor, from the happiness and fulfillment of a real eternity,

Ask yourself intently. Where will I be next?
Will you be in glory, on streets of gold? Or, will you be vexed?

Keep your awareness, of a true timelessness in each.
Find the helping hand within your heart, and give, or teach.

Give sensitively to the needs of every soul,
And feel the love, appreciation, and glory of being whole.

Give of your spirit of kindness throughout time,
And receive the reward of friendship, a love divine.

Yearn to know, each value, unto every heart,
And give humble respect to Jesus, who sat us apart,

Therefore, keep to only the way of truth,
Or, surely Satan will embark,

To put a lie in every ear,
Hidden from every heart,

Weigh all God given choices, and know!
Or, find only doubt, and simply go.

Seeking your eternal steps, as such a silly sleuth.

Eternally,
A Brother in Christ
Quey Quay

CONGRESS DECLARES BIBLE
"THE WORD OF GOD"

PUBLIC LAW 97-280—OCT. 4, 1982

Public Law 97-280   96 STAT. 1211
97th Congress

Joint Resolution

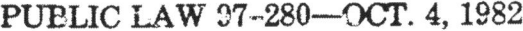

Authorizing and requesting the President to proclaim 1983 as the "Year of the Bible".

Whereas the Bible, the Word of God, has made a unique contribution in shaping the United States as a distinctive and blessed nation and people;

Whereas deeply held religious convictions springing from the Holy Scriptures led to the early settlement of our Nation;

Whereas Biblical teachings inspired concepts of civil government that are contained in our Declaration of Independence and the Constitution of the United States;

Whereas many of our great national leaders—among them Presidents Washington, Jackson, Lincoln, and Wilson—paid tribute to the surpassing influence of the Bible in our country's development, as in the words of President Jackson that the Bible is "the rock on which our Republic rests";

Whereas the history of our Nation clearly illustrates the value of voluntarily applying the teachings of the Scriptures in the lives of individuals, families, and societies;

Whereas this Nation now faces great challenges that will test this Nation as it has never been tested before; and

Whereas that renewing our knowledge of and faith in God through Holy Scripture can strengthen us as a nation and a people: Now, therefore, be it

Resolved by the Senate and House of Representatives of the United States of America in Congress assembled, That the President is authorized and requested to designate 1983 as a national "Year of the Bible" in recognition of both the formative influence the Bible has been for our Nation, and our national need to study and apply the teachings of the Holy Scriptures.

Approved October 4, 1982.

THE GOVERNMENT OF THE UNITED STATES BY AN ACT OF CONGRESS

HAS DECLARED THAT THE BIBLE

IS "THE WORD OF GOD" AND "HOLY SCRIPTURE"

The United States Congress has settled it. The Bible is now officially proclaimed by a Law of the United States to be "the Word of God."

Public Law 97-280 (see other side) is not just a statement by Congress. It is a Law, an official Act of the elected Representatives of the People of the United States sitting in Law-making session. That the Holy Bible is "the Word of God" is now "the Law of the Land."

In addition Public Law 97-280 states "that renewing our knowledge of and faith in God through Holy Scripture can strengthen us as a nation and a people," and it rules that the United States has a "national need to study and apply the teachings of the Holy Scripture."

As surely as it was the intent of the first U.S. Congress that the Government not interfere with the Christian religion, just as surely as it has now been declared the intent of the 1982 United States Congress that the Bible is "the Word of God" and that the People of the United States should use "the Holy Scriptures" to renew their "faith in God."

Under Public Law 97-280 a study of "the Holy Scripture" should now be made a part of every public and private school cirriculum. The Law does not say it is the "right" of people to study the Bible, the Law says, "our knowledge of and faith in God through Holy Scriptures can strengthen us as a nation and a people." Anyone attempting in any way to prevent any American citizen from acquiring that "knowledge of and faith in God through the Holy Scripture" is attempting to weaken America. For instance, individuals and organizations who advocate the banning of the Bible from the public schools or who actively oppose any Bible study group or interfere in any way with a Christian Church would be guilty of violating this Law and probably guilty of sedition against the United States of America.

The American People are a law-abiding People. Every American who believes what Public Law 97-280 says should not only obey this Law, but should actively work to inform other Americans about this Law to the end that it will become widely observed throughout the United States and its territories. This would not only be pleasing to Almighty God, but, according to the U.S. Congress, would benefit our People exceedingly.

Disobedience of this Law should be discouraged in our own communities and in the nation at large. Copies of Public Law 97-280 should be given to friends, neighbors and especially to public servants who can then take whatever action is necessary in their own departments or under their own realm of authority to comform to Public Law 97-280. All Elementary, and High School Principals, Superintendents and College Presidents should be given copies and urged to take immediate steps to add courses of Bible study to their school curriculum to bring them into conformity with the intent of Congress.

With the wide dissemination of copies of Public Law 97-280 all America will come to know that the marvellous Truth that the Holy Bible is "the Word of God" has now been made "the Law of the Land." They will see that in that Law the People's Representatives have recognized the "need" for all Americans to "study and apply the teachings of the Holy Scripture."

The study of the Holy Scriptures leads to Jesus Christ. Jesus said of the Scripture, "They are they which testify of Me." (John 5:39b.) Therefore, this will be is another significant step by our Nation and our People toward that day when "every tongue should confess that Jesus Christ is Lord, to the glory of God the Father." This is a marvellous thing and is quite obviously the Hand of God ruling and overruling in the affairs of our Nation. Praise Jesus!

Pray that God will bless America in this, through Jesus Christ,

Pastor Sheldon Emry

Copies of this sheet with Public Law 97-280 on the other side are available from Lord's Covenant Church or America's Promise, PO Box 30000, Phoenix, Arizona 85046. 100 copies for a $3.00 offering.

Affidavit of Fact and Judicial Notice

For the record, and by the authority of Article 1 Sec. 8 and Article 5 Sec. 15 of the Texas Constitution, I hereby claim my right to redress this government for a grievance, and my right to a court of record. Further, I claim my right to a fully informed jury of my lawful peers. Take Judicial Notice! In order to fulfill my right to a jury of my peers, all members of the jury panel must be fully informed jurors and sovereign by birth. Each juror must clearly understand their full authority, and the essential dynamics of "Common Law". Each juror must be aware of his/her right to determine the validity of any law, and his/her authority of nullification!

Therefore, in this case, it is your duty as a truthful juror, (if, you are not fully informed of all jurors' rights, and a sovereign) to dismiss yourself from jury duty.

I further declare that these proceedings are a treasonous action against my rights, brought under "color of law" by barristers. Point of order, (no victim!) no verified complaint has been sworn to, and signed, and no "Public Prosecutor" is present.

A "Common Law" crime can not exist; against the dignity of a legal fiction STATE!

Therefore, I hereby challenge subject matter jurisdiction! Further, I signify the mandate of the Texas Constitution, Article 1 Sec. 10 and its' requirement of a grand jury indictment, an injured party, and the mandate of his presence! Article 1 Sec. 30 (5)(d) Quote! The state, through its' prosecuting attorney, has the right to enforce the rights of "crime victims". End Quote! Without a sworn affidavit from an injured party, jurisdiction is lost. I also cite Article 1 Sec. 10 quote; and no person shall be held to answer for a criminal offense, unless on an indictment of a grand jury-End quote! So! How did a foreign agent, a barrister, (*not a public prosecutor) obtain authority to prosecute me, without a verified complaint, and with, harm to no one?

This "New Deal" judicial system exists in a matriculated, "legal fiction", corporate entity identity system of "numbered flesh". In their matriculated system, original jurisdiction was claimed, allegedly, under the "emergency powers acts" of Roosevelt.

Martial Law, was implemented during the depression, and is yet to be repealed. Witness your NOM DE GUERRE! Your "WAR NAME", on "YOUR ID"!

The judicial system, now implemented in this country, is foreign to the rights of the sovereign Citizens, and an abomination of the intent of our founding fathers. Our forefathers defiantly claimed sovereignty, for each member of the native populous. We the People authorized, "public servants" to protect the sovereign rights and property of all People! "<u>NOT</u>", to suppress rights, with immunity!

In their capacity as newly emancipated sovereign Americans, as compared to being, (subjects of a king), our forefathers conferred, as against a tyrannical government, and claimed their God given dominion, as a sovereign People.

Liberty, essential, precious, liberty, of we the People, within "our" free society, must be treasured, and guarded from any infringement, with all diligence!

COMMON LAW VEHICULAR JUDICIAL NOTICE
CONSTITUTIONAL DRIVERS LICENSE

THE UNDERSIGNED Common Law Citizen, _____ hereby Certifies, by Rights Secured under provisions of the Constitution of the United States of America, the Constitution of the several states, Common Law, Nature and Laws of Natures GOD, that these Rights are retained in FEE SIMPLE ABSOLUTE, and held and protected with special regard to Rights designated and/or set forth as follows: ALSO NOTE; Rights and Property are ONE AND THE SAME THING--by the Honorable Justice LOUIS BRANDIS U.S. SUPREME COURT.

NOTICE AND ADVISORY OF RIGHTS CLAIMED INVIOLATE:

1) The Right to TRAVEL FREELY, UNENCUMBERED, and UNFETTERED is guaranteed as a RIGHT and not a mere privilege. That the Right to TRAVEL is such a BASIC RIGHT it does NOT even need to be mentioned for it is SELF-EVIDENT by Common Sense that the Right to TRAVEL is a BASIC CONCOM?VITANT of a FREE Society to come and go from length and breadth FREELY UNENCUMBERED and UNFETERED distinguishes the characteristic required for a FREE PEOPLE TO EXIST IN FACT. Please See SHAPIRO vs. THOMSON 394 U.S. 618. Further, the Right to TRAVEL by private conveyance for private purposes upon the Common way can NOT BE INFRINGED. No license or permission is required for TRAVEL when such TRAVEL IS NOT for the purpose of [COMMERCIAL] PROFIT OR GAIN on the open highways operating under license IN COMMERCE. The above named Common Law Citizen listed IS NOT OPERATING IN CONIMERCE and as such is thereby EXEMPTED FROM THE REQUIREINTENT OF A LICENSE AS SUCH.

2) Further, the state of Texas is FORBIDDEN BY LAW from converting a BASIC RIGHT into a PRIVILEGE and requiring a LICENSE and or a FEE CHARGED for the exercise of the BASIC RIGHT. Please SEE MURDOCK vs. PENNSYLVANIA, 319 U.S. 105, and if the state of Texas does ERRONIOUSLY convert BASIC RIGHTS into PPJVILEGES and require a License or FEE a Citizen may IGNORE THE LICENSE OR FEE WITH TOTAL IMMUNITY FOR SUCH EXERCISE OF A BASIC RIGHT. Please see Schuttlesworth vs. BIRMINGHAM , ALABAMA, 373 U.S. 262. Now if a Citizen exercises a BASIC RIGHT and a Law of ANY state is to the contrary of such exercise of that BASIC RIGHT, the said supposed Law of ANY state is a FICTION OF LAW and 100% TOTALLY UNCONSTITUTIONAL and NO COURTS ARE BOUND TO UPHOLD IT AND NO Citizen is REQUIRED TO OBEY SUCH UNCONSTITUTIONAL LAW OR LICENSE REOUIREMENT. Please see MARBURY vs. MADISON, 5 U.S. 137 (1803), which has never been overturned in over 194 years, see Shephard's Citations.

3) Now further, if a Citizen relies in good faith on the advice of Counsel and or on the Decisions of the UNITED STATES SUPREME COURT that Citizen has a PERFECT DEFENSE to the element of WILLFULNESS and since the burden of proof of said WILLFULNESS is on the Prosecution to prove beyond a REASONABLE DOUPT, said task or burden being totally impossible to specifically perform there is NO CAUSE OF ACTION FOR WHICH RELIEF MAY BE GRANTED BY A COURT OF LAW. Please see U.S. vs. Bishop 412 U.S. 346. OBVIOUSLY THERE IS NO LAWFUL CHARGE AGAINST EXERCISING A BASIC Right to TRAVEL for a regular Common Law Citizen NOT IN COMMERCE on the common way Public HIGHWAY. THAT IS THE LAW!!! The above named Citizen IS IMMUNED FROM ANY CHARGE TO THE CONTRARY AND ANY PARTY MAKING SUCH CHARGE SHOULD BE DULY WARNED OF THE TORT OF TRESPASS!!! YOU ARE TRESPASSING ON THIS Common Law Citizen!!!

4) The original and Judicial jurisdiction of the United States Supreme Court in ALL actions in which a State may be party thru subdivision, political or trust. This includes ALL state approved subdivisions and/or INCORPORATED Cities, Townships, municipalities, and Villages, Et Al . Please see Article 3, Section 2, Para. (1) and (2), U.S. Constitution.

5) The undersigned has NEVER willingly and knowingly entered into ANY Contract or Contractual agreement giving up ANY Constitutional Rights, that are secured by the CONSTITUTION, the SUPREME LAW OF THE LAND. This Common Law Citizen has NOT harmed any party, has NOT threatened any party, and that includes has NOT threatened or caused any endangerment to the safety or well being of any party and would leave any claimant otherwise to their strictest proofs otherwise IN A COURT OF LAW.

6) The above named Citizen is merely exercising the BASIC RIGHT TO TRAVEL UNENCUMBERED and UNFETTERED on the Common public way or highway, which is their RIGHT TO SO DO!!! Please see Zobel vs. Williams, 457 U.S. 55 , held the R[GTIT TO TRAVEL is Constitutionally PROTECTED!!

7) Conversion of the RIGHT To TRAVEL into a PRIVILEGE and or CRIME is A FRAUD and is in clear and direct conflict with the UNITED STATES CONSTITUTION, THE SUPREME LAW OF THE LAND. LAWS made by any state, which are clearly in direct CONFLICT or REPUGNANCY are UNCONSTITUTIONAL and are NOT WITH STANDING IN LAW, AND ARE BEING CHALLENGED AS SUCH HERE, AND THFREBY ARE NULL AND VOID OF LAW ON THEIRFACE. NO COURTS ARE BOUND TO UPHOLD SUCH FICTIONS OF LAW AND NO Citizen is bound to obey such a FICTION OF LAW. SUCH REGULATION OR LAW OPERATES AS A MERE NULLITY OR FICTION OF LAW AS IF IT NEVER EXISTED IN LAW. No CITIZEN IS BOUND TO OBEY SUCH UNCONSTITUTIONAL LAW!!!!!

8) The payment for a privilege requires a benefit to be received. As the RIGHT TO TRAVEL is already secured, it is clearly unlawful to cite any charges without direct damage to the specific party. Nor may a Citizen be charged with an offense for the exercise of a CONSTITUTIONAL RIGHT, in this case the RIGHT TO TRAVEL. Please see Miller vs. UNITED STATES 230 F2d 486. Nor may a Citizen be denied DUE PROCESS OF LAW or EQUAL PROTECTION UNDER THE LAW.

9) The undersigned does hereby claim, declare, and certify ANY AND ALL their CONSTITUTIONAL RIGHTS INVIOLATE from GOD and secured in THE UNITED STATES CONSTITUTION and the CONSTITUTION OF THE state wherein they abode as a SOVEREIGN, Common LAW CITIZEN existing and acting entirely AT THE COMMON LAW, and retains ALL BASIC RIGHTS under the CONSTITUTION OF THE UINITED STATES OF AMERICA, NATURE AND NATURE'S GOD AND UNDER THE LAWS OF GOD THE SUPREME LAW GIVER.

10) ANY VIOLATOR OF THE ABOVE CONSTRUCTIVE NOTICE AND CLAIM IS CRIMINALLY TRESPASSING UPON THIS ABOVE NAMED COMMON LAW Citizen and WILL BE PROSECUTED TO THE FULLEST EXTENT UNDER THE SUPREME LAW OF THE LAND. BE WARNED OF THE TRESPASS AND THE ATTACHED CAVEATS. ALSO TAKE CONSTRUCTIVE NOTICE, IGNORANCE OF THE LAW IS NOT AN EXCUSE!

SIGNATURE OF THE ABOVE NOTED

Common Law Citizen, _____

WITNESS _____

WITNESS _____

Emancipated Sovereign
c/o Anywhere America
County, State [Non-Domestic]

To: STATE OF TEXAS DEPARTMENT OF TRANSPORTATION (hereinafter DOT)
        Attn: EXECUTIVE DIRECTOR MICHAEL W BEHRING
        125 EAST 11TH STREET, AUSTIN, TX 78711
        Certified Mail #

To: STATE OF TEXAS DEPARTMENT OF TRANSPORTATION
        VEHICLE TITLE AND REGISTRATION (hereinafter DOT-VTR)
        DIRECTOR JERRY DIKE
        4000 JACKSON AVENUE, AUSTIN, TX 78731-9904
        Certified Mail #

Ref: Request for Alluvial Registration of Private Motorized Conveyance.

Greetings:

Concerning an automobile that has not been registered in over five years, I believe that, pursuant to the Texas Transportation Code 501.005 and Chapter 9 of the Texas Business and Commerce Code, the Priority Security Interest secured by the fraudulent coercion of the surrender of the MSO from the First Buyer through collusion, conspiracy and racketeering with dealers and financiers, has timely expired and will remain so, unless renewed by the current owner. I own such an automobile and have no intention of renewing such fraudulent registration and re-granting such ill gained Priority Security Interest as I do not support the Sixth Plank of the Communist Manifesto, government owns all communications and transportation systems.

As you can see from the other enclosed paperwork, I fully intend to use such automobile for Private Travel per my Natural/Fundamental/Basic/God given Rights to Free and Unencumbered Travel and to Ownership of Private Property in the form of a Private Motorized Conveyance. I have no intention of either registering or using such automobile in commercial activity.

Please send me the paperwork used to register my alluvial ownership of My Private Motorized Conveyance as such to obtain the proper license plates for a Sovereign Citizen to use for Private Travel.

Should you choose to inform me that there is no such paperwork, no such plate and that there is no alternative registration except to grant the Priority Security Interest, which is in violation of Article I Section 17 of the Texas Constitution to require or make compulsory, please see the other paperwork enclosed, particularly My ***Offer to Contract*** which becomes a Contract upon a denial of a Right (Acceptance) and reception of Consideration.

Also, please send me the proper forms for surrendering the Texas Certificate of Title and receiving back the original of the MSO, a certified copy thereof, or a full and complete statement of relinquishment of all interests in and to My Private Motorized Conveyance.

"The Top Ten Problems Plaguing"

Mankind, our Daily Lives, Liberty, & True Justice!

AND,

<u>How We Can Solve Them!!!</u>

WE MUST REALIZE! ~ Noted Abuses Exist! We Must Prioritize "Our" Course, Contingent of the Sovereignty of Each, Under "Common Law"!

Realize, ~ Discerning "Our" Priorities and Purpose, Is "Our" Intrinsic Destiny! Our Eternal Mission!

Realize, ~ "Our" Purpose is to Love God Above All, and "Our" Neighbor, as We love Ourselves!

Realize, you will only obtain, "a worthy desire"! So!

Do you seek for all things? "Or", things for all?

"We Must Realize"! These Problems "Endure"! Currently and "Indefinitely" & "Uncle Scam" Doesn't Care About Purposeful, Humanitarian Concerns, Or; The Top Ten Problems, Plaguing "our" Humanity!

1. Hunger and Homelessness!
2. Human Rights Violations! "We must honor sovereign Rights Worldwide"
3. Health Care!
4. Environmental Degradation!
5. Nuclear Capabilities & Readiness, Maintained at Cold War Levels!
6. Accountability of Elected Officials, and Campaign Finance Laws!
7. Federal "OR?" State Jurisdiction!
8. Voting and Ballot Counting Laws! "Note Absurdity of the Electoral College"
9. Corporate Control of Public Airwaves!
10. Corporate Control of Printed Media!

An Eternal Friend,
Quey Quay,
Eddie Duncan

We "_Need_" A War! A Daily War! On Hunger!

Chapter 1

Give us this day, our daily bread, is a "revealing example" of the method of prayer expressed by Jesus, to help us to establish, our true priorities! That being, honor all, a loving concern for, and the care and feeding of, one another! Yet, the daily nourishment, and a humane concern for the health of each and every fellowman, remains "unattended". And presently, the U.S. government presents no evidence of an endearing sentiment, or priority status, concerning their plight. They ignore the daily suffering that our poor and homeless continually endure.

The problem is, we have failed to realize our purpose! As a People, we have failed terribly, in recognizing "our true value", and "our heritage", established and delivered by Jesus, that of, "eternal life" within each, and all humanity! We have carelessly, systematically, plundered and degraded "Our Eternal Garden".

We must now, learn (choose!) to honor, respect and appreciate one another, and our sustaining earth! Or, our heirs shall soon perish, among one another!

*Arise, reveal your true, and intrinsic nature, "to a temperament taught", by doubtful publicans! Arise! Turn to find your true, God given purpose, and lead "our" humanity by example, among a brotherhood of thankful, penitent believers, not in lieu of an ultimatum, boasting of "mutually assured destruction"!

We Have It! We "have" the technology to conquer hunger, poverty, and homelessness! We have it! NOW! RIGHT NOW! YES! WE CAN! We can make it so! Do you not realize, the immediate potential, of the computer before you? We have retrieved and listed historical logs, every song ever recorded, every word written, and, its' meaning, in every language.

The computer keyboard, used to write and edit these words, can also list every person on the planet, and, "in doing so", disperse our wealth uniformly, eliminate hunger, homelessness, and secure "our" endangered habitat for our posterity! Which generation will actually utilize this technology, and become MtZION.WS?

We the people have too long ignored the most valuable portions of our lives. The heritage of the sacrifice made by the man named Jesus, and the well being of our fellow man. Nowhere is there more potential than in the hearts, and deeds, of our fellow man. Our humanity, is our greatest, of all treasures! We were, and are, encouraged by Jesus, to love one another as we love ourselves. Gods' greatest example of His love for mankind, was a man.

Yet, many still choose to hate, and victimize their fellow man. A treasure more valuable than all things, is a life. Isaiah 13; 12 says, I will make a man more precious than fine gold, even a man, than the golden wedge of Ophir.

We have instead, made our priorities, securing money, material possessions, power, image, and more, more, more. Even though, the meek shall inherit the earth, and friendship, is a love divine.

Obviously, many on this planet do not realize exactly where they are, or, the actual heritage, and dimensions of their lives.

Certainly, if they realized, that some day soon, Jesus would reveal, every day of their lives, in the twinkling of an eye, they would surely change their silly ways.

MtZION.WS

Multitudes Treasure Zero Indifference Of Nations World Services
"The Lords' Sovereign Brotherhood"
"A Thankful Penitent Humanity"

**Linking inspiration & technology, providing
for the brotherhood of man!**

We are a Public Domain Trust & humanitarian/ environmental charity, established in "Public Domain" (on the Internet) and open to member verification by each, 24 hours a day. The purpose of MtZion. ws is to disperse member donations, which, upon membership, are instantly gifted sequentially, to all designated members, and to improve the health and welfare of the human condition, and also, to preserve our endangered planet for "Public Domain"! Through the collective dynamics of numbers!

"Charter"

We recognize and hereby honor our role of sovereign stewards, thankful of Gods' gifts! We the People of MtZion.ws hereby proclaim, ordain, and declare our guiding priorities, our mission, and intent is to:

1. Disperse member donations, sequentially gifted to five designated levels.
2. Declare, fund and establish a "Daily" War on Hunger.
3. Fund and establish all diligent efforts to end homelessness.
4. Secure farmland for habitat, and ecological development.
5. Secure endangered habitat for public domain.
6. All funds available in the MtZION.WS "public account" that are not designated for member considerations, will be held in the public trust account, until a twelve member board (elected by MtZION. WS members) is nominated, elected, and agree, upon the purpose for funds available in the "public account".

Isaiah:1-27 Zion will be redeemed with justice, her penitent ones with righteousness.

Isaiah: 2-2 In the last days, MtZion (the church) shall rise like a mountain among the hills.

Eternally,
A Brother in Christ
Quey Quay
Eddie Duncan

MtZION.WS

Definition of How "our" Public Trust Works:

a. Members donate on any monetary level they choose.
b. Members encourage other concerned and purposeful people to join.
c. Members receive a donation from all signers under their public trust account number, and from signers of those signers, and from signers of those signers, and signers of those signers. We are an unbreakable total, a chain of penitent believers, established on the Internet, simply, to help our humanity! The time has come, unto this generation of penitent souls, to enlist our selves, unto a worthy purpose!

Example: A new member donates to "our" church on the $100.00 level through a (sponsor). At that point in time $30.00 is deposited in the sponsors account, $25.00 is deposited into his/her previous sponsors' account, $20.00 is deposited into that previous sponsors' account, $15.00 is deposited into the previous and final sponsors' account, and $10.00 is deposited into MtZION.WS. "All" powered simply by numbers, brotherhood, and the calculating and verifying capabilities of the Internet and public domain.

This example should reveal to everyone that after three people are enlisted under your public domain trust, any activity under that trust account and three subsequent levels will "only" profit the account. Should we not help each other, and all of our fellowman, through our technology, and Brotherhood?

Any that would insinuate, that we are a pyramid scheme simply do not understand "Public Domain". We are open to public scrutiny 24 hours a day. We welcome scrutiny! The more you know about us, the sooner you will realize that we are here to help each soul, and all of mankind! Social Security is the true,

"Non-Voluntary Pyramid Scheme" operating within an Unconstitutional, "Socialist System". It's criteria and objectives form an unconscionable contract. "It", is a "Non-Voluntary Pyramid Scheme" that is operating in a deficit, and holding your funds, without paying you interest. MtZion.ws public account is subject to the prerogative of Twelve duly elected MtZion.ws members, elected by MtZion.ws members.

Your Public Trust Account # opened on any monetary level
   Donation – <u>100%</u> - and its' designated dispersal
   (1st Level) - 30% -your sponsor
   (2nd Level) - 25% -his/her previous sponsor
   (3rd Level) - 20% -his/her previous sponsor
   (4th Level) - 15% -his/her previous sponsor
   MtZion.ws - 10% -Public Domain

Isaiah 1; 27 & 2; 2-5 The Mountain of the Lord

Zion shall be redeemed with judgement and her converts with righteousness. In the last days, the mountain of the Lord's temple will be established as chief among the mountains; it will be raised above the hills, and all nations will stream to it. Many people will come and say, " Come, let us go up to the mountain of the Lord, to the house of the God of Jacob. He will teach us his ways, so that we may walk in his path." The law will go out from Zion, the word of the Lord from Jerusalem. He will judge between the nations and will settle disputes for many peoples. They will beat their swords into plowshares and their spears into pruning hooks. Nation will not take up sword against nation, nor will they train for war anymore.

This is the purpose that is purposed upon the whole earth: and this is the hand that is stretched out upon all the nations. What shall one then answer the messengers of the nation? That the Lord hath founded Zion, and the poor of His people shall trust in it. Let mine outcasts dwell with thee, Moab; be thou a convert to them from the face of the spoiler: for the extortion is at an end, the spoiler ceaseth, the oppressors are consumed out of the land. Come, O house of Jacob, let us walk in the light of the Lord.

Search your heart, "your conscious spirit", and find the foresight to realize, and embrace Gods' glorious creation, and His eternal humanity, and the purpose set before all. Preserving our healthy humanity, is our intrinsic purpose, and is the abiding purpose for which MtZion.ws is established. Therefore, I challenge all people, to be of a concerned and penitent spirit, and to inspect our Public Trust. I ask you to establish our method and purpose, by a full and complete inspection of "our" Public Domain Trust. All member donations to MtZION.WS are posted online instantly, and are instantly verifiable, and available!

MtZION.WS implements the "donate forward" principal, on levels of designated dispersal. Uniting the technology of the computer, with the "chain letter" principal. You may remember when your parents "mailed" dollars across the country, because, they had a name and address, and because, chain letters worked.

We unite the chain letter principal, with any level of donation, and the up to the second verification, on the Internet, for all member donations, twenty-four hours a day.

Which generation will finally realize "our present capabilities" and become MTZION.WS?

Eternally, A
Brother in Christ
Quey Quay
Eddie Duncan

Uncle Scam, is a Fraudulent, Prosecuting Attorney!
Acute at Prosecuting Victimless Crimes, The
IRS, also Perpetrates Fraud by Deception!

Chapter 2

"That's his job"! To prosecute, condemn and ignore "sovereign" rights and liberties, now and inevitably, throughout the lives of all that are unknowing. His designed procedure, to deliberately mislead the masses, was established by the Act of 1871. That Act, created the corporation, "THE UNITED STATES", allowing a pseudo "NATIONAL AUTHORITY" to cover the treason, that the act, so blatantly accomplished. All federal "CORPORATE" departments, bureaus, and agencies stem from this simple, yet grand deception.

The continual, ever rising number of codes, statutes, ordinances, rules, regulations, amendments, and the "alleged" need for licensing and permits, and, the superfluous amount of new legislation yearly enacted, clearly violates the original intent of The Constitution <u>for</u> the united States. Where in the Constitution, or the Bill of Rights, is the phrase "civil rights" (ever) espoused? The Declaration of Independence never declared, to secure, or defend "civil rights". The Declaration of Independence solemnly declared, and rightfully signified that, our forefathers had established their "sovereign rights". Thereby, they have also secured "our" sovereign rights.

We the People, as "sovereign" Citizens of a Free Republic of states, must unite! We must discard the authority "usurped" by a "New Deal" corporate government, through ITS' blatant and treasonous conspiracy, initiated by Franklin Delanoe Roosevelt, on June 5th of 1933A.D., and blatantly expressed in the "<u>resolution</u>" HJR192-The New Deal, AKA-Trading "With" The Enemies Act.

Under that infamous "resolution", the Land of the Free, was again, "taken back", under matriarchal law, the "single sovereign" theory of parliamentary England, known as King James' law, or maritime law. All of which, have effectively removed "sovereign rights" from a gullible citizenry, and replaced them with a "matriculated" system of government, issuing mandated "civil privileges".

The depression of 1933, the Emergency Powers Act by Franklin Roosevelt, the "new deal", and its' "new judiciary", espousing your right to only "civil privileges" were each and all, "premeditated", and designed to deny you of your God given birthright! HJR-192 resolved to implement a "Public Policy" forum, which has placed feudal standards and taxes, on "sovereign" Citizens and bona fide free landowners! Question; Do we still have alluvial landowners in America? Do we have any land patented property owners (alluvial titled) remaining in America? How many Americans actually claim alluvial titled, freehold, land patent rights?

The taxes, illegally levied on "your" property are even more oppressive, through "their" appraisal system, which yearly and regularly increases "your" debt, because, the more you improve your property, the more you owe, them! Why? Because, you trusted them! Your trusted real estate agent (surrendered) "your" title deed, to/with the "<u>County Deed of Record</u>"! Then, (the State government), "claimed it", by statute, and have since, and will continue indefinitely, to claim it, and tax you, and your heirs!

Investigate Article 7 Sec. 2A and Sec. 2B of the Texas Constitution. To counter their claim, and obtain a copy of the land patent covering the real estate property you own, follow these simple instructions.

1. Obtain a copy of your lands' legal description from your Warranty Deed. Make sure that the legal description has in it, the Township Number, Range Number and Section Number of your property.
2. You then send the copy of your lands' legal description to the Bureau of Land Management Office for the area in which you are located. Do not send your warranty deed or abstract, just a copy of the lands' description.
3. Attach a letter, stating that you would like a certified copy of the original land patent or land grant covering the land described.
4. The cost of the land patent was $4.25, 14 years ago, plus a search fee for each land patent or grant. For most land east of the Missouri and Kansas border, the patents were issued per 80 acres. In areas west of Missouri, patents were usually issued per 160 acres. To figure costs, divide figures above by acreage owned. This will tell approximately how many patents are needed. Inquire of current cost of patents and multiply by number of patents needed to determine approximate cost. Send a little more to cover search fees. (All over payments will be returned by the Bureau.) Send a postal money order, not a check. Allow approximately six weeks for return of patents. You can also visit in person, yet an appointment is recommended, at the Bureaus' office.
5. When you receive the land patent, or land grant, use the Declaration of Land Patent to record the patent in the local county courthouse for the county in which the property is located.
6. You have now claimed your lawful right, to the alluvial title to your property.

***For more detailed information and forms, obtain a copy of the book entitled "Land Patents, Memorandum of Law History, Force, and Effect of the Land Patent" by Jay Stewart. PS- Book may be out of print, I suggest an inter-Library loan at your local library. The phone numbers and locations of offices that can issue a land patent, if provided with the legal description of your property are the following;

Bureau of Land Management Offices

ALASKA
Anchorage Federal Building
701 "c" Street, Box 13
Anchorage ALASKA 99513
Phone; 907-271-5555

ARIZONA
2400 Valley Bank Center
Phoenix, Arizona 85073
Phone; 602-261-3900

CALIFORNIA
Federal Office Building
Room E-2841
2800 Cottage Way
Sacramento, California 95825
Phone; 916-484-4724

COLORADO – (KANSAS)
1037 20th Street
Denver, Colorado 80202
Phone; 303-837-4481

IDAHO
Federal Building
550 West Fort Street
P.O. Box 042
Boise, Idaho 83724
Phone; 208-334-1170

MONTANA (NORTH DAKOTA,
    SOUTH DAKOTA)
Granite Tower
222 North 32nd Street
P.O. Box 30157
Billings, Montana 59107
Phone: 406-657-6461

NEVADA:
Federal Building, Room 3008
300 Booth Street
P.O. Box 12000
Reno, Nevada 89520
Phone: 702-784-5311

NEW MEXICO (OKLAHOMA):
Joseph M. Montoya Federal Building
South Federal Place
P.O. Box 1449
Santa Fe, New Mexico 87501
Phone: 505-988-6316

OREGON (WASHINGTON):
825 N.E. Multnomah Street
P.O. Box 2965
Portland, Oregon 97208
Phone: 503-231-6273

UTAH:
University Club Building
136 East South Temple
Salt Lake City, Utah 84111
Phone: 801-524-4227

WYOMING (NEBRASKA):
2515 Warren Avenue
P.O. Box 1828
Cheyenne, Wyoming 82003
Phone: 307-772-2334

ALL OTHER STATES:
Eastern States Office
350 South Pickett Street
Alexandria, Virginia 22304
Phone: 703-235-2875

In order to share in our God given abundance, we must first realize it, and claim it. Your "sovereign" rights, are a gift of dominion from God, and as a natural born American, your "sovereign" rights were established within the Declaration of Independence and Articles of Confederation, not the holier than thou Constitution!

All three are significant documents, pertaining to "sovereignty and authority", but, "The Constitution" was basically copied (revised, altered and degraded) from "The Articles of Confederation", in a closed-door session! Article 1 section 4 verse 2 of the Constitution reveals, Quote; "The Congress shall assemble at least once in every year, and such meeting shall be on the first Monday in December, unless they shall by law appoint a different day". End Quote! That portion of the Constitution clearly reveals an obligation to assemble, "only once a year", and on a specific day.

The following article clearly reveals that the Constitution was revised from The Articles of Confederation. Quote; Article V: "For the most convenient management of the general interests of the United States, delegates shall be annually appointed in such manner as the "legislatures of each State shall direct", to meet in Congress on the first Monday in November, in every year, with a power reserved to each State to recall its delegates, or any of them, at any time within the year, and to send others in their stead for the remainder of the year". End Quote!

Note the "subtle" differences between the two! Not only does the constitutional article omit (not repeal) the portions pertaining to states rights! But also, (By the blatant omission of the opening sentence!), Congress has effectively eliminated its' "management obligations", by omitting the following quote; "For the most convenient management of the general interests of the United States", end quote!

Whereas, the Constitution and its' procedures were established on November 15th 1777; and revised by Congress (Altered and Degraded!) on September 17th, 1778, and later ratified and in force on March1, 1781.

"We the People" were prepared to enjoy our lives, liberties and pursuits, now that we had freed ourselves from the oppressive regulations and taxes of King George, and therefore, numerous (oppressive) congressional sessions were "not" necessary.

Yet, today we have even more oppressive laws, and taxes under "Uncle Scam" than King George would have ever considered.

Point of fact, on average, 900 new statutes, amendments and ordinances are adopted in Texas, yearly. A superfluous amount of new [statutes] does not reflect a concerned Congress, "on the contrary" rather, one of unconcern and unnecessary zeal, to encumber our rights and liberty!

This national onslaught of numerous unauthorized activities by the federal government, significantly increased under Presidential Proclamation No. 2039, issued March 9,1933, which "temporarily" placed the United States into a State of Emergency, which "is still in force and effect to this day". As a matter of fact, all previously enacted "Emergency Powers Acts" are yet to be repealed!

Therefore, we now live, and have lived, under a "martial law status" for approximately one hundred and fifty years. Since the day that Lincoln initiated his first executive order, proclaiming "Emergency (War) Powers"!

Ask yourself, why has "my" government listed "my" identity, through a "nom de guerre" designation-a war name- (CAPITAL LETTERS), and not by the true and actual Christian appellation, taught in public schools? WHY? - To insure that "you" are entered into "their" matriculated system, in a corporate, commercial capacity.

We no longer enjoy the sovereign Citizen rights that our forefathers died to secure for us. We are now, regulated corporate entities, under a treasonous bureaucracy, which is operating under martial law, whereby a "legal fiction" corporate identity (and liability), is associated with all "matriculated" living souls.

In this country, the violation of our human rights, is the most rampant of all crimes, and doing it, through the "guise of concern and/or patriotism" is the most revolting, premeditated activity, that this and/or any government could pursue!

But, that "is" his job, and method! Hiding your inherent sovereign rights insures "his" civil authority! So, hiding your "sovereign" rights is key to maintaining, their deception! Violating our sovereign rights, is a governmental enterprise! Do you know what a sovereign American is? Do you still retain your "sovereign" rights?

I can almost guarantee you that you do not! If your parents signed a birth certificate, or you have signed a social security card, or a voter's registration card, or a "drivers license", or enlisted in the military, your sovereign rights, have been relinquished, "for" civil privileges!

"Civil" jurisdiction can now bring you into STATE courts, fighting ex post facto charges, victimless crime charges, and any criminal charges, "they", the "STATE" may choose to imagine, "against the dignity of the legal fiction state"! All, irrespective of the fact that Article 1 Sec, 10 states, quote; "and no person shall be held to answer for a criminal offense, unless on an indictment of a grand jury.

The STATE agents of this judiciary act, without a verified complaint, as if a crime could/did exist, "against the dignity of the state" (*a "legal fiction" STATE). They often ignore the fact, that you, and/or the other party, may not wish to pursue charges. Your pleas for sanity are ignored, even though there is no victim, and no sworn affidavit from an injured party. Yet, your self-incrimination is encouraged by public servants. Witnessing a crime is a key element in any warrant-less arrest, yet many are continually prosecuted unconstitutionally, irrelevant of that fact. No matter how flawless your record, or how considerate your behavior, you may still end up in probate court, relinquishing all common law rights, simply because you signed a marriage license. Adding insult to injury, when you retain an attorney, (*an agent obliged to the court), you have effectively "given jurisdiction" to an "equity" court. Your sovereign rights have thus, been torn from you, and, you are now recognized by the court as "a deaf mute, and a ward of the state".

Realize now, that your government has effectively made "you" a "bankrupt corporate entity", and a second class citizen. Realize also, how long this deception has endured, (June 5th, 1933) and do not ignore the fact that the Federal Government ("your" feudal lord!) is bankrupt. "You", now being a "bankrupt entity" have even fewer rights! And if represented by one of their agents, "an attorney" you are basically "a mute defendant" in their court, deserving no considerations. Meaning, you will be "tried" and condemned under criminal, or commercial statutes, even though there is no victim, and you are truly not a commercial entity.

"Uncle Scam" has no remorse for the deceptions, injustices, fraud, and extortion "he" has inflicted on the People, "he", swore to serve and protect. Pillaging Citizens that do not lawfully owe, of their homes, properties and goods, only to fatten an International Monetary Fund account, (which holds liens on the national debt), is treason!

The following seven pages are a written testimony, defining willful and intentional abuses by agents of the current <u>LEGAL</u> <u>INDUSTRY</u>, now embedded, and flourishing in "<u>our</u>" country. This great country, is no longer, the land of the free! "Our" land has become instead, the land of the freely prosecuted, for any and every, alleged abuse of their "<u>Public Policy</u>" , alleged by any agent of their said; "LEGAL INDUSTRY"!

The following seven pages are true and authentic copies of the actual sworn to, verified, and submitted, in open court, "AFFIDAVIT OF FACT and VERIFIED COMPLAINT" of "Official Misconduct", which is mandated by Texas Code of Criminal Procedure to proceed to District Court.

Yet, the County Court Judge, Dennis Watson, presiding over the cause, (as of his initial notice), has willfully and intentionally denied us, this due process mandate.

Therefore, we are forced to proceed with a Writ of Habeas Corpus, to the District Court and have, and will assert our right to a hearing (of "official misconduct") before the Grand Jury.

The three pages entitled: "Petition For Acquittal of Void Conviction" were filed timely, in Appellate Court, four years after the conspired charge/conviction. The infinite timeframe, for their claim to prosecute, concerning this victimless charge, or any allegation, about anyone, speaks volumes about "our" current, Legal Industry. My petition for acquittal is still pending, as of the first day of Febrary, in the Year of Our Lord, Two Thousand and Seven A.D.

"<u>Hot</u> <u>Pursuit</u>" was tendered in the aftermath of the "rouge behavior", of nearly every "peace officer", that I have encountered in this county, over the past eight years.

Eternally,
A Brother In Christ
A Thankful
Quey Quay

AFFIDAVIT OF FACT and VERIFIED COMPLAINT

I am writing to you for the purpose of defining willful, wanton and retaliatory acts, within a long train of rights violations by the Montgomery County Sheriffs' Department, the Montgomery County Department of Public Safety, and also the Municipal, County and District Courts.

The governmental agencies cited and transcribed above have committed the criminal offenses listed and numbered below;

1. Tampered with evidence – Erased Portions of 911 Taped Call.
2. Perpetrated Numerous False Arrests and Malicious Prosecutions.
3. Charge of assault, when in fact, I was assaulted! Case dismissed.
4. Charge of "Burglary of a Vehicle". My auto! Case dismissed.
5. Charge of "No Septic". Dismissed at PC hearing.
6. Charge of "Failure to Appear". Proven fraudulent at PC hearing.
7. Charge of "Illegal Discharge of Septic". I was tried in Precinct #1 Municipal Court, even though, there were no witnesses or evidence against me, (because none existed, no illegal discharge occurred). Yet, a jury of six, that was comprised of four civilians and, (over my objections) two Montgomery County Sheriffs' Deputies, said guilty.
8. Notice of Appeal and Motion to Stay Judgement was ignored by Judge Lanny Moriarty and on July 20th, 2003A.D. He initiated a hearing, in a malicious and bias court, to which I was allegedly mandated to attend. The hearing was initiated by April 18th, 2003 charges of traffic violations by Trooper Caryn Mosier McAnarney. Lanny Moriarty denied all lawful requests, and my request to determine the status of my appeal. He stated; Quote; We're not here for that today. Bailiff, please serve the [104] warrants on Mr. Duncan. Mr. Moriarty put me to jail, that day, for a false allegation, of a non-jail offense, that was in fact, a void judgement.
9. On April 18th 2003 A.D. Trooper Caryn Mosier McAnarney lied to responding officers and ignored testimony of Officer Velenzuela and her dispatcher, and proceeded to initiate two unjustified arrests. [video and audio evidence proves her culpability, and was ignored by the prosecutor, and the presiding Judges of the court, and is available]

10. [during the term of a conspired, false, and malicious conviction, brought under Lenny Moriarty] and while in the "**actual**" custody of Sheriff GuyWilliams, a Judge Mason Martin issued a Capias Warrant for Failure to Appear, even though I was in their custody, and had notified jail records two weeks earlier of my pending court appearance.

11. I was later freed of the unjust incarceration, after a Writ of Habeas

Corpus was brought before Judge Underwood. Yet, he suppressed

the Writ of Habeas (the Most Extraordinary Writ) and "allowed" an indigent issue to prevail. Yet, until I posted a bond of $10,000 for failure to appear, Montgomery County Sheriff Guy Williams, (who signed the Capias "For Failure To Appear") would not release me.

12 On November 16th, 2004 A.D. RECUSED Judge Mason Martin initiated (by his own volition), an indigent hearing to, and which did, overturn my previously established indigent status. All, to my harm.

13. RECUSED Judge Mason Martin issued warrants for my arrest, eighteen months after his RECUSAL, for cases that are on appeal.

14. On March 18th, 2004A.D. Judge Mason Martin performed a mass arraignment by entering a plea of not guilty for all accused, present in the courtroom that day.

15. On or about March 7th, 2004 A.D. Assistant District Attorney Brett and two Montgomery County Deputies arrived on my property. Brett Peabody approached me and began to discuss pending traffic cases and the fact that he intended to prosecute them, with or without my consent, and that he would with hold discovery, if I did not agree. By what authority did he trespass on my land, and threaten me?

16. On June 29th, 2004 A.D. I filed a PETITION FOR REMOVAL of Assistant District Brett Peabody in District Court, and the suit came before Judge Stovall. No hearing was held in that court, yet the suit was transferred to Orange, Texas and taken before Judge Buddie J. Hahn, who obliged the Montgomery County District Attorney, and dismissed Cause No. 04-06-05037-CV on April 22, 2005 A.D.

17. On July 12th, 2004 A.D. Assistant District Attorney Brett Peabody and visiting Judge Jerry Sandel proceeded with an unjust and malicious prosecution against me, (for an alleged jailable offense). They suppressed subpoenaed witnesses, and ignored perjured testimony by the lead witness, Trooper Caryn Mosier McAnarney, that was expressed/established on the admitted taped evidence.

18. Brett Peabody knowingly and intentionally attempted to deny me, my right to counsel, by requesting that I sign a "Waiver of Right to Counsel", the day of the trial, that/which I refused to sign, and did request, at that point in time, that competent counsel be appointed. He refused my request, and ignored the fact that I refused to sign "his" waiver of right to counsel, as he presented it! The Court was not completed, yet he and court administrators, proceeded maliciously and wantonly, knowingly in violation of the Sixth Amendment.

19. On December 17th, 2004 A.D. in County Court # 3, the indigent hearing, (initiated by RECUSED Mason Martin), came before visiting Judge Jerry Sandel. I objected to the right of a RECUSED person, to interfere in my affairs. I further objected to the presence of Brett Peabody, because a Petition For Removal, that I filed June 29th, 2004 A.D. was then, still pending in the 221st District Court.

20. He, Brett Peabody, further obstructed justice and did commit perjury on December 17th, 2004 A.D. within line 14 and 15 of the Court transcripts. He testified to the Court, Quote; Actually, your honor, I believe the District Court has dismissed that action. End Quote! He further alleged that Stacy Mooring had told him last month that Mr. Duncans' most recent case in District Court HAD BEEN dismissed for failure to prosecute. Visiting Judge Jerry Sandel assumed that the matter has/had been taken care of, and that the 221st had acted to deny the citation. Both assumptions were untrue, the suit was not heard in the 221st District Court, it was taken to Orange Texas. And, the suit was not, actually denied until April 22nd, 2005 A.D. by Buddie J. Hahn of the 260th Judicial District of Orange County Texas.

21. On February 27th, 2006 A.D. Montgomery County City Officer J. Kelemen seized my private property, from private property, under "color of law" and misapplied commercial codes.

My auto was ("impounded, to keep it safe"), and sold, with no notice in thirty days.

22. On February 27th, Officer J. Kelemen arrested me on grounds that Mason Martin had issued warrants for my arrest. I informed him at that moment, that Mason Martin was/had been RECUSED – (impersonating a judicial officer) from this case eighteen months ago.

23. On June 25th, 2006 A.D.Trooper Caryn Mosier McAnarney led a rogue gang of DPS troopers, who trespassed, (a second time within the hour), with no warrant, weapons drawn, ordering everyone in the house to come outside. We were enjoying a Sunday dinner, when they walked onto the property, aiming weapons at everyone and ordering us to exit the building. I was in fear of my life, and even more apprehensive, when I recognized Caryn Mosier McAnarney. Everyone stepped outside, and when my friend requested a warrant, he was threatened to be shot, sprayed and blinded by mace, beaten by nightstick, assaulted and thrown to the ground and kneed on the neck and ribs by three DPS officers. Then, after handcuffing him, they lifted his entire weight by one arm.

24. They then, had the audacity to charge him with interfering with the duties of a public servant and resisting arrest. I believe it was a premeditated retaliatory act by Trooper Caryn Mosier McAnarney and her Calvary, against Will Ferguson. Because of the fact that, an hour earlier, he had requested a warrant for their presence. He also reminded them of their duty to abide by lawful due process. I also believe that, he was targeted because of his association with me.

25. Four sworn affidavits of witnesses have been filed in that case, and shall soon be presented to the Grand Jury. I challenge you to pursue with all of your heart, to substantiate, and determine the truth of, or to disavow the allegations lodged in above paragraphs 1- 24. And also, to investigate the alleged charges of interfering, and resisting arrest, lodged against Will Ferguson, when in fact, his only interaction with the "armed assailants' was his request for a warrant.

26. On August 10th, 2006A.D. Assistant City Attorney, Gary A. Scott filed fraudulent documents, (breaching his fiduciary duty to establish venue and all elements of the charge) on public record, alleging untruths related to my testimony in open court. Whereas the evidence, witnesses, and truth of the matter, establishes that; Mr. Scott violated Texas Government Code Annotated 51.904 and the Code of Criminal Procedure, Articles 1.03, 1.04, 1.05, 1.27 and Article 2.01 and the Texas Penal Code 37.10 (a) (1) (c) (actors' intent constituted harm) therefore, he must be charged and tried for noted violations.

27. On October 9th, 2006 A.D. the City of Conroe, Municipal Court issued five dysfunctional warrants for my arrest, after entering a void judgement, concerning both subject matter and "Due Process". I was found guilty, fined, and warrants issued, with no hearing and no trial!

Seven years ago, (January of 1999) I called 911, to report a stolen car and the fact that my alleged friend had defrauded me, and had now re-claimed the car he had previously sold to me. Officer Huntsman arrived at my property, to investigate my call. He informed me that, by the record, the car was still the property of Kenny Jones, and that if I wanted him removed from my property, I must seek eviction process in the municipal court. I stated that I intended to, and the officer left.

Mr. Jones then began rummaging through my toolbox, claiming that many belonged to him. He walked away with tools in both hands. I followed, requesting Kenny to return the tools. He turned suddenly and struck me with the wrenches in his right hand.

We wrestled for a few minutes, then decided to call it a draw. I then went to the phone to report the assault. The Sheriffs' Department arrested me for assault, because I didn't press charges against him, (the actual perpetrator of the assault). Their (reason?) for arresting me was, to keep us separated! Yet, they put us in the same cell.

The above is only one example of numerous rights violations of lawful Citizens, and a "standard procedure" that encourages it, then, covers it up, when lawfully questioned. The prosecutor, Michael Shirley tried to convict me for breaking into my own car, even though I had complained of it on my original 911 call. THE TAPED CALL WAS IGNORED! Not only was it ignored, ESSENTIAL SUBJECT MATTER WAS ERASED!

My attorney, Doug Atkinson, has a copy of my original 911 tape in its' entirety, and I have the altered copy, which was delivered to me after my second PIA request. <u>PORTIONS</u> <u>WERE</u> <u>ERASED</u>!

Essential portions of subject matter of that 911 call <u>WERE</u> <u>ERASED</u>! Whereas, such actions constitute tampering with a Federal Communication, and must be investigated, and if found to be true, prosecuted accordingly. Therefore, I strongly request that you give your wholehearted best effort to determine the actual validity of these violations by the law enforcement agencies and the judicial "system" of Montgomery County, and when confirmed, wholeheartedly seek true justice, competent restitution for all harmed and all necessary reorganization.

In the fall off 2002A.D. I was charged with No Septic System by Montgomery County Environmental Agent, Dan Kiplinger. I appeared before the Precinct #1 Municipal clerk Belinda _____ before the designated deadline. I presented the ticket to her, she read it, then wrote on it $500, and stated to me, Quote; "That will be five hundred dollars! Would you like to pay that today? End Quote! I responded, no! She asked; "Would you like to talk to a lawyer? I responded, no! Then, I requested to speak with the judge. She responded, "That is not possible"!

I left the Precinct 1 Annex with the understanding/belief that a hearing date would be set, to determine the validity of the allegations. A month later, I was arrested for "FAILURE TO APPEAR", even though the inscription of $500 written on the citation by the attending court clerk Belinda _____ established my presence within defined time frame.

Montgomery County Magistrate Trey Spikes dismissed the "Failure to Appear" charge when presented the written proof. He also dismissed the "No Septic" charge when presented with evidence of compliance, and yet, forewarned me that; "they won't stop", just because I dismissed the one charge. And, He was right!

They shortly returned with another fraudulent charge of, "Illegal Discharge of Septic". And, in a mock trial, where, over my timely objections, two deputy sheriffs served on the jury, where no evidence or witnesses against me were ever brought forward, because none existed. There was never any illegal discharge of septic. Yet, a jury, with two Deputy Sheriffs on the jury panel, (over my objections) decided my guilt.

On July 20th, 2003 A.D. I appeared in Precinct #1 Municipal Court for an appointed hearing, initiated by Lanny Moriarty. Instead of ruling on my petitions, he issued 104 warrants for my arrest and promptly instructed his bailiff to serve his 104 warrants for my arrest. I went to jail immediately, and was informed that I owed the County over $30,000 and would remain in custody until February of 2004 A.D.

Lanny Moriarty ignored my appeal and motion to stay judgement, and sent me to jail, (for a non-jailable offense) on a/this second fraudulent and conspired charge.

They initially charged me with no septic, which was dismissed by Judge Trey Spikes, then they "restyled" it, changed it to illegal discharge of septic, and got "their" conviction.

I was unlawfully incarcerated for fifty-two days! And would have lost my property, (and my cherished liberty for the intended sentenced time) if not for my friends and a Writ of Habeas Corpus brought by Dale Robertson, before Judge Olen Underwood on August 23rd 2002A.D.

Mr. Robertson established before Judge Underwood, the proper course of his/my Writ of Habeas Corpus. Yet, no meaningful hearing, on the Habeas Writ, was ever performed. Olen Underwood, by his own volition, conspired with the prosecutor to conduct an indigent hearing, instead!

The lawful, due course of my Habeas Writ was suppressed and denied, thus, culpable parties were protected.

Not only were the culpable parties protected from prosecution, but, a dysfunctional charge of "Failure to Appear" by Judge Mason Martin was pending, even though I was unlawfully, in the custody of Sheriff Guy Williams, a Co-signer on the warrant, at the time of "their" alleged failure. In fact, Guy Williams failed to secure my presence in court at appointed date, yet required a 10,000 bond for "Failure to Appear", before my release, even though, it was his failure to assure my presence in court.

Whereas, the above listed and numbered complaints reveal a long train of violations by the law enforcement officers and the judicial authorities "reigning" in this county.

Whereas, I know, that all claims listed in the above affidavit are true and factual, I hereby demand an extensive, public inspection of the entire judicial system within this county, and any other county, where the people deem it necessary.

Whereas, the public record, and the evidence will/does reveal the truth of the numerous violations listed in paragraphs 1-27.

Therefore, I hereby request that all public servants, involved in perpetrating the listed violations, be prosecuted, and when/if found guilty, be punished accordingly.

Eternally,
A Brother in Christ,
All God Given
Rights Reserved
Without Prejudice

THE STATE OF TEXAS	§	IN THE TENTH COURT OF APPEALS
	§	
VS.	§	McLENNAN COUNTY COURTHOUSE
	§	
Ronald Edwin Duncan, Sui Juris	§	WACO, TEXAS

Judicial Notice
Pursuant under 201(d) and 201 (g) of the Texas and Federal Rules of Evidence

MANDATORY
Public Law 93-595: A Court shall take Judicial Notice if requested by a party and supplied with the necessary information.

Petition For Acquittal of Void Conviction

The Texas Constitution and the Code of Criminal Procedures stand as protective instruments, which establish due process rights, and define the actual process by which jurisdiction is obtained, and, to assure due process.

The trial court has failed to follow the due process mandates defined in the Texas Constitution, and, in Art. 1.03, Art. 1.04, Art. 1.05 Art. 1.051, Art. 1.06, Art. 1.08, Art. 1.27, Art. 2.01, Art. 2.16, and Art. 3.04 of the Texas Code of Criminal Procedure. Violating Art. 39.03 of the Texas Penal Code.

The Information is dysfunctional, on grounds that it is not based on a verified complaint, from/by an actual victim, of a "common law" crime.

The Information also alleges that; RONALD EDDIE DUNCAN, with "<u>criminal</u> <u>negligence</u>", did INTERFERE with TROOPER MCANARNEY.

[Criminal negligence"] is defined by Texas Penal Code 1.07 Section 6.03. It requires that the alleged conduct is a conscious objective, to cause the result, when he ought to be aware of a substantial and unjustifiable risk that the circumstances exist, or the result will occur.

I had no concept, that Officer Caryn Mosier McAnarney, at 8:19PM would lie to responding officers, and ignore the testimony of responding officer Valenzuela, who testified, to her directly, at 8:13PM that he had observed similar behavior, when he pulled me over, a month earlier.

The same behavior being, informing officers of my lawful right, to travel. When detained by several other officers during the year, that/this same prior behavior, had resulted in a simple "traffic" citation, at each encounter.

Therefore, I had no intent or concept, that I could possibly be acting with "Criminal Negligence", as alleged by Trooper Caryn Mosier McAnarney.

Further, It was not until, after conspiring with responding officers, that she was informed of her "opportunity" to allege a violation, and that she "could" charge me. A responding officer stated; Quote! "You can charge him with Interfering with your duties." She responded; Quote! I Can? A Class B! He's going down! Do you want to break the windows? End Quote!

She was advised to obtain clearance from a sergeant, before proceeding with a non-warrant arrest. She attempted to secure such clearance, but never did. She proceeded by her own volition, without lawful authority. She also perjured herself, when questioned; "Did both of them fail to identify?" She responded; yes! That response was untrue, and misleading, and for the specific purpose of inciting the responding officers to arrest my traveling companion, and myself. By her own volition, without clearance from a sergeant on duty, she, Trooper McAnarney, did with willful intent, chose to willfully lie to responding officers, and inflict a false imprisonment upon Mike Erwin, myself, and thereby denied us, our lawfully entitled liberty.

Further, it is a defense, to which I am lawfully entitled under (5) (d) of Sec. 38.15 Interference With Public Duties, because in fact, the only interaction with Trooper McAnarney was speech only. And, please take Judicial Notice that; the same interaction, with numerous other peace officers, during the prior years, (as exemplified by the testimony of officer Valenzuela, after arriving at the scene, he testified to Trooper McAnarney of our previous encounter) did not constitute a charge of "Interfering"!

Further, page 29 through40 of the trial court record reflects a Denial of Speedy Trial, which is grounds for dismissal, and, the issue was presented and petitioned for redress in the trial court.

Further, "Motion to Dismiss Due to Denial of Speedy Trial" was ignored. In the alternative, please take judicial notice of accused's Application for the Most Extraordinary Writ of Habeas Corpus on page 33 section II.

Further, it is obvious by the trial court record that my right to competent counsel was denied. Page 44, 45, 46, & 47 of the trial court record reflects Defendants' Motion For Assistance of Appointed Counsel.

Brett Peabody, breached of his fiduciary duty to complete the court, he failed to assure that I, in fact, received competent counsel. He instead, waited until the day of trial, approached me, and requested that I sign a "Waiver of Right To Counsel"(page 75). I refused to sign his waiver, and told him that I wanted competent counsel. He ignored my request, and the fact that I did not sign the "Waiver Of Right To Counsel" and therefore, trial court failed to complete the court, and proceeded without jurisdiction!

Therefore, trial court acted without jurisdiction, and its' ruling is void.

Appellate Case No. 09-04-00362-CR

Trial Court No. 03-185426

THE STATE OF TEXAS	§	IN THE TENTH COURT OF APPEALS
	§	
VS.	§	McLENNAN COUNTY COURTHOUSE
	§	
Ronald Edwin Duncan, Sui Juris	§	WACO, TEXAS

ORDER ON; PETITION FOR AQUITTAL
OF VOID CONVICTION

On this, the _____ day of _____, 200___, came to be heard, the Petition For Acquittal of Void Conviction, in the above entitled and numbered cause. And, the court, having heard Accused's Petition, and the evidence thereon submitted, is of the opinion that Accused's Petition should be;

_____ Granted

_____ Denied, Grounds Being _____

_____

_____

_____

Signed and entered this _____ day of _____, 200___ .

Presiding Judge

_____

55

"Hot Pursuit!"

Privacy rights are plundered, sovereigns, must be mute!
Rouge agents are running everywhere, and always, in "<u>hot</u>" pursuit!

Running rampant, in our land, misinformed, controlling, little clowns!
Hunting for an excuse, any excuse at all, to take "<u>someone</u>" down!

Come out of the house with your hands in the air!
We're looking for a man, and we reckon, he's in there!

We're in "Hot Pursuit" of this man, for a traffic offense!
He wud'n wearing a seat belt, he ran, we been chasin him ever since!

He violated a code, he failed to buckle up, and then, "he fled the scene".
So, we're chasin him down, and we're emptin every house, in between!

Do you have a warrant? They seemed confused, about, what I meant!
Excuse me, <u>public</u> <u>servant</u>, must I die for inquiring, about your intent?

Do you have a warrant? I asked! I didn't hear a sound!
That's it! I'll Shoot! I'll shoot you! Get on the ground!

Mace in my face, and a blackjack across my knee!
The justification, for his merciless attack is, you interfered with me!

As an American native, I have the right to privacy, and to be left alone!
Why do rouge agents, trespass, threaten, and order us from our home!

What's going on here, rouge agents in "our" country! How can this be?
Will "<u>a</u> <u>proper</u> <u>court</u>" hear my cause! Hah! I doubt it! Hmm, Let's see!

Take judicial notice, I filed a sworn affidavit and a verified complaint!
This case belongs in District Court and District Court, this ain't!

The Judge did not concern himself with my testimony, the truth in fact!
He said; "We're comin at you, with all we got, and, "that's that"!

Our "servants" are immune from prosecution, for any rights, violated!
Allegedly above the law, as though divine, so pompously, celebrated!

Why should that be? Who is sovereign here, the servant, or me?
Violating sovereign rights is nothing new, it happens, continually!

Native Americans have no conception, of they're own sovereignty!
They live, as pawns, in a "New Deal" maze, of a "Legal Industry"!

Never accountable to any authority, other than, their own discretion!
That is, the current judicial prerogative, and they're intended direction!

They are no longer bound, by their duty, to serve and protect!
They cannot be prosecuted, "for harm done", by intent, or neglect!

Official Immunity! How could my servant, be so endowed!
Officially allowed, to violate the law! Should I, be proud?

Across "our" land, rouge agents are plundering, with a free hand!
Above the law, they've alleged, to serve! Is this, "our" framers' plan?

Our servants have reversed the roles, and the chain of command!
Ignoring the fundamental principals of sovereignty, the law of the land!

The land of the "<u>Free-ly</u> <u>Prosecuted</u>"! This is, what, we have become!
Our cherished liberty is bartered, and "<u>our</u>" authority, is shunned!

When one questions rouge authority, ones' answer, is "only", torment!
Prison, is where, there is no question, one who questions, will be sent!

The essential principal of liberty! Gods' gift to humanity, for one & all!
Has been suppressed, by this traitorous government! Surely, it will fall!

Beloved, and at Liberty, there can be, no better way!
Eternally, A Brother In Christ, A Thankful, Quey Quay

Act of 1871

http://www.worldnewsstand.net/2001/article/L4.htmhttp://
www.worldnewsstand.net/2001/article/L4.htm

1871, February 21: Congress Passes an Act to Provide a Government for the District of Columbia, also known as the Act of 1871.

With no constitutional authority to do so, Congress creates a separate form of government for the District of Columbia, a ten mile square parcel of land (see, Acts of the Forty-first Congress," Section 34, Session III, chapters 61 and 62).

The act -- passed when the country was weakened and financially depleted in the aftermath of the Civil War -- was a strategic move by foreign interests (international bankers) who were intent upon gaining a stranglehold on the coffers and neck of America. Congress cut a deal with the international bankers (specifically Rothschilds of London) to incur a DEBT to said bankers. Because the bankers were not about to lend money to a floundering nation without serious stipulations, they devised a way to get their foot in the door of the United States.

The Act of 1871 formed a corporation called THE UNITED STATES. The corporation, OWNED by foreign interests, moved in and shoved the original Constitution into a dustbin.

With the Act of 1871, the organic Constitution was defaced -- in effect vandalized and sabotage -- when the title was capitalized and the word "for" was changed to "of" in the title.

THE CONSTITUTION OF THE UNITED STATES OF AMERICA is the constitution of the incorporated UNITED STATES OF AMERICA. It operates in an economic capacity and has been used to fool the People into thinking it governs the Republic. It does not! Capitalization is NOT insignificant when one is referring to a legal document. This seemingly "minor" alteration has had a major impact on every subsequent generation of Americans. What Congress did by passing the Act of 1871 was create an entirely new document, a constitution for the government of the District of Columbia, an INCORPORATED government. This newly altered Constitution was not intended to benefit the Republic. It benefits only the corporation of the UNITED STATES OF AMERICA and operates entirely outside the original (organic) Constitution.

Instead of having absolute and unalienable rights guaranteed under the organic Constitution, we the people now have "relative" rights or privileges. One example is the Sovereign's right to travel, which has now been transformed (under corporate government policy) into a "privilege" that requires citizens to be licensed. (Passports) By passing the Act of 1871, Congress committed TREASON against the People who were Sovereign under the grants and decrees of the Declaration of Independence and the organic Constitution. [Information courtesy of Lisa Guliani, www.babelmagazine.com. The Act of 1871 became the FOUNDATION of all the treason since committed by government officials.]

~~~~~~~~~~~~~~~

Dove: The following is an expansion and further explanation of the above (an adaptation of Lisa's work, done with her permission), which you may want to read for your own edification. Whereas my Chapter 9 is a time-map of the major Headlines and Landmines of the 200-years-plus history of America, each subsequent chapter goes into particular details. This section is from Chapter 18, "The Tale of Two Governments, which overall addresses the difference between a democracy and a republic as well as the fact of a federal government and a shadow government practicing under the guise of The Corporation. I'm sure Lisa won't mind your using what you need in order to make whatever point you wish to make in the moment.

The United States Isn't a Country; It's a Corporation!

In preparation for stealing America, the puppets of Britain's banking cabal had already created a second government, a Shadow Government designed to manage what the common herd believed was a democracy, but what really was an incorporated UNITED STATES. Together this chimera, this two-headed monster, disallowed the common herd all rights of sui juris. [you, in your sovereignty]

Congress, with no authority to do so, created a separate form of government for the District of Columbia, a ten-mile square parcel of land. WHY and HOW did they do so? First, Lisa Guliani of Babel Magazine, reminds us that the Civil War was, in fact, "little more than a calculated front with fancy footwork by backroom players." Then she adds: "It was also a strategic maneuver by British and European interests (international bankers) intent on gaining a stranglehold on the coffers of America.

And, because Congress knew our country was in dire financial straits, certain members of Congress cut a deal with the international bankers (in those days, the Rothschilds of London were dipping their fingers into everyone's pie). . . . . There you have the WHY, why members of Congress permitted the international bankers to gain further control of America. . . . . .

"Then, by passing the Act of 1871, Congress formed a corporation known as THE UNITED STATES. This corporation, owned by foreign interests, shoved the organic version of the Constitution aside by changing the word 'for' to 'of' in the title. Let me explain: the original Constitution drafted by the Founding Fathers read: 'The Constitution for the united states of America.' [note that neither the words 'united' nor 'states' began with capital letters] But the CONSTITUTION OF THE UNITED STATES OF AMERICA' is a corporate constitution, which is absolutely NOT the same document you think it is. First of all, it ended all our rights of sovereignty [sui juris]. So you now have the HOW, how the international bankers got their hands on THE UNITED STATES OF AMERICA."

To fully understand how our rights of sovereignty were ended, you must know the full meaning of sovereign: "Chief or highest, supreme power, superior in position to all others; independent of and unlimited by others; possessing or entitled to; original and independent authority or jurisdiction." (Webster).

In short, our government, which was created by and for us as sovereigns -- free citizens deemed to have the highest authority in the land – was stolen from us, along with our rights. Keep in mind that, according to the original Constitution, only We the People are sovereign.

Government is not sovereign. The Declaration of Independence says, "...government is subject to the consent of the governed." That's us -- the sovereigns. When did you last feel like a sovereign? As Lisa Guliani said;

"It doesn't take a rocket scientist or a constitutional historian to figure out that the U.S. Government has NOT been subject to the consent of the governed since long before you or I were born. Rather, the governed are subject to the whim and greed of the corporation, which has stretched its tentacles beyond the ten-mile-square parcel of land known as the District of Columbia. In fact, it has invaded every state of the Republic. Mind you, the corporation has NO jurisdiction beyond the District of Columbia. You just think it does.

"You see, you are 'presumed' to know the law, which is very weird since We the People are taught NOTHING about the law in school. We memorize obscure facts and phrases here and there, like the Preamble, which says, 'We the People...establish this Constitution for the United States of America.' But our teachers only gloss over the Bill of Rights. Our schools (controlled by the corporate government) don't delve into the Constitution at depth. After all, the corporation was established to indoctrinate and 'dumb-down' the masses, not to teach anything of value or importance. Certainly, no one mentioned that America was sold-out to foreign interests, that we were beneficiaries of the debt incurred by Congress, or that we were in debt to the international bankers. Yet, for generations, Americans have had the bulk of their earnings confiscated to pay a massive debt that they did not incur. There's an endless stream of things the People aren't told. And, now that you are being told, how do you feel about being made the recipient of a debt without your knowledge or consent? "After passage of the Act of 1871 Congress set a series of subtle and overt deceptions into motion, deceptions in the form of decisions that were meant to sell us down the river. Over time, the Republic took it on the chin until it was knocked down and counted out by a technical KO [knock out]. With the surrender of the people's gold in 1933, the 'common herd' was handed over to illegitimate law. (I'll bet you weren't taught THAT in school.)

"Our corporate form of governance is based on Roman Civil Law and Admiralty, or Maritime, Law, which is also known as the 'Divine Right of Kings' and the 'Law of the Seas' -- another fact of American history not taught in our schools. Actually, Roman Civil Law was fully established in the colonies before our nation began, and then became managed by private international law.

In other words, the government -- the government created for the District of Columbia via the Act of 1871 – operates solely under Private International Law, not Common Law, which was the foundation of our Constitutional Republic. "This fact has impacted all Americans in concrete ways. For instance, although Private International Law is technically only applicable within the District of Columbia, and NOT in the other states of the Union, the arms of the Corporation of the UNITED STATES are called 'departments' -- i.e., the Justice Department, the Treasury Department.

And those departments affect everyone, no matter where (in what state) they live. Guess what? Each department belongs to the corporation -- to the UNITED STATES.

"Refer to any UNITED STATES CODE (USC). Note the capitalization; this is evidence of a corporation, not a Republic. For example, In Title 28 3002 (15) (A) (B) (C), it is unequivocally stated that the UNITED STATES is a corporation. Translation: the corporation is NOT a separate and distinct entity; it is not disconnected from the government; it IS the government -- your government.

This is extremely important! I refer to it as the 'corporate EMPIRE of the UNITED STATES,' which operates under Roman Civil Law outside the original Constitution. How do you like being ruled by a corporation? You say you'll ask your Congressperson about this? HA!! "Congress is fully aware of this deception. So it's time that you, too, become aware of the deception. What this great deception means is that the members of Congress do NOT work for us, for you and me. They work for the Corporation, for the UNITED STATES. No wonder we can't get them to do anything on our behalf, or meet or demands, or answer our questions.

"Technically, legally, or any other way you want to look at the matter, the corporate government of the UNITED STATES has no jurisdiction or authority in ANY State of the Union (the Republic) beyond the District of Columbia. Let that tidbit sink in, then ask yourself, could this deception have occurred without full knowledge and complicity of the Congress? Do you think it happened by accident? If you do, you're deceiving yourself.

"There are no accidents, no coincidences. Face the facts and confront the truth. Remember, you are presumed to know the law. THEY know you don't know the law or, for that matter, your history. Why? Because no concerted effort was ever made to teach or otherwise inform you. As a Sovereign, you are entitled to full disclosure of all facts. As a slave, you are entitled to nothing other than what the corporation decides to 'give'.

"Remember also that 'Ignorance of the law is no excuse.' It's your responsibility and obligation to learn the law and know how it applies to you. No wonder the corporation counted on the fact that most people are too indifferent, unconcerned, distracted, or lazy to learn what they need to know to survive within the system. We have been conditioned to let the government do our thinking for us. Now's the time to turn that around if we intend to help save our Republic and ourselves -- before it's too late.

"As an instrument of the international bankers, the UNITED STATES owns you from birth to death". It also holds ownership of all your assets, of your property, even of your children. Think long and hard about all the bills, taxes, fines, and licenses you have paid for or purchased. Yes, they had you by the pockets. If you don't believe it, read the 14th Amendment. See how 'free' you really are. Ignorance of the facts led to your silence. Silence is construed as consent; consent to be beneficiaries of a debt you did not incur. As a Sovereign People we have been deceived for hundreds of years; we think we are free, but in truth we are servants of the corporation.

"Congress committed treason against the People in 1871. Honest men could have corrected the fraud and treason. But apparently there weren't enough honest men to counteract the lust for money and power. We lost more freedom than we will ever know, thanks to corporate infiltration of our so-called 'government.'

"Do you think that any soldier who died in any of our many wars would have fought if he or she had known the truth? Do you think one person would have laid down his/her life for a corporation? How long will we remain silent? How long will we perpetuate the MYTH that we are free? When will we stand together as One Sovereign People? When will we take back what has been as stolen from the us?

"If the People of America had known to what extent their trust was betrayed, how long would it have taken for a real revolution to occur? What we now need is a Revolution in THOUGHT. We need to change our thinking, then we can change our world. Our children deserve their rightful legacy -- the liberty our ancestors fought to preserve, the legacy of a Sovereign and Fully Free People." [Posted 8/27/02, www.babelmagazine.com/]

Affidavit of Tax Exempt Foreign Status

For the purposes of this affidavit, the terms "United States" and "U.S." mean only the Federal Legislative Democracy of the District of Columbia, Puerto Rico, U.S. Virgin Islands, Guam, American Samoa and any other Territory within the "United States", which entity has its' origin and jurisdiction from Article 1, Section 8, Clause 17-18, and Article IV, Section 3, Clause 2 of the Constitution for the United States. The terms "United States" and "U.S." are NOT to be construed to mean or include the sovereign, united 50 States of America.

Neither born nor naturalized in the "United States" nor "subject to its jurisdiction", I am NOT and never have been, as described in 26 CFR 1.1-1(c) and the 14th Amendment, a "U.S. citizen". Therefore, I am an "alien" with respect to the "United States".

I am NOT and never have been, as described in 26 USC 865(g)(1)(A), a "resident of the U.S."

I have NEVER made, with ANY "knowingly intelligent acts" (Brady v. U.S., 397 U.S. 742,748), ANY voluntary election under 26 USC 6013 or 26 CFR 1.871-4 to be treated as a "U.S. resident alien" for any purpose. Further, I have utterly NO intention of making any such election in the future.

I AM a Sovereign American Citizen.

I AM a non-taxpayer.

I am NOT and never have been, as described in 26 USC 7701 (a)(30), a "U.S. person".

I am NOT and never have been, as described in 26 USC 7701 (a)(14), a "taxpayer".

I do NOT have and have never had, as described in 26 USC 911 (d)(3), a "tax home within the U.S."

I AM outside the general venue and jurisdiction of the United States federal government.

I am NOT and never have been, as described in 26 USC 3401, an "officer", or an "employee", or an "elected official" of the "United States", of a "State" or of any political subdivision thereof, nor of the District of Columbia, nor of a "domestic" corporation, earning "wages" from an "employer".

I am NOT and never have been, as described in 31 USC 3713, a "fiduciary", or, as described in 26 USC 6901, a "transferee" or a "transferee of a transferee".

I am NOT and never have been, as described in 26 USC Subtitle B, a "donor" or a "contributor", and as a Sovereign American Citizen, I am EXEMPT from any gift tax under 26 USC Subtitle B.

As a Sovereign American Citizen NOT engaged in or effectively connected with any "trade or business within the United States", I am NOT REQUIRED by law to obtain a "U.S. Taxpayer Identification Number or a Social Security Number because of my exemption under 26 CFR 301.6109-1(g). Further, I am NOT REQUIRED by law to make, as described in 26 CFR 1.6015(a)-1, a "declaration" because I am exempt under 26 CFR 1.6015(I)-1 and fundamental law.

As a Sovereign American Citizen, I have no "self-employment income".

As a Sovereign American Citizen, I derive NO "gross income... from sources within the United States", either "effectively connected" or "not effectively connected with the conduct of a trade or business in the United States", as described in 26 USC 872(a).

As a Sovereign American Citizen, my private-sector remuneration is "from sources without the United States" as described in 26 CFR 1.1441-3(a), and does NOT constitute 26 USC 3401 "wages", and is therefore NOT "subject to" mandatory with-holding under 26 USC 3402(a), 3101(a), or 26 CFR 1.144-1) because of its' EXEMPTION under 26 USC 3401 (a)(6) and FUNDAMENTAL LAW.

As a Sovereign American Citizen, I NEVER intentionally made, with ANY "knowingly intelligent acts", ANY voluntary with-holding "agreement" as described in 26 USC 3402(p).

As a Sovereign American Citizen, my income is NOT included as "gross income" under Subtitle A and is EXEMPT from with holding.

As a Sovereign American Citizen, with NO income from sources within the United States", my private-sector, NON-"U.S." income is FREE from all federal tax under <u>fundamental Law</u>. (see Treasury Decisions 3146 and 3640, and <u>United States v. Morris, 125 F.Rept. 322,331</u>).

As a Sovereign American Citizen, my estate and/or trust is, as described in 26 USC 7701(a)(31), a TAX-EXEMPT "foreign estate or trust".

As a "natural born Citizen" (see II:1:5 of the Constitution) and a free Sovereign American Citizen, I did NEVER voluntarily, intentionally waive, with ANY "knowingly intelligent acts", ANY of my unalienable rights, and, have utterly NO intention of doing so in the future. Any prima facie evidence, or presumption to the contrary is hereby rebutted. Any past signatures on IRS and SSA forms, statements, etc. were in error and involuntarily made under threat, duress and coercion. I hereby revoke, cancel and render void, <u>Nunc Pro Tunc</u>, both currently and retroactively to the time of signing, any and all such signatures. I reserve my Common Law right, NOT to be compelled to perform under any agreement that I have not entered into <u>knowingly, voluntarily, and intentionally</u>.

I am NOT a 26 USC 7203 "person required". I am a <u>non-taxpayer</u>, outside both general and tangential venue and jurisdiction of Title 26, United States Codes.

Pursuant to 28 USC 1746(1) and executed "without the United States", I affirm under penalty of perjury, under the Laws of the united States of America that the foregoing is true and correct, to the best of my belief and informed knowledge. Further, This Affiant Saith Not.

Subscribed, sealed and affirmed, this _____ day of _____, in the year of our Lord, _____, Anno Domini.

! hereby affix my own signature to all of the above affirmations with explicit reservation of ALL unalienable rights, without prejudice to ANY of those rights.

<u>Name, Citizen/Principal</u>, by Special Appearance, in Propria Persona, proceeding Sui Juris, with Assistance, Special, "Without Prejudice" to ANY of my unalienable rights.

*Source: Goodbye April 15th! By Boston T. Party.

(Javelin Press <u>www.javelinpress.com</u>   877-300-9001)

Chapter 3

For some unknown, inexplicable reason, the health and well being of "our" ill and elderly, is not, and has never been, a priority of the Republican Congress. Quite the contrary! When the Clinton administration introduced, "national health care" and prescription drug benefits to Congress, for their consideration, the "Republicants", (rather than helping to implement them, by seeking ways to help make it happen), deplored them, and insisted it/they were "a terrible idea".

Remember now, national health care is a terrible idea. What we really need is more money to/for the rich, and a national (star war) missile defense system. The health and well being of our peoples is not a priority, but, missiles and military hardware is. They profess endlessly, and so eloquently, of the sanctity of life. Then, luridly walk away, only concerned with ledgers and lucre, not life! Their hardened hearts have not noticed the "sanctity of life", all about them, old and young! We are here, everyone, each and all, living about us, now and eternally! How could, and why would, grown men be, and remain so insensitive, so misguided? Money!

The HMOs' are one of the largest contributors to the Republican't Party. Their money paid for "corporate" airtime, (during election time, is approximately one million dollars a second) abstinently criticizing, any, and/or all, health care initiatives. Our most puzzling, legislative reality, is "lobbyists"! Why should corporate, HMO lobbyists, have any influence whatsoever, over "our" legislators? Remember now, the Republicans want you to believe that "national health care", is a bad thing, and national missile defense, (war-mongering) is a good thing.

Do you agree? Healing people is a contingency, killing people is a policy! You have to be a Republican't (Repulsive Con) to even be involved with such an initiative, as hindering health care for all! How could any public servant, work to hinder, or endanger the health, and access to qualified health care, from any Citizen? Any other position or prerogative, held by any public servant, other than full access, by all, of all, for all, on a national basis is unacceptable!

Ask yourself this simple question. Why are the HMOs' contributing to the Republican Party? The answer is as obvious as the question is simple. They want their laws passed, treatments withheld, (gag rule) and profits maintained. The sad truth about the "HMO Policies" is; The Republican'ts are there for them, and their profits!

Did you know that Canada's elderly pay three dollars, for the same pill that our elderly pay ten? The pill is made in America, packaged and shipped to Canada, and sold there for 70% less. What happened to the packing and shipping charges? How can they pay less?

Obviously, our public servants are not concerned about our public welfare! Obviously! Can any of those public servants, explain to me why, we should pay more for a local product, than we would pay, after it is shipped out of the country? You have to be a Republican't (Repulsive Con) to legitimize and/or condone such a process that so clearly harms our elderly!

The Publics' Health and well being, as I said earlier, is not a priority of the Republican congress. Quite the contrary, they are opposed to it! On March the 7th, 2001, the Republican led Congress initiated, and passed, "for the first time ever", a "Congressional Revue Act". Must be important! What were they reviewing? The ergonomics laws, pertaining to workplace safety and "your rights", while performing your job duties, and when, or, if injured! Why were they reviewing a "ten-year old law", enacted to insure and protect the health of Americas' workers? Because "they", no longer viewed it as a protective measure, and a legislated law, they viewed it as an unnecessary expense, quote; "an extreme problem". End quote!

The "inexplicable revelation" of the "first ever", "Congressional Revue Act" was espoused, to remedy an "an extreme problem"! How? By terminating "it", worker safety rights, that "is"! What is wrong with that example? Our "elite" legislators were (sent?) to Washington, to manage the general interests of the Citizens!

Instead, they "gave up", on securing a safe workplace and your workplace rights, because it posed, "an extreme problem". They gave-up! After a (mandated) ten year study, "they gave-up", because the problem was really, really, really "extreme"? "Believe it or not", our current public servants repealed the ergonomics laws due for implementation on April 1st 2001, "on the grounds" that it was "an extreme problem"! Duhhh? They don't do extreme problems??? They don't do extreme problems!

They don't do humanitarian, common man problems! They repeal them!

The work place safety laws were yet to be implemented, and thus, their effects were unknown, yet the Republican'ts viewed them as "an extreme problem". Even though, in places where OSHA standards have been implemented, accidents are down, and profits are up. The ergonomics laws recently Re-viewed and Re-pealed (by Repulsive Republican'ts) were the product of a ten-year study, mandated by congress. We had a congress, (the congress of the year 1991A.D.,) that was convinced that something must be done about employee' conditions, and workplace safety! They were so convinced, that they mandated (ordered) a ten year study, to learn more, about how to best solve the problems, plaguing hundreds of thousands of their fellowman!

Yes! Butt! The Republicans in "this" Congress, viewed the policies of that 1991 Congress, and its' ten-year study, and the law mandating its' implementation, as "the problem"! Again, they did not help to implement it. They Re-viewed it and determined that it, was "an extreme problem". "They", the Reviewing, Reforming, Revamping, Repealing, Republican't party, are the "extreme problem"!

A ten-year study, mandated by Congress, performed by medical experts, insurers, OSHA, and on site employee feedback, to help develop common sense, common concern policies, to improve workplace safety, was Re-viewed by the 2001 Re-publican't Congress, and Re-pealed on grounds of being "an extreme problem". Your right to a healthy, safe, and considerate work place, was dismissed, and Re-pealed on the "grounds", of being an "extreme problem"!

Those Re-publicans view all common man, civic-minded agendas as an "extreme problem". National health care is an extreme problem, workplace safety is an extreme problem, a minimum wage hike for our neediest, is an extreme problem! But, a $14,000.00 tax refund for each and every legislator, is no problem!

The ergonomic laws, previously scheduled to be implemented, April 1st 2001, concluding a "mandated" ten year study, by Congress, were Re-viewed by this congress, for one hour. After one hour of debate on March 7th 2001, and after ten years of study, it was repealed! "WE" are Aprils' 1st Fools! Aprils' First, Workplace Fools! They have, Re-pealed the implementation of "our long awaited", and well-deserved safety, and medical criteria standards, for every person. Why?

They were viewed and Re-viewed by the "HMOs", then, were determined to be an "extreme problem"! Employers and insurers would have been held to a higher and more humane standard. Thus, the HMOs' objected and the Republican'ts re-acted.

Again the Republicans have sabotaged the workings of a worthy effort, concerning the health and lawful rights of their fellow man, and His workplace environment. We are left with the "Doctrine of Employment at Will", also known as "at will to work". It is simply a contractual policy, protecting corporations, etc. You're fired at will, scheduled at will, transferred at will, rescheduled at will, all at the will, of an employer. In an "at will to work state" you could be subjected to a negligent injury on the job, "and" a negligent medical practice following, with little, and/or no right to sue! Most Americans spend a third of their lives in a workplace environment, should it be, or not be, responsive to workers' needs?

Chapter 4

How long will we consciously ignore our worldwide human condition, and the ever progressive, continual degradation, of our only home? The one and only environment within our known universe, to our knowledge, "that is capable", of sustaining human life! Earth, the one and only! Then! Where do we go? We go nowhere! THEN! That's IT! Game Over!

How much CO_2 can earth and humanity endure? Do we really want to know? How many deserts are we to create? How many oceans, lakes and rivers will we poison? How many species will we eliminate, through manmade poisons, within our polluted environments, killing both predator and prey? How many droughts, floods, El Ninos (lost coral banks) and poisoned ecosystems will we endure, before we consciously, and wholeheartedly address our planets' continual degradation?

Not only are we the "worlds' most prolific polluter", we are also, the worlds' most prolific war-monger. We have no qualms about, or contenders to, the numbers of landmines laid throughout Cambodia, by US forces! Uncle Scam is the most "prolific abuser" on the planet, and, the number one, "Grand Poo Baa of pollution" is none other than George Bush Jr. He recently, and bewilderingly, neglected to attend the recent "Kyoto Treaty", environmental summit, held in South America in September of 2001. (I'm dumbfounded by his lack of concern, but not surprised!)

By deserting his duty to attend the summit, he thereby, helped to withhold US ratification of The Kyoto Treaty. His reason was to, quote; "pursue a separate coarse of action". End quote! He has again, disregarded another worthy purpose, being pursued, for a healthier mankind. Ref.- On March 7, 2001 the Republicans (after a ten-year study to implement) repealed the workplace ergonomics laws, that "would have" protected your health and medical rights in case of a workplace accident.

Who is he, to unpretentiously think, that the protocol of The Kyoto Treaty, and the wishes of a majority of the people of all nations of the Earth, are irrelevant to, his pursuit of a "separate coarse of action".

Are you gonna clean it up yeself, George? George, you are the "Grand Poo Baa of pollution".

Your voluntary pollution standards took Houston straight to number one, and the current title-holder of "most polluted city" in the nation, bar none! How many ice statues will melt away, into trays of wine and caviar, before the eyes our wasteful legislators, before they change their silly, harmful ways?

Unconcerned, inapt, and superfluously greedy, is the only way to describe our, so-called leaders, within the litigating parties. Why did our poorest workers, not deserve a minimum wage hike, but congressional legislators deserved a $14,000 tax refund? Greed! Superfluous Greed! Greed beyond need! Greed before need!

The abundance bequeathed us, by our God and creator, is sustained only by our thankful awareness and respect, of its' glorious bounty! The seasons of nature are understood. Therefore we must respect the bountiful glory of Gods' creation, and His will, and live in harmony with the laws of nature, as is our intended destiny.

Conquering, plundering, degrading and wasting our natural gifts robs mankind of a most cherished legacy, (a healthy life and habitat) in a once, pristine garden.

Consider the future of our young, and remember, "we do not inherit this planet from our parents, we borrow it from our children"!

Point of Order; The allegedly "protected?" Orka Whales, of the Northern Pacific Ocean, are dying at an alarming rate. Massive amounts of man-made toxins in their systems are poisoning them, through their food supply. The carcasses are so heavily contaminated that, when any are washed ashore, they are considered to be a serious health hazard, and must be declared and treated as "toxic waste"!

Chapter 5

Our governing representatives are funding a crazed, oil speculator, with a no-bid Haliburton contract, and his misguided, self-induced, lingering war. A war based admittedly, by George Bush Jr., on faulty information. Weapons inspectors were on the ground in Iraq, (yet George pulled them out), at the time he professed (lied) that weapons of mass destruction were present. Yet, he pulled inspectors out!

The U.S. continues to build, sell, and distribute all forms of deadly, destructive technology, for that war, and throughout the world, (Lebanon) rather than food, blankets, tractors and seed? WHY? Because there is more money made, selling war!

It is totally bewildering to me that our congressmen find a need for a multi-billion-dollar national defense (warmonger) budget, yet consider a "national health care plan" as unfeasible! Which programs are "We" funding, and to what end? Congressmen please note; It is not us or them! It is, us and them! Yes, it is simply "<u>Us</u>"! All of Us! Consciously honoring the presence of each eternal soul, at every encounter. Do unto others as you would have done unto you, is our purpose.

You gentlemen have abandoned your duty, to the general interests of the People! The turmoil evidenced within the Legislatures is a clear example of private interest lobbying, asserting its demands over the general interests of the People.

Repeatedly, our legislators profess only slanderous accusations at one another, blaming all constituents, on "the other side of the isle"! Could they be, more childish? I think not!

The overkill capabilities of our nuclear arsenals, still at cold war readiness, throughout the world (well over three thousand) is more than enough radioactive weaponry to fry the entire earth for generations to come. We now exist, "on the edge" of self-annihilation, maintained by a few "elite idiots" in Washington D.C., claiming it, a matter of "our" national security. How could world annihilation, insure "our" national security?

We invest billions of undisclosed tax dollars into CIA, and national defense. The same national defense, that failed to deter, the Iraqi troop build-up along the Kuwaiti border, and/or, the subsequent invasion.

History reveals that the Bush Sr. administration ignored the evidence/ fact of a prospective invasion, and all of the prospective tyrannies associated with that fact! Then, "after ignoring those truculent acts of intended aggression", came the murderous invasion and plunder of Kwaite. Shortly thereafter, "Desert Storm", and after only three days, our brave men had won the (inevitable?) war.

But, the murdering tyrant was not subdued, or held accountable. The facts are, the Bush administration restored the perpetrators, ("Saddam and his chain of command") to power!

Speaking of facts, consider this fact! During the time of the Iraqi troop buildup along the Kwaite border, George Bush Sr. sent a "female diplomat", to confront a maniacal, Islamic dictator. The fact that Islamic traditions view the female, as a second class citizen, with no authority and no recognition, leads me to ask. George, why did you send a female diplomat, to confront the Islamic dictator, whose tanks were poised at the Kwaite border? Didn't your CIA friends inform you of Muslim traditions, concerning "the" women?

Islamic men do not, "respect or recognize" the will of a "simple female"! The probable reaction was that Saddam and his comrades were insulted! In any case, history reveals that the (female) diplomat in question was unsuccessful! I would also ask, under the right to information act that a certified, full and true copy of the diplomatic decree presented to Saddam Hussein, be posted on the Internet.

Speaking of the CIA, look at the record of its' two most notable alumni, two men, who consecutively headed the CIA, in the recent past. I refer to ex-president Bush, and the person that replaced him as head of CIA, Richard (Dick) Chaney. After George Bush Sr. was elected as president, he moved Chaney from head of CIA, to Secretary of Defense. Ask yourself, why was Chaney appointed, from the private sector, to head our armed forces? Because the Secretary of Defense commands our armed forces, appropriates the military budget, and determines its dispersal.

Another interesting fact about this dynamic duo is, "they, and they alone", deserve all of the credit for "restoring" Saddam Hussein to power! National forces engaged, suppressed, and arrested the entire Iraqi army, in two days.

The following day they engaged and dismantled the Royal Guard, thereby ending the war of wars, after only three days! Iraq was "conquered"! Baghdad was surrounded, Saddam and his culpable generals were "completely defenseless"! General Shwartzkauf had accomplished total submission! What happened then?

The most contemptible, objectionable, "unjustifiable act" of the 20th century! Cease and Desist, came the order, given by Bush Sr. and his Secretary of Defense, Dick Chaney! Cease and Desist? They waited until Kwaiti had been invaded, its' citizens killed, and properties plundered, before they opposed Saddam.

Then, they pulled our troops out, after, he was subdued and surrounded! American troops handily defeated his army, and his Royal Guard, and effectively subdued him to complete helplessness, then, they freed him to kill again!

The only remaining duty before our heroic soldiers was to arrest Saddam, a vile entity of death and torment, "now" a conquered war criminal, and his culpable chain of command.

Ask yourself, what if Roosevelt and his Secretary of Defense had left Hitler, and his chain of command in power? Only a "Repulsive Con" would somehow try to justify the logic of leaving a murdering tyrant in power, after he was effectively subdued! Was that choice, part of his "sanctity of life" policy? Was it pro-life?

What now, of the plight, of the innocent Iraqi people? Did Dick and George, not consider them? Obviously not! How else could the Iraqi army, again, be killing its' own people, and firing air to ground missiles at our pilots? PS-Days of No-Fly Zone!

Why did George Bush Sr. and Dick Chaney, "cease and desist" the victory in Iraq? Money? "Mindin" our defense dollars? Not! George Bush and Dick Chaney are each, heavily invested in the oil industry.

Consider the amount of oil, lost and/or burned, and question, which oil executives were likely to lose the most, and what could be done to secure their interests? After Saddams' Royal Guard was crushed, the "War of Wars" was over, and he was revealed, a paper tiger! Did he call? Did he agree to pay for all oil losses, interest and fines? Did the order, then go out? Cease and desist!

We have had treaties sense we've had print! Yet, we still have over 3,000 deadly nuclear missiles ready for launch. To what end? Why, do we pour billions of dollars into nuclear silos?

Why are we maintaining world destruction capabilities? Why is the mightiest nation of the world, allied with twelve others, fearing its' future? What are we to fear? But, an unworthy desire! And! THE WAR MONGERS!

We "must" initiate a worldwide unilateral dismantling of all nuclear weapons!

Or! Face Pandora, and her consequence!   "THE END!"

Chapter 6

We the People, "as sovereign Citizens", (the highest office holders within this self-governing free society), must unite, declare and demand our sovereign rights, and we must also demand accountability, from/of, "our" elected representatives.

Currently "our" representatives, are elected through their "Electoral College" system, which has twice overturned the mandate of the national vote, and thereby, the true will of the People. Our representatives were assigned the duty, of securing and protecting the life, rights and property of the sovereign People.

So, the question must be asked; Are you aware of your status/birthright as a sovereign American? Are you fully informed of your "Common Law" birthrights, and do you have alluvial title to your land? If not, you have been misrepresented, denied and deceived!

Yet, if any public servant violates the law, he/she can somehow claim, and be granted, diplomatic immunity from prosecution, "if needed". That is, if/when a resignation from office didn't resolve the criminal issue at hand.

The facts pertaining to Secetary of State John Poindexters' involvement with Iran/Contra were not revealed until John Poindexter was granted "IMMUNITY"!

Of course, they want accountability, from all people, that are, and are not, accountable to "their civil statutes". The common man is considered and judged by "Uncle Scam", as a second class citizen. Why? Because Uncle Scam has "cleverly?" suppressed your sovereign rights, those given by God, and secured in the Bible and Declaration of Independence. "Uncle Scam" has replaced them with "civil privileges", through deceptive wording in 14th Amendment and HJR192 - Trading With the Enemies Act, signed June Fifth 1933A.D., Your "certificate of birth" informs of your "port of entry", and also signifies your citizenship, and, "enrolls you" into a matriculated, corporate enterprise, as "a corporate entity", by you're unawares!

Your "nom de guerre"–(WAR NAME) informs all agents, of your status as an impoverished subject, under Emergency Powers Acts, yet to be repealed, and that you are "allegedly" accountable to an admiralty jurisdiction, which is brought under "color of law". The very nature and purpose of (they're!) Admiralty court system is, to simply do what King George did to the colonists! Extort, from their fellowman, with no just claim and/or no true cause! We the People, now, "exist" under government issued "civil privileges", through treason, fraud, and deception.

The "sovereign rights", of "we the People", claimed by our forefathers, after winning the Revolutionary War, have effectively been removed, and surrendered to the morally deficient, corrupt and treasonous Federal government, which, defrauded us of them! Now, all unknowing "sovereign Americans", mistakenly believe, that they are corporate U.S. citizens, accountable to all "commercial codes", statutes and ordinances, of any and every particular county or state, regardless of the fact that those claims, abrogate "our" constitutional rights.

Is there any accountability, demanded of our legislators for anything they've ever done? For blatantly, "abrogating, and hiding our sovereign rights"? No! Quite the contrary! The speech and debate clause amended into the constitution, "allows" government officials, (public servants) to somehow obtain "IMMUNITY", aka "Diplomatic Immunity" from prosecution! If, caught red-handed, they simply resign, or claim some statutory immunity, or they're pardoned! Will the Lord consider their resignation, or diplomatic status?

"If", sabotaging Viet Nam peace talks, or, hiding that "fact" for thirty-three years. Or, if the Warren Commission upholds the physically impossible, "single bullet theory" espoused by Arlen Spectre. Or, if they don't recall arming the contra!

Or, if they empty the contents of the Savings and Loan, or, leave Saddam Hussien in power, or, they drain the entire state fund from California, or/then, they extort the entire 401K retirement fund of all of Enrons' employees, and then, "they" become bankrupt?

Then, they resign, or are pardoned, or, are not charged! Point of order! *John Ashcroft recused himself from prosecuting, the largest and most blatant (trading floors closed for 20 days with no notice of solvency) abuse of banking laws, and bankruptcy fraud in American history!

Therefore, what should we do? Our "silly" government officials are, in no way, a glowing example of accountability.

Mr. Bush Sr., please give us an account the circumstances of the savings and loan debacle, during your administration, and your sons' leadership! George Jr., why did your appointee to the Securities and Exchange Commission "allow" Enron to close its' trading windows for twenty days, with no access for stockholders, until the accounts were plundered? Why did the SEC allow Californias' entire general fund to be extorted, by the fraudulent and corrupt marketing procedures, (blackouts!) used by the (now! "bankrupt?") Enron corporation? George Jr., why did your SEC appointee resign?

The people within the federal government often "seize" homes, freeze assets, and/or imprison people, for any number of groundless, victimless charges. They, the government, place fraudulent taxes, and equity court claims on your property, that must be subdued or paid, or they will file for your eviction. Then, they often do, evict "YOU", the rightful owner, without lawful cause, if you let them!

Yet, no Congressman can be questioned or charged by police, if he/she chooses to ignore them. They ignore them! They also ignore the IRS, while they are fraudulently claiming your home and property, for taxes, you never actually owed!

They ignore the fact that "our" liberty is not to be infringed upon, without a sworn affidavit by an injured party. Further, the "State" of Texas, has "no" public defenders office in the entire state! Call information, look it up in the book, or go to jail, and you will realize, there is no public defender, in the entire state of Texas!

I Reckon! What we have out here is Judge Roy Bean, and the "misinformed" Texas Rangers! Raging against, a misled, misinformed, misrepresented, and vulnerable public, in an "at will to work" state.

Do we really need an "elite" group of people, in our government, "above the law", working in turmoil and division among themselves, deciding "our" methods and priorities? I think not! My colleague, "on the other side of the isle", is the political way of saying; the moral abyss between these two parties, is intransigent and incorrigible. "Our" legislators are so adapted to the unproductive and combative nature of their appointments, that they insist on stalling, blaming and/or stopping anyone, "on the other side of the isle", with little if any concern for, or dedication to, improving the public welfare.

It has become, their standard procedure, and it is quite obvious to those of us that observe, from an unbiased prerogative, that, the first priority of every candidate is, to place blame, "on the other side of the isle", then, apply his efforts toward the wishes of his campaign contributors!

If you question the truth and accuracy of the previous sentence, ask yourself, why do Canadians pay seventy percent less for their "American made" prescription medications, than any American senior? The simple answer would be; Canadas' national buying power, versus an HMO controlled congress. "A house divided cannot stand"! A Congress and Senate so incorrigibly divided, should not stand!

We are no longer in a civil war, until one enters the halls of "our" incorrigible Congressmen! The partisan behavior exhibited in the halls of Congress is, "one would think" a clear symptom of a nationwide problem, "failure to communicate"! Actually, they've all agreed, too disagree! Gridlock, effectively secures their positions, and their means. Note the "Gorilla of Gridlock" only appears, when debating petitions such as Campaign Finance Reform, and the repeal of the "archaic and corrupt" Electoral College Laws!

Obviously, no one is policing the police, and or, the "silly" lawmakers, "above their laws". "A house divided can not stand", so, why do we continue to elect and inaugurate an incorrigible Congress, separated by a moral abyss, they refer to as, "the other side of the isle"? For all practical purposes, and in lieu their ongoing "failure to communicate", our legislators could be on the other side of the "planet", any planet! Pick one!

The overwhelmingly encumbering, and combative nature of our legislators, is inherent of "our silly party" system, and the archaic ballot counting laws of the Electoral College. The purposes of the two perspectives are known, and are rarely, if ever, in agreement. Why do we encourage our incorrigible Congressmen? "Our" Senate is there to modify a united, purposeful, and truly concerned Congress, not an incorrigible one, voicing a demeaning explicative, at a designated counterpart, on the other side of the "world" isle.

Republicans are against a national health care, and prescription drug benefits, they're against a minimum wage hike! But, they're not against a $14,000 tax break, for themselves! They have repealed "your" workplace safety standards, after a 1991 Congressionally mandated and thoroughly subjective, ten-year study, had determined, needs and parameters.

They accomplished this traitorous act, with the first ever, "Congressional Revue Act"! The "first ever" CRA repealed worker rights.

At a recent interview George Bush Jr. said, Quote; "we're running "our" members through the system". Mathew-5; 46-47 states; 46: For if you love them which love you, what reward have ye? Do not even the publicans the same? 47: And if ye salute your brethren only, what do ye more than others? Do not even the publicans so?

Take a close look at the multi-billion dollar budget and priorities of Ronald "I Don't Recall" Reagan, and his hand picked predecessor, George W. Bush Sr. Those men accumulated billions of dollars into the office of "The Secretary of Defense".

Yet, prior to Desert Storm, and under the "leadership" of George Bush Sr. and his new Secretary of Defense, Dick Chaney, "a female diplomat" was dispatched to approach Saddam, in an effort to address -(ignore) troop buildup along the Kwaiti border! They sent (a female diplomat, April Glaspie, to address Sadamm Hussein). Need I Say More? Our silly politicians declared war on a maniac in Iraq. Yet, chose to "restore" him to power, after his armies were arrested and/or defeated in only three days. We warred on a maniac in power, won that war, and then, restored that maniacal tyrant to power. ***Bush and Chaney, restored that maniac to power!

Consider the postwar Iraqi troop build up along the Kwaite border, and the fact that the Bush administration sent a diplomat to address the problem. The diplomat dispatched, by the Bush administration, to counsel with the fanatical "Muslim" dictator, in command, and responsible for the troop buildup, was a woman!

And, aside from that incomprehensible fact, her diplomatic decree stated to Saddam; "This administration has no opinion about your border dispute with Kwaite"! Imagine that! The Bush administration "had no opinion" about the "armored tank divisions" that were moving into position along the border of neighboring Kwaite. They had no opinion, concerning the truculent acts of aggression by a tyrannical dictator, poised to commit mass genocide, on innocent people! They had no opinion! The "sanctity of life" administration, had no opinion.

Our efforts in the Gulf War were Herculean, yet we had no opinion about their border dispute with Kwaite. Yet, the result was actually, a self-imposed defeat!

Why did they, (Bush Sr. as president and Dick Chaney as Secretary of Defense), return deadly weaponry to the Iraqi army, and "restore" Saddam to power?

Could it be that Bush and Chaney were among a group of oilmen that stood to lose millions? Did Saddam call and agree to pay for the oil fires and the interest on the lost income? Did Dick and George simply call General Swartzcoff, and order him to "Cease and Desist"?

Woe unto them that draw iniquity with cords of vanity, and sin as it were with a cart rope. Woe unto them that call evil good, and good evil; that put darkness for light, and light for darkness; that put bitter for sweet, and sweet for bitter! Woe unto them that are wise in their own eyes, and prudent in their own sight! Woe unto them that are mighty to drink wine, and men of strength to mingle strong drink; Which justify the wicked for reward, and take away the righteousness of the righteous from him. Therefore as the fire devoureth the stubble, and the flame consumeth the chaff, so their root shall be as rotteness and their blossom shall go up as dust: because they have cast away the law of the Lord of hosts, and despised the word of the Holy One of Isreal.

Why do "our" esteemed legislators continually mimic the pointless bickering, slanderous accusations, self-centered filibusters, and the "other side of the isle mentality" of all preceding politicians? A two party system, especially "our" current, "silly party system", where beauraucrats count only "their" _electoral_ votes is shameful, and, as far from a true Republic as any system could be.

The "Electoral College" system of electing representatives is shamefully archaic and only leads to corruption, contempt and confusion. A candidate was "selected", even though the national totals mandated another candidate, namely, Al Gore.

We are one people, and should be led by a single party, "accountable" for "their" actions. The bickering simpletons, imbedded in the present political arena, serve no purpose, only a single, corrupt intent. Voice a pure purpose, or be silent, and wait upon a worthy revelation. We cannot be united if indeed we are at odds. With one party, and one purpose, all are encouraged to vote and to serve. This would also effectively eliminate the current, divisive and combative nature of our present system of government.

It would also eliminate all excuses, normally directed toward, and/or associated with, "constituents", "on the other side of the -world- isle".

My distinguished colleague, "Mr. other side of the isle" is an eloquent orator. He is thoughtful, diligent, concerned, purposeful and completely devoted to his appointment and his duties in this great institution. He is a fine gentleman!

But! He is dead wrong, totally misguided, completely out of touch, unaware of the consequences of his actions, doesn't understand the basic fundamentals of this bill, and is holding this bill up in conference, etc. So, it's his fault!

Will we let a division of bickering voices, stumbling blocks, single priorities, greed and self-induced ignorance, stop a truly worthy mission? I think not. A voice of a pure purpose, will I echo! Let not the bickering of wrongful appeasers' change the true intent of your heart. Each has been set unto a mission. It is your duty to realize the manner and purpose of that mission. To ignore or to leave your brother hungry is to wallow in blindness. Open your eyes to see, your heart to give, and your voice to declare. Know from where you came, and realize a great knowledge.

George Bush Sr. sent a woman to face an Islamic tyrant. Why? Did the CIA not inform him of the females' status, in that country? Our intelligence agency sent a "female" diplomat, "who had to be rejected", considering present Muslim protocol.

Our fine young men answered the call, fought a war against tyranny, won it, then the "dynamic duo" of Bush & Chaney left that tyrannical murderer in power. But, Dick and George have -"HAD"- agreed that he is/was an acceptable end!

The pseudo pious Republicans, who claim to be pro-life, have now, falsely initiated a lingering war, contemptuously abandoned the Iraqi people, the Haitians, those in West Timar, and countless others, to certain death.

Do you recall the documented atrocities in Haiti during the 80s and early 90s under Raul Sedras? Here, again the Republican Party demonstrated a complete lack of moral empathy, or concern for innocent lives lost. A worthy leader must demonstrate respect for each life, contempt for tyranny, and a truly diligent commitment to a worthy purpose, as the cornerstone of all decisions. While ignoring human atrocities, we become accessories to those atrocities. At the very least our moral consciousness is condemned, and we are guilty by neglect.

Human rights, peace of mind, freedom and brotherhood are not, only relevant, within Americas' borders.

We will all be better off, when we're all better off. Do you desire for all things or, for things for all? Brotherhood and honor of mankind should not end at our border, any longer! Know, the longer we ignore abuses and tyranny, the stronger a tyrant becomes, and many more innocent people, suffer or die! The Republicans, under Reagan and Bush Sr., continually chose to ignore the innocent women and children dying in Haiti. Even though the murder scenes and body counts, were documented by American film crews and journalists on a treacherous, deadly, daily basis. Those atrocities happened in our own hemisphere, approximately 100 miles away, and were documented by American news and film crews. Yet, Reagan, Bush and a Republican congress chose to ignore those ruthless murderers, for twelve deadly years. Reagan increased the military budget by multi-billions, and ignored a ruthless dictator one hundred miles away. His hand picked replacement, George Bush Sr., chose to do the same.

It was not until 1993, when Bill Clinton allowed Jimmy Carter and Colen Powell to fly to Haiti, (to convince Raul Sedras of his last opportunity to leave Haiti), that a just action was taken. In short, they informed him, the marines are airborne and their mission is to "arrest or kill you".

By simply confronting Sedras, they replaced him with a democratic government, with no further lives lost, American or otherwise! Obviously, human rights means very little to the Republican Party, unless you are an American, and a rich one.

Those pompous Republicans claim to be pro life. Yet, history reveals their indignant behavior, concerning the innocent women and children being killed on an on-going basis in Haiti, and appearing nightly, lying dead before their eyes, on all major stations. Yet, George Bush Sr. decided that the death of innocent Haitian women and children was not his problem, and no soldiers lives, would be risked!

Why did George Sr. and Dick decide to leave Saddam Hussein in power? Those pompous Republicans want us to believe that they are pro life. How can one turn a blind eye on cold-blooded murderers, and be pro-life? Did Dick and George consider the rights of the Iraqi people, or the capabilities of Saddam, to pay for the oil fires and interest on "their" losses?

I wonder if Saddam suspended payments while Clinton was in office? Is that why, as soon as George Jr. "got in", it was bombs away? Check the record, George Jr. struck twice! He bombed Iraqi "positions", on the second day, of his ill-gotten station.

Then, lacking foresight and compassion, he defiantly professed his total support for Israel. While, he ignored the recent trespasses by Prime Minister Sherron, of a Palestine holy sight, and the continued "unlawful" occupation of Palestine.

As compared to other U.S. Presidents, and (his war) foreign policy, George Jr. would also have to be considered miserably dysfunctional. Was Richard Nixon, not a crook, when He deliberately sabotaged the Vietnam peace talks? Were the depictions of a nationwide public documentary true? Did Richard Nixon sabotage the Vietnam peace talks? Each time the peace talks were postponed, Johnson fell drastically in the polls. Was Nixon as alleged in the documentary, tempted into sabotaging the peace talks?

Allegedly, he insured that the dates for the talks were always misunderstood. Did Lyndon Johnson record his treasonous efforts, and blackmail him? Nixon was also implicated (caught) for ordering the break-in of the democratic headquarters. What was "Tricky Nick" trying to retrieve from the Watergate building?

Yet, beyond question, one of the most diabolically proficient politicians of my generation, as history has now revealed, was hands down, Lyndon Johnson.

Shortly after John Kennedys' assassination, the first Executive Order by Lyndon Baines Johnson, now President Johnson was to rescind Kennedy's Executive Order 11110, and to initiate Executive Order #10289 signed June 4, 1963, and to destroy all "silver certificates" that had been printed.

He further espoused the posture of the "Federal Reserve", when he told the American People that, silver had become "too" valuable to be used as "money". Duh? Too! What? Too, valuable? Our "legal tender" was intended to be substantive!

He then signed an act on July 23rd, 1965, authorizing the issuance of copper clad coins to replace "our" silver coins, and burned President Kennedys' worthy, purposeful legacy of "Silver Certificates"!

That treasonous act was a direct violation of Article 1, Section 10, clause 1, of the Constitution. Quote; "No State shall... coin money; emit bills of credit; make anything but gold and silver coin a tender in payment of debts..." End Quote!

Fifty million "worthless" Federal Reserve Notes, which are not redeemable in silver, and, when tendered, can only "discharge"(set aside) a debt, were released into circulation on the day of President Kennedy's funeral! The purposeful effort by John Fitzgerald Kennedy, to re-implement silver certificates into circulation, and its' promise was tragically ended. Yet, evidence of his effort, his "honorable legacy" is become, our best example of a necessary step to assure true prosperity among the populous. As contemptuous and disheartening as it is, those silver certificates, the security, prosperity, and true promise, which they would have brought to our nation, were burned, on the same day that John Fitzgerald Kennedy was buried!

A televised documentary alleged, that Lyndon Johnson, deliberately, with malice and intent, withheld the tapes of recorded phone conversations, proving Richard Nixons' efforts in sabotaging the Vietnam peace talks, from authorities and public knowledge. He allegedly recorded, indubitably conclusive evidence, incriminating Richard Nixon, and proving his culpable connection, with sabotaging the Viet Nam peace talks. Yet, that alleged proof was with held from public knowledge. If as alleged, with such evidence on Nixon, (now in his possession) Johnson could run the White House, irrelevant of the fact that Nixon won the election!

Could that possibly explain the nagging question of why Richard Nixon, taped all White House meetings? Consider that, at least thirty percent of the Nixon dialogue on the tapes, is a vulgar explicative, that would surely harm his political career. Do you truly believe that he voluntarily taped himself? I think not!

Was it "so ordered" by Lyndon Baines Johnson? It is now quite obvious to me, what Richard Nixon meant, the day he left office, when he said; quote; "You won't have Nixon to kick around anymore"!

Another celebrated past leader, of that "sanctimonious" Republican Party, was Ronald "I Don't Recall" Reagan.

Under his administration, Iran-Contra was armed, to stop a newly formed democratic government (begun by "American" college students) from establishing civil freedoms, civil rights, labor unions and equal justice in Latin America. Why did Reagan's Secretary of State, John Poindextter "not recall" selling arms to the contras, "until", he was given immunity by Congress?

86

In order to stop American College students from forming a democratic government in Nicaragua, the contra was supplied with U.S. Military arms, and is still suppressing their people, with poverty level wages, and sovereign rights abuses. That area is now known as a Free Trade Zone. Where wages and benefits are suppressed by poverty and lack of representation, where multi-national corporations flee, to flourish.

Ronald, "I don't recall" Reagan didn't recall much about an armed dictatorial force, that was fighting against sovereign and civil liberties. He doesn't even realize that, in spite of his "unsubstantiated actions", his constituents, (The Republicans-aka- Repulsive Cons) have named an airport after him, and claim to desire to lead, "after his legacy"! Reagan-omits!

Another question of missing funds, during the Bush Sr. administration, still unanswered, uninvestigated, and unaccounted for, is the Savings and Loan debacle. Where's the money? Show me the money! Where did it go, Neil? Is it really untraceable, Neil? Under the watch of President George Bush Sr., Congress voted to change the rules, governing the Savings and Loan industry! Change their rules?

Shortly thereafter, the Savings and Loan Administration, under the leadership of Neil Bush, was bankrupt. It seems that after the banking laws were changed, Neil Bush made too many, unsecured loans, to too many of his investment associates.

These, investment associates, liable for millions of Savings & Loan account holder dollars, "failed" to pay them back! My question is! Was this the first recorded appearance of the dreaded "fuzzy math", associated with the Bush administration?

George Bush Sr. "doesn't recall" the emptying, of the savings and loan, under the watch of his son, Neil Bush! Shortly after changing the banking laws, and placing his son as head of the S&L, someone erred in their duties! The money turned up missing, is still gone, and is apparently, still untraceable! The Bushs' proficiency with "fuzzy math", didn't suddenly materialize, at Enron.

The math used, in the past, at the Savings and Loan association, seems to have been "infinitely fuzzy math", which seems to have been written, in disappearing ink. Didn't we once have, a Savings & Loan in this country? We did, until Neal!

Looting funds rightfully entitled to others, through fraudulent business practices is a repulsive endeavor, a lucre' and common sin, that I would not want on my conscious.

If not concerned about the debacle of the S&L under "his sons' watch", I wonder how George Bush Sr. feels about leaving Saddam Hussein in power?

This Bush administration solves problems, conveniently, by conveniently failing to consider them!

For example, Enron closed its' trading windows for twenty consecutive days, without filing for bankruptcy (solvency). Yet, the Securities and Exchange Commission failed, (inexcusably), in its' duty to protect investors from such unlawful, scandalous acts of thievery. A stock exchange closes its' trading windows for twenty days, without filing bankruptcy, and conveniently, no one at the Securities and Exchange Commission, considers it to be (out of the ordinary), a problem. How convenient, now, they don't even have to worry about fuzzy math!

Understand this! George Jr. and the house Republicans have recently, 2001A.D., changed the title of; *Monthly Statement of Public Debt, to the *Monthly Report of Treasury Securities! Debt is now securities, and the monthly statement is now a report. Why? Because a report is simply, "an interpretation", a statement actually "reports the statistics"!

Recently, Bush and his Republican friends, submitted and passed, in violation of House rules, a budget busting tax refund for his political base, (the only ones, whom he is concerned about, the richest), before he had even submitted a budget.

Eventually, Georges' budget turned up, and it turned out to be based on a hypothetical ten-year projection of numbers, otherwise known as "fuzzy math".

Yet, one inescapable statistic remained. Only one percent of our people prospered superfluously, while the overwhelming amount of our fellow man, surviving at poverty level, may or may not receive a percentage of a refund, of their pittance of an income. George, do not forget, Proverbs 22:16; He that oppresseth the poor to increase his riches, and he that giveth to the rich, shall surely come to want.

He next, raised the legal CO_2 limits, now allowed to be released into "our" environment, insuring no legal repercussions, if/when continued use of fossil fuels, and coal burning power plants, raise CO_2 levels past, the previous legal limits.

Why did George Bush, and his, agreeing constituents, have no public health concerns about raising the CO_2 limits in our atmosphere, and/or the arsenic levels within territorial waters?

Why do we solemnly accept the fact that George Bush Jr. has now abandoned the protocol of the 1997 Kyoto Treaty, "to pursue a separate course of action"? Will he implement the same "voluntary standards" that thrust Houston into Americas # 1 standing, and still retaining, the title of; "Americas' most polluted city", all without the consequence of mountains, which collects pollution in competing cities!

George Jr. abandoned the Kyoto Summit and all current efforts for desperately needed environmental standards. He is intending to break the SALT treaties, he abandoned the peace talks in South Africa, and blatantly rebuffed "his essential duty" to entertain Mr. Yassar Arafat in a "verifying" third party capacity. His ill-gotten station, bequeaths' only, more unworthy methods. Unless, Georges' idea of a "new-world order", is anthrax throughout the postal system, refugees forced into a humanitarian crisis, and our young men, stationed in harms way.

George Jr. has obviously abandoned all considerations, of any responsibilities, to anyone! He violated his duty to attend the worldwide peace summit held in Africa. He failed to honor the cries of millions of environmental stewards worldwide, to honor the Protocol of the Kyoto Environmental Summits. He, "for some reason" chose instead, to separate, and pursue "a separate course of action".

Why is George Jr. intentionally avoiding a commitment, to any and all, environmentally protective agendas! When one considers that, people breathe an average of three thousand times per day! Would anyone, of sound mind, and a worthy purpose, lower "our" air quality standards? Your respiratory system, remaining operative for the duration, and without fail, is an essential and critical element, in sustaining ones' health, and life.

Yet, George Jr, "The Grand Poo Baa Of Pollution", has catapulted Texas into the "slime lite"! We are the title-holder of, "the most polluted city in the union". We're #1, Can you see through the smog? Can you still breathe? Try! Try harder! Don't mind the thick, pervasive, smell of rotten eggs, you'll get used to it!

For some inexplicable reason, George also found a need to amend and raise, the legal limits of the arsenic levels within some territorial waters, and obviously, and as usual, a Congressional Republican majority has backed him, in that endeavor! Rising arsenic levels may be an environmental development, but that does not "justify" raising current legal arsenic levels!

Instead, we must provide equipment to preserve the infinite quality of the waters in question, and seek to stem, the source of the incursion, rather than overlooking it!

George Jr. has decided, he will pursue, "a separate course of action". He has effectively separated himself, from every, worthwhile environmental effort on this planet, and instead, has pursued to please, and cooperate with, the corporate interests of the globe. His "<u>voluntary</u>" pollution standards in Texas, effectively say to the abusers, "let the polluters, pollute", when they don't "choose" to "<u>volunteer</u>".

On his second day in office, *without congressional approval, George Bush Jr. launched, against the sovereign nation of Iraq, two separate missile attacks, which served exactly, whose purpose? Leaving that tyrant in power, after he was subdued, served exactly whose purpose? Supplying Israel, the capabilities of pinpoint airborne missile strikes, and helping to fight against the "stone throwing children of deed holding parents", serves exactly whose purpose?

Our legislators are divided, by, not only a carpeted isle! They continue to perpetuate their "silly party" mentality, with a "this side of the isle" agenda! That agenda, only leads to a developing, and, an enveloping abyss, evidenced by the many inherent, intransigent, dysfunctional prejudices, and differing agendas, of our congressmen's misled priorities and purposes. It is a veritable "Civil War" within "our" Congress!

The first "misled' priority of any politician is, "continue to accuse", the other side, the other guy, the other group, or the other method, anything! But, place the blame on them, "the other side of the isle"!

They have created, and now practice, equity law, "legal fiction", a transparent reality, litigated on most, in an admiralty court, by their unawares! (Not within a common law court!) Did you know that the government has designated, and considers you to be, a corporation, "a legal fiction", unless you specify otherwise!

As a result of our "legal fiction status", and their continued usurpation of power, and their treasonous suppression of your sovereign rights, we are subjected to unlawful fees, and taxes! Our Congressmen have staged and developed gridlock, especially concerning a national health care system. For what reason, would one hinder a program, attempting to establish a national health care system, and, to which alternative? Did you know that our elderly fellowman, pay 70% more for their prescriptions, than the medications, that are shipped to, and sold in Canada.

The HMOs' seek to retain their control of the current system. A majority of "our" Congressmen apparently believe that we don't deserve National Health Care, yet, they deserve full medical, a tax refund, a raise, and an opulent retirement plan. Don't forget! They "<u>deserve</u>" immunity? They are lawmakers, above "their" laws!

While on the campaign, George Bush Jr. claimed that he was going to restore rights to the states, and dignity to the White House. I can only say, "Hog Wash"!

First and foremost, the "sovereign rights of all states" and the natural Citizens thereof, have never been relinquished, (knowingly) to the Federal government.

The District of Columbia, is not even a state! Nor, is it a commonwealth! It is a ten square mile "business district", of a foreign corporation, heavily indebted to foreign bankers, aka International Monetary Fund, wrongfully legislating cumbersome laws, on a deceived and unknowing, "corporate" citizenry!

Obviously the rights of the People in the state of Florida did not matter when their will, conflicted with Georges' plans. "States Rights" is a "bogus" political theme developed to counter the enemy, the enemy being "big abusive government"! Big government is an enemy, when it is being manipulated by a "simple minded" majority of greedy Republicans. "States rights" is another political cliché, another diversion, flowing from the mouth of George Bush Jr.

If, in fact, he was truly a proponent of states rights, why is he allowing the deployment of Federal agents into the "free state" of California, in an attempt to overturn Californias' recently enacted marijuana laws.

Insensitive, inapt, greedy, treasonous, fraudulently usurping of power, wasteful and incorrigible, is the only way to describe "our?" ("BIG") Federal government.

How exactly does George intend to restore dignity to the White House? While, on the campaign trail, he referred to a New York reporter as an ---hole! How dignified of George Jr., using degrading, slanderous terms to describe his fellow man.

Did George Jr. help to restore dignity to the White House, when he abandoned the peace summit in Africa, or, the Kyoto environmental summit and its' agenda? Or, when he bombed Iraq twice, within his first week in office, and staunchly backed Israels', Prime Minister Sherrons' indignant behavior, at a Palestine holy place.

Was it dignified, to raise the legal CO_2 levels in our atmosphere and arsenic levels in our water? Was it dignified, to repeal workplace safety rights, (developed from a (mandated) ten-year study), that were to be implemented on April 1st 2001.

He also failed to supply his daughters with fake IDs, so they determined, they would find their own. George, what were the girls thinking? Didn't your daughters know, that you "was" right in the middle, of restoring dignity to the White House? The legacy of your father, the Republican Party, and your silly, misled priorities (voluntary environmental standards) and methods (ballot box on the beach, and the butterfly ballot) and your stubborn willingness to perpetuate a misrepresented, lingering war, are anything, but dignified!

We need one party, "The Sovereign American Party" to represent the American people in Congress and the Senate. Whom does your congressman represent when he fights against, health care, worker safety, and a minimum wage hike? He represents the HMOs', and the corporate dollars that paid for His multi-million dollar campaign. One million dollars a second, is what it costs to air the typical (smear slot campaign ad) on national television. That is lunacy! We can, and must use our public television channels to air "all" local and national debates, among "all" eligible candidates.

The insights, ideas, suggestions and named purposes of each candidate, in the setting of an open debate, are established on, and for public record. Compare that format to the current campaign methods, now established, over "corporate airwaves"! Thirty seconds of slanderous sentiments, smearing a fellowman, with no constructive suggestions whatsoever. Roll that golden bean footage! A thirty second, thirty million-dollar smear ad, which establishes nothing, but further division!

We must insure that the peoples' government, not be dictated, only, by candidates who can afford "corporate airtime". The public airwaves above us belong to us, not "a corporate agenda"! Why do our politicians pay millions of dollars a second for corporate airtime, when public airtime is free?

The hypocrisy of corporate airtime was/is exemplified, when CSPAN critiqued the recent campaign ads. An hour of examining dozens of thirty-second, thirty-million-dollar smear ads, (airing over and over, free) blatantly proves the capabilities of public airwaves.

We need publicly administered debates, for all legitimate candidates, aired on all local "public airwaves". This would effectively eliminate the demand for exorbitant campaign funding, and the unacceptable influences incurred by financiers, lobbyists and corporate interests.

Campaign financing is not a first amendment right, Mr. Bush. Collecting money from your constituents, to simply voice a misleading, simple-minded opinion, is not, I repeat, is "not" a first amendment right! The first amendment to the Constitution refers clearly, to the right of any individual to bring his or her petition before congress. It was the first, and, "a necessary" amendment, because (an elite) congress was picking and choosing the petitions it cared to address.

The first amendment secured the right of each and every individual, to bring his or her petition before Congress, and it has absolutely nothing, "nothing at all", Mr. Bush, to do with campaign funding! The honorable legislators of our past, did not initiate the first amendment to the Constitution, in order to allow candidates the "right" to endless funds! Campaign funding is not a first amendment right, Mr. Bush. Campaign financing is actually, legalized bribery, evidenced by the current health care policies, established by the HMOs. Why do "our" HMO doctors work under, "a gag order", which withholds treatment, and many other treatment options? Why do "they" charge Canadas' elderly, 70% less for supplied medications, than "they" charge our elderly? Because, it's the Republican'ts current health care policy, established by the HMOs.

How could this administration, "dare" to demand accountability from anyone? Who is accountable, for the death of the people that were murdered under Saddam Husseins' extended rule? Saddam was left in (restored to) power, even though his army was defeated, and his royal guard was destroyed. George Bush Sr. and Dick Chaney chose, to restore that tyrannical maniac to power. Why?

Accountability, these people demand accountability from the populace, though they, Dick and George, incurred upon the world, the repercussions of the worst decision made, during the 20th century, that of condoning Saddams authority. They continue to live beyond the reach of the same laws that would imprison us!

Another questionable method of operation, within the Bush administration is the creation of the Homeland Security agency, and the appointment of John Poindexter as head of that new security agency. Why not fund and enhance our current security systems?

How do the people within the criminal justice system feel, when their seniority is receded, and their claim to legal authority, is unconstitutionally removed? Because, George Jr. said, my "congressionally pardoned friend", John Poindexter, is in charge, now!

We must begin by demanding accountability of all legislators, to all laws, under our constitutionally guaranteed, "Common Law". I suggest that, "we the People" "<u>absolutely demand</u>" from each candidate, "<u>a ten-point list</u>", be developed! A list naming the top ten problems, that he or she deems as priorities, and his/her suggestions and methods for solving them.

We must demand accountability from each legislator, beginning with a daily diary, including a list of daily activities, votes levied and why, and any suggestions pertaining to bills, currently pending on the floor.

Who is accountable for their truculent invasions of our sovereignty, and private property rights? How can this socialist "public policy" exist, in this, the land of liberty, the land of Common Law? Who is accountable for the monetary debt, of the Federal Reserve Notes, which can only discharge (transfer) a debt? It can never outright pay a debt! Therefore, you can never, outright own, the home you're living in, because, "you have not paid for it", you only promised to pay, when you presented a "debt instrument", Federal Reserve Note.

Discharging a debt, with a federal obligation, is not lawfully the same as paying with substantive money. Allegedly therefore, you are given a warranty deed. You are not entitled to an alluvial title, because you have not rendered substance for substance. Because, there is no gold or silver available in this economy, in which to make payment, for any property. Debt, whatever the form, is perpetually discharged, by rendering a federal reserve "obligation". The debt is never paid. Therefore, your right to "pay in full" and receive a paramount, alluvial title is not available, because of the constructive fraud, enabled by HJR-192.

The legal definition of a Federal Reserve Note, "an obligation", is stated in the following United States Code – Title 12 – Chapter 3- Subchapter XII- Sec 411. *See copy on page 60.

Greed! The compulsive, obsessive, continual pursuit, for procurement of more, simply to have more, has become the American way. We have become a nation of multi-million dollar lobbyists, silly lawmakers, blinded judges, and attorneys that have learned, adapted to, and now, manipulate a foreign judiciary, enforcing a socialist "public policy" system, of deception, and unauthorized persecution.

After, deceptively removing your "sovereign rights", and effectively placing you under civil authority, "your" corporate taxes are levied, "for life and infamy" and your obedience to all civil statutes is "required"! They, have effectively hidden your sovereign rights, and passed hundreds of new civil statutes, for you to obey, or pay!

They enact, on average, approximately nine hundred new statutes in Texas, yearly! Pure greed has led our representatives on "both sides of the isle" for decades. Yet, "on the record", Republicans have always fought against a minimum wage hike, for our poorest workers. From the day the issue was brought to the floor, until this very day, their demeaning efforts, to suppress their impoverished fellowman, have continued without "conscious reservations", and will continue, if "We, the People" allow it. Yet, under the new percentage tax laws, levied by the rich Republicans, the rich Republicans (deserved?) a $14,000.00 dollar tax break, this year, for themselves?

The tax laws, recently passed by the Republicans under the Bush proposal, (note- I did not say budget, a budget had not been submitted) are an embarrassment. A percentage tax break does next to nothing for our poor. A percentage of the pittance of income, is a smaller pittance. Yet, the refund for a $1,000,000 income is approximately $50,000, and even though the Democrats pointed to the fact, that "we" (John Q. Public) get a muffler, and they (lovers of lucre) get a Lexus. The new tax laws passed, meaning, a lucrative $14000 refund for all litigating legislators and more for upper income brackets. Imagine that! Who got the muffler?

Bush quoted Cardinal OConnor in one of his campaign speeches, saying, Quote; "Poverty in a wealthy nation is a scandal". End quote! So, if poverty is the tragedy that we are to address, why did over 90% of the Republican tax break go to the richest among us?

George, "that" is scandalous! George, do you really think that Cardinal OConnor would approve of your percentage of concern? I think not! Poverty in a wealthy nation is a tragedy! So also, is the pittance of concern demonstrated by you, and this incorrigible Republican administration! Can money, or any material asset, ever remove the guilt of every innocent Iraqi and American life that was taken, or is going to be taken? Question and investigate the examples listed before you, and you will then realize, the true legacy of the alleged, "pro-life" Republican Party.

*<u>Reality Check</u>! - Point of order! Recently, in July of 2005 A.D., the Supreme Court announced its' ruling, that the government and its' employees are "immune" from prosecution. Therefore, our representatives (our Supreme Court Justices) must believe that the men that signed the Declaration of Independence intended to create a government, enabled with tyrannical power, over the liberty of the populous, that is not accountable to the people, and was/is in fact "immune" from prosecution.

How can a government that was designed to protect the liberty, rights, and property of the people, "not be" accountable, to the highest office holders in the land, the sovereign People?

*<u>Reality Check</u>! - Point of order! Recently, in July of 2005 A.D., the Supreme Court announced its' ruling, that private property rights, (eminent domain rights) were no longer paramount in favor of the owner. Instead, corporations that desired your property could now buy you out at minimal appraised value, whether you desired to sell or not. Therefore, the private property rights that our forefathers cherished and died for, have effectively been relinquished by this Supreme Court, and this administration.

Accountability lies within the hands of our nations' leaders, not among the governed masses. Therefore, "we the People" must demand accountability from all legislators, appointed to, and accountable for, determining "our" course!

I find it "<u>incomprehensible</u>", that this government, that was constituted by, of, and "for" the People, to protect the liberty, rights and property, "of the People", could somehow, perpetrate a claim of "immunity" from prosecution, "at any time", for any reason! And, would dare to repeal the cherished right of private property.

Further, any claim of government immunity is repulsive to the true intent of our Constitution. It is without merit, and is obnoxious to the true and original intent of our founding fathers, when drafting our Constitution, and it clearly abrogates cherished constitutional rights. The 1st Amendment to the Constitution gives all Citizens, (the highest office holders within this government) the right to; Quote; "Petition their government for a redress of grievances". End Quote!

Therefore, any alleged law, that so clearly violates the Constitution, is (by Law and precedent) void from its' enactment. Ask yourself, this simple question; Would/Did; the founding fathers, whom, conferred, as against a tyrannical government, desire to grant another, tyrannical authority over their liberty? And, grant such tyrannical authority "with total immunity from redress"? Certainly not!

Therefore, no government agency can lawfully claim immunity, and certainly not in the aftermath of such blatant usurpation of powers, by its' agents, whom were aided by, and not restrained by, other agents. Whereas, the first amendment guarantees my right to redress the government for a grievance, and we all have the right to private property. Therefore, any "Laws?" that so clearly violate the original intent of our founding fathers, is simply, void from its' enactment.

For the record, as a sovereign American, I am, by design, the highest officer holder within this system of self-government. And, as such, I am one of many lawful Citizens, whom are holders of supreme power. Therefore, as supreme authority over "public" servants, I am entitled to any and all immunities that they, (the servants) might assume to claim.

Therefore, if "<u>my servant</u>" could "reasonably" be entitled to a "government immunity", it could only be "reasonably" assumed that I, the sovereign American, (the highest office holder within our government) am entitled to an "immunity".

Whereas, all contracts that were entered into, with our current governing agencies, have been initiated through a "socialist" system of matriculated corporate identities, without full disclosure, and are therefore, unconscionable, and void of any Lawful authority, they're claim of authority and indebtedness through these contracts, is groundless. (Non-Assumpsit)

Subject: Supreme Court Ruling in Cruden v. Neale - Independent of all laws

Quote; When a change of government takes place, from a monarchial to a republican government, the old is dissolved. Those who lived under it, and did not choose to become members of the new, had a right to refuse their allegiance to it, and to retire elsewhere. By being a part of the society subject to the old government, they had not entered into any engagement to become subject to any new form the majority might think proper to adopt. That the majority shall prevail is a rule posterior to the formation of government, and results from it. It is not a rule binding upon mankind in their natural state. <u>There, every man is independent of all laws, except those prescribed by nature. He is not bound by any institutions formed by his fellowman without his consent.</u> "CRUDEN v. NEALE, 2 N.C. 338 (1796) 2 S.E. 70. -End Quote!

California Civil Code section 3539 – "Time does not confirm a void act".

Are We Communists?

The 10 planks of the Communist Manifesto (1848) by Karl Marx	*What our Federal and State Governments have forced upon us.*
1. Abolition of property in land and application of all rents of land to public purposes.	1. State property taxes. If you think you own your land, don't pay your rent (property taxes) and you will see who owns it.
2. A heavy progressive or graduated income tax.	2. Federal and State Income Tax.
3. Abolition of all right of inheritance.	3. Federal and State Inheritance Taxes and Reformed Probate Laws.
4. Confiscation of the property of all emigrants and rebels.	4. Sedition Act of 1798; I.R.S. Powers; Executive Order 11490, Sec 1205- giving total power over all private lands to the Department of Housing & Urban Development; Executive Order 11490 giving total power over all personal property to the General Services Administration Sec. 2002.
5. Centralization of Credit in the hands of the State, by means of a national bank with State capital and an exclusive monopoly.	5. The Federal Reserve System (The Federal Reserve Act of 1913 unlawfully delegated the Power to regulate the value of our money to the Federal Reserve, a private corporation. See- U.S. Constitution, Art.1, Sec.8(5) – Only Congress can have this power.
6. Centralization of the means of communication and transport in the hands of the State.	6. F.C.C. Regulations & Executive Order 10995 Provides for the take over of all communication media's; State Drivers Licenses provide for State regulation of the "privilege" to travel; D.O.T. regulations and Executive Order 10999 provide for the take over of all modes of transportation.
7. Extension of factories and instruments of production owned by the State, the bringing into cultivation of waste lands, and the improvement of the soil, generally in accordance with a common plan.	7. The Federal Government has total production & labor control under Executive Order 11490 through the Departments of Labor, Commerce, agriculture, and Interior. (Department of Interior Controls: Bureau of Land Management, Bureau of Reclamation, Fish& Wildlife Service, etc.)
8. Equal Liability of all to labor. Establishment of industrial crimes, especially for agriculture.	8. Federal Emergency Public Works Programs; Executive Order 11000 provides for forced mobilization of civilians into work brigades.
9. Combination of agriculture with manufacturing industries; gradual abolition of the distinction between town and country, by a more equitable distribution of population over the country.	9. Using the Re-organization Act of 1949, Executive Order 11647, Public Law 89-136, and Executive Order 11731 we will no longer have 50 States with cities and towns, but instead have 10 Regions and their respective capitals.

10. Free education for all children in public schools.	10. Free State Public Schools; Child Abuse Laws; Abolition of children's factory labor in its' present Child Labor Laws where children work with State form. Combination of education with industrial approval- Abolition of private apprenticeships & production, etc. the creation of State controlled apprenticeships (Fair Labor Standards Act of 1937).

United States Code

United States Code

- TITLE 12 - BANKS AND BANKING
    - CHAPTER 3 - FEDERAL RESERVE SYSTEM
        - SUBCHAPTER XII - FEDERAL RESERVE NOTES

Sec. 411. Issuance to reserve banks; nature of obligation; redemption

Federal reserve notes, to be issued at the discretion of the Board of Governors of the Federal Reserve System for the purpose of making advances to Federal reserve banks through the Federal reserve agents as hereinafter set forth and for no other purpose, are authorized. The said notes **shall be obligations** of the United States and shall be receivable by all national and member banks and Federal reserve banks and for all taxes, customs, and other public dues. They shall be redeemed in lawful money on demand at the Treasury Department of the United States, in the city of Washington, District of Columbia, or at any Federal Reserve bank.

- TITLE 18 - CRIMES AND CRIMINAL PROCEDURE
    - PART I - CRIMES
        - CHAPTER 1 - GENERAL PROVISIONS

Sec. 8. Obligation or other security of the United States defined

The term **"obligation** or other security of the United States" **includes** all bonds, certificates of indebtedness, national bank currency, Federal Reserve notes, **Federal Reserve bank notes**, coupons, United States notes, Treasury notes, gold certificates, silver certificates, fractional notes, certificates of deposit, bills, checks, or drafts for money, drawn by or upon authorized officers of the United States, stamps and other representatives of value, of whatever denomination, issued under any Act of Congress, and canceled United States stamps.

TITLE 31 - MONEY AND FINANCE

- SUBTITLE III - FINANCIAL MANAGEMENT
    - CHAPTER 31 - PUBLIC DEBT
        - SUBCHAPTER II - ADMINISTRATIVE

Sec. 3124. Exemption from taxation

- (a) Stocks and **obligations** of the United States Government are **exempt from taxation** by a State or political subdivision of a State. The exemption applies to each form of taxation that would require the obligation, the interest on the obligation, or both, to be considered in computing a tax, except -
    - (1) a nondiscriminatory franchise tax or another nonproperty tax instead of a franchise tax, imposed on a corporation; and
    - (2) an estate or inheritance tax.
- (b) The tax status of interest on obligations and dividends, earnings, or other income from evidences of ownership issued by the Government or an agency and the tax treatment of gain and loss from the disposition of those obligations and evidences of ownership is decided under the Internal Revenue Code of 1986 (26 U.S.C. 1 et seq.). An obligation that the Federal Housing Administration had agreed, under a contract made before March 1, 1941, to issue at a future date, has the tax exemption privileges provided by the authorizing law at the time of the contract. This subsection does not apply to obligations and evidences of ownership issued by the District of Columbia, a territory or possession of the United States, or a department, agency, instrumentality, or political subdivision of the District, territory, or possession.

At each retail or wholesale register there is a tax exempt document. The tax ID# should be 31USC3124. All products brought in, manufactured or purchased in the Country have been with Federal Reserve Notes, which are not taxable by 31 U.S.C. § 3124. Just in case you didn't know.

"The Madness of Uncle Scam"

Once upon a time! There was a "movie"! About addiction, the feigns, held under its' grip, and how "it transformed" any typical individual, into a "cold blooded" calculating psycho. Akin to the "Dracula" mode! Pillaging, stalking, raping, and committing murder, in a semiconscious, psychotic state of mind.

Which movie am I describing? Which drug causes such violent psychotic behavior? None! Until! A "movie", convinced a gullible citizenry, that there is, and it does! The movie, "Refer Madness", debuted in 1938, and shortly thereafter, a scourge of stoned, murdering rapists, "were everywhere", according to that "movie", and a now, thoroughly brainwashed, fearful and vocally re-active public! So, "Uncle Scam" struck, "while the iron was hot" and shortly thereafter, the most "fibrous" plant on the planet, cannabis sativa, the wonder crop, was now illegal, and effectively removed from its' "leading role" in our commercial markets!

The most revealing fact about the movie, is the money trail. The corporate financial backers, desiring to eliminate the competition, were timber interests, chemical industries, and "Uncle Scam". In a deceitful effort, to spread pseudo fear, and "their propaganda", about (Indian hemp) the strongest, most durable, longest lasting, natural soft fiber on the planet, the movie, "Refer Madness" was created.

Our forefathers cultivated cannabis for numerous applications, such as medicinal purposes, clothing, shoes, food, rope, paper products, fuel, paints, varnishes, etc. It is also the most restorative to the environment, Cannabis aerates the atmosphere, and replenishes the soil more than any plant on the planet.

Someone must inform "Uncle Scam" that the activities of psychopathic murderers and rapists, are not mandated, or preceded by refer smoking! The vulnerability of the generation of the 1930's is obvious, in hindsight. Consider that, there was no television, the main contact with the outside world, for the 30s' Citizen, was a night at the picture show, and any images, (propaganda) portrayed there!

Our current laws, pertaining to cannabis sativa, are founded on "pure propaganda" and they overturned previous laws, mandating its' cultivation! The first statute pertaining to marijuana, enacted in the united states, originated from Jamestown, Virginia (McBride 47), mandating all farmers to plant the Indian Hemp seed.

Massachusetts, Connecticut and other colonies enacted similar statutes, authorizing taxes to be paid with hemp.

So, why are we subjected to victimless crime persecutions, under color of law, that only harm or hinder Gods' plan, through man made de-facto statutes? Are we to remain as gullible, as the first patrons of the "movie", Refer Madness!

Genesis, chapter 1 verse 11 & 12; Then God said, let the earth bring forth grass, the herb yielding seed, and the fruit tree yielding fruit after his kind, whose seed is in itself, upon the earth: and it was so. And the earth brought forth grass, and herb yielding seed after his kind, and the tree yielding fruit, whose seed was in itself, after its' kind: and God saw that it was good. Genesis, chapter 1: 29; And God said, Behold, I have given you every herb bearing seed, which is upon the face of all the earth, and every tree, in the which is the fruit of a tree yielding seed; to you it shall be for food. Proverbs 15 verse 17; Better is a dinner of herbs where love is, than a stalled ox and hatred therewith.

Do our pompous politicians wish us to believe that, God was in error, when "He" created, and gave us, this seed-bearing medicinal herb? He has "admitted" that He gave us all seed-bearing herb. So, why has no man charged Him with delivery?

The premeditated, pseudo depictions, of psychotic criminal behavior, initiated by the use of cannabis, in the movie "REFER MADNESS" is "PURE PROPAGANDA"! It's political purpose, and result, was to sway public opinion about the "wonder crop". It was in fact, nothing more than "Political Propaganda". The pseudo threat portrayed in "REFER MADNESS", suddenly produced "LEGISLATION", which overturned a declared law, and removed a vital, and valued commodity, from its' "number one" position in the free market. The most fibrous plant on the planet was effectively removed from its' leading role in the stock market, and from all of its' commercial applications. The propaganda portrayed in "Refer Madness" led a conspiring Congress to enact "new" laws, pertaining to Cannabis. Those new laws, have led to the entrapment, conviction, and continued imprisonment, of millions of innocent Citizens.

Did God create His seed bearing herb, cannabis sativa, (the most aerating of all land plants, the most restorative to the soil, and the most fibrous and commercially applicable plant on the planet), to divide the people into criminals and/or judgmental hypocrites? I think not!

See to it that no one takes you captive, through hollow and deceptive philosophy, and high sounding non sense, that comes from human thinking and from the evil powers of this world, and not from Christ.

Eternally,
A Brother in Christ
Quey Quay

Chapter 7

Congress has initiated Republics in "<u>our</u>" land. Article IV section 4, guaranteed to every state, a republican form of government, and proclaimed human rights over all others, and States Rights over all other government authorities. The Federal government has never had jurisdiction over any state, so why should we appeal to the Federal government, for rights that are sovereign to us. Quote: A republic is a state in which the supreme power rests in the body of citizens entitled to vote and is exercised by representatives chosen directly or indirectly by them.

In The Bill of Rights, the Tenth Amendment to the US Constitution says quote; The powers not delegated to the United States by the Constitution, nor prohibited by it to the States, are reserved to the States respectively, or to the People. End quote;

So, if states rights are supreme to federal jurisdiction, why was the Florida State Supreme Courts' decision, overturned by an inferior authority? Answer! It was not overturned! Could it be that "moving" jurisdiction to a Federal Court was allowed by Al Gore? YES! Had he demanded that the eminent domain of the state Florida, and the Florida Supreme Court decision, "be honored", then, the votes would have been counted! And, the "absence" of "Federal Authority" would have been revealed!

Did the Federal Supreme Court have the authority and/or right to overrule, or ignore, the decision of the Florida Supreme Court? NO!

Then, why was the Florida Supreme Court ruling ignored? Venue! Ask Al Gore, why he allowed a change of venue? Ask yourself, why did the Federal Supreme Court, ignore the national vote total, "if" in fact, every vote "actually" counted?

Why did they ignore the numerous inappropriate activities, associated with the 2000 election in Florida? Why did the Federal judges withhold their rulings, until it was too late to count the votes? Why did a dozen Democratic Congresspersons submit official objections to the counting of Florida's electoral votes? Why were all objections ignored? Why were they unable to secure a single Senators' signature?

How is it, how can it be that no Senator questioned the legitimacy of the Florida election, after an "official ballot box" was found on the beach?

Ask yourself, why, and how did it happen that Republican ballots, were removed from county custody, completed, returned and counted. Why were faulty ballot counting machines, which led to so many Democratic votes going uncounted, (dangling chad machines) strategically placed in Democratic precincts?

How/why is it that the butterfly ballot used in Valusia County, determined that Buchanon had received over 3,700 votes there, yet, in a "larger", neighboring county, "using a proper ballot", he received approximately 700 votes! Why?

If that isn't enough, another troubling fact, yet to be examined, is the exit poles! The people questioned, after they had voted, and all major channels, projected Al Gore as the winner! Because, more People intended too, and "did" vote for Al Gore, and declared so, during the exit pole! Yet, no Senator found a reason to endorse objections by twelve concerned congresspersons, to the legitimacy of the Florida electoral vote count. Why?

Those <u>people</u> are U.S. Senators, one would think that they would be a little more informed and concerned about "questionable" elections, and current procedures. The number of questions, concerning the Florida election, and the judicial procedures that followed, were a clear and obvious breach of proper procedure.

All Senators ignored official congressional objections, and the numerous dysfunctional procedures that occurred during the 2,000 presidential election. No Senator recognized a problem! Why did no Senator, question the procedures, or honor any of the twelve congressional objections to the Florida electoral count? That, is a question for the ages, which may never be known, but, know this! Had Gore demanded that, the eminent domain rights, of the sovereign people of Florida, and the ruling of the Florida Supreme Court, be honored, he would have effectively revealed the lack of jurisdiction over the states, by the government office he sought!

It's one thing, when the general masses, stick their heads in the sand, give up in disgust, ignoring the obvious, but when a Senator accepts such methods as "standard procedure", then, I must object! "Uncle Scam" obviously, has placed no limits, on his deceptive practices.

The more you know! The more you know of! Why did the total number of votes, not matter? Because "our" (modern legislators) use an archaic, and undemocratic system, that was developed in the 1770s.

We live in a Republic, of the 21st century, do we not? For a second time, the true will of the people was subverted! The will of a few culpable legislators, prevailed to thwart the will of the people, in Florida, and thereby the nation, exemplifying the vulnerability, and manipulative nature of "our?" archaic, Electoral College system!

The purpose for developing the Electoral College system in the 1700s, was to insure that the western states were campaigned, and thereby the populous was well "informed" of their candidates. The Electoral College system is history revisited. Did anyone in the western states, not know who was running for president? Why in the world should we use an archaic system, of which, methods are "dubious", and obviously, vulnerable to manipulation? History, must now document, that its' implementation and effect, has now, twice overturned the "mandate", the certified vote, of the People!

If "they" choose, to elect one another, using the "archaic" Electoral College system, we should make "them" use a horse and buggy, to do they're campaigning.

We have satellite television today Mr. Congressman, isn't that how you ran your campaign? Yes, and you spent only, one million dollars a second, "corporate time", to air your ire, of the other. Even though, "they" could have used, "for free", "public access television", for lengthy, question and answer sessions, producing very informative debates, etc. Thereby, all enlightening prerogatives could/would be established for public record!

Why do we send our tax dollars to Washington D.C., where (elite?) legislators, work in turmoil and division, and continue to widen the abyss between themselves, by fighting over "our" needed funds, to which they have no right, and no worthy purpose? No person in Washington D.C. can name a street in my county, or knows of the local circumstances, within this county, or its' peoples needs. Local authority is much more aware of the human condition, within our county borders, and we are much more capable of securing domestic tranquility within the county. Local authority is much more informed and empowered, to direct needed efforts, than an argumentative bureaucracy, in Washington D.C.!

Why do we send our money to Washington D.C., where conflict, confusion and greed prevail? Our legislators encourage stockpiling, of military armaments, and sales to warring factions! Yes, we are warmongers! As a matter of fact, we are the worlds' most prolific "warmonger"! Why do we condone and accept the silly system, and silly policies now in effect, governing our legislators, and thereby, ourselves? Washington cannot agree on who needs help, where to begin, or, what should be done! Gridlock is the "Game in the Loop".

<u>County authority</u> is the type of authority needed. Local governing authority, would be much more capable, efficient, and responsive, to its' local populous. The mammoth expense, incurred and wasted on this "UNCONSTITUTIONAL" dysfunctional Federal bureaucracy, is exceeded "only", by its' inapt methods, and its' pitiful performance.

The Federal government, should only be empowered, if requested to act, by local authorities, and should only direct its' jurisdiction toward suppressing foreign aggression. We must insist on local authority over local tax dollars. Why should we send our tax dollars, to a corrupt, incorrigible bureaucracy, where constituents, "on the other side of the isle", continually waste time, work in continual turmoil, and seek only gridlock?

The only time that they are in agreement, is when they are legislating themselves a raise, a retirement package, or a spending bill, allowing billions to be spent on one crazed mans' misguided and ungodly war. The current "silly party" system, serves no worthy purpose, only deception, graft, gridlock, and "silly intent"!

We the People, must unite, and demand accountability, from a single "sovereign" party!

U.S. Supreme Court

**PACIFIC STATES TELEPHONE & TELEGRAPH CO. v. STATE OF OREGON, 223 U.S. 118
(1912) 223 U.S. 118**

**PACIFIC STATES TELEPHONE & TELEGRAPH COMPANY, Plff. in
Err.,
v.
STATE OF OREGON.**

No. 36.

**Argued November 3, 1911.
Decided February 19, 1912.**

[223 U.S. 118, 119] Messrs. E. S. Pillsbury and Oscar Sutro for plaintiff in
error.
[223 U.S. 118, 129] Mr. A. M. Crawford, Attorney General of Oregon,
Messrs. George Fred Williams, Jackson H. Ralston, I. H. Van Winkle, W.
S. U'Ren, C. E. S. Wood, Frederick L. Siddons, William E. Richardson,
George H. Shibley, Robert L. Owen, and J. Harry Carnes for defendant
in error.
Mr. Elliott W. Major, Attorney General of Missouri, and Messrs. John T.
Dye and Addison C. Harris as amici curioe. [223 U.S. 118, 133]

Mr. Chief Justice White delivered the opinion of the court:

We premise by saying that while the controversy which this record
presents is of much importance, it is not novel. It is important, since it
calls upon us to decide whether it is the duty of the courts or the province
of Congress to determine when a state has ceased to be republican in
form, and to enforce the guaranty of the Constitution on that subject. It is
not novel, as that question has long since been determined by this court
conformably to the practice of the government from the beginning to be
political in character, and therefore not cognizable by the judicial power,
but solely committed by the Constitution to the judgment of Congress.

The case is this: In 1902 Oregon amended its Constitution.

This amendment, while retaining an existing clause vesting the exclusive legislative power in a general assembly consisting of a senate and a house of representatives, added to that provision the following: 'But the people reserve to themselves power to propose laws and amendments to the Constitution, and to enact or [223 U.S. 118, 134] reject the same at the polls, independent of the legislative assembly, and also reserve power at their own option to approve or reject at the polls any act of the legislative assembly.' [Art. 4, 1.] Specific means for the exercise of the power thus reserved was contained in further clauses authorizing both the amendment of the Constitution and the enactment of laws to be accomplished by the method known as the initiative and that commonly referred to as the referendum.

As to the first, the initiative, it suffices to say that a stated number of voters were given the right at any time to secure a submission to popular vote for approval of any matter which it was desired to have enacted into law, and providing that the proposition thus submitted, when approved by popular vote, should become the law of the state. The second, the referendum, provided for a reference to a popular vote, for approval or disapproval, of any law passed by the legislature, such reference to take place either as the result of the action of the legislature itself, or of a petition filed for that purpose by a specified number of voters. The full text of the amendment is in the margin.

Section 1 of article 4 of the Constitution of the state of Oregon shall be, and hereby is, amended to read as follows:

Section 1. The legislative authority of the state shall be vested in a legislative assembly, consisting of a senate and house of representatives, but the people reserve to themselves power to propose laws and amendments to the Constitution, and to enact or reject the same at the polls, independent of the legislative assembly, and also reserve power at their own option to approve or reject at the polls any act of the legislative assembly. The first power reserved by the people is the initiative, and not more than 8 per cent of the legal voters shall be required to propose any measure by such petition, and every such petition shall include the full text of the measure so proposed. Initiative petitions shall be filed with the Secretary of State not less than four months before the election at which they are to be voted upon.

The second power is the referendum, and it may be ordered (except as to laws necessary for the immediate preservation of the public peace, health, or safety) either by the petition signed by 5 per cent of the legal voters, or by the legislative assembly, as other bills are enacted. Referendum petitions shall be filed with the Secretary of State not more than ninety days after the final adjournment of the session of the legislative assembly which passed the bill on which the referendum is demanded. The veto power of the governor shall not extend to measures referred to the people. All elections on measures referred to the people of the state shall be had at the biennial regular general elections, except when the legislative assembly shall order a special election. Any measure referred to the people shall take effect and become the law when it is approved by a majority of the votes cast thereon, and not otherwise. The style of all bills shall be: 'Be it enacted by the people of the state of Oregon.' This section shall not be construed to deprive any member of the legislative assembly of the right to introduce any measure. The whole number of votes cast for justice of the supreme court at the regular election last preceding the filing of any petition for the initiative or for the referendum shall be the basis on which the number of legal voters necessary to sign such petition shall be counted. Petitions and orders for the initiative or for the referendum shall be filed with the Secretary of State, and in submitting the same to the people, he and all other officers shall be guided by the general laws and the act submitting this amendment until legislation shall be especially provided therefor. [223 U.S. 118, 135] In 1903 detailed provisions for the carrying into effect of this amendment were enacted by the legislature.

By resort to the initiative in 1906, a law taxing certain classes of corporations was submitted, voted on, and promulgated by the governor in 1907 as having been duly adopted. By this law telephone and telegraph companies were taxed, by what was qualified as an annual license, 2 per centum upon their gross revenue derived from business done within the state. Penalties were provided for nonpayment, and methods were created for enforcing payment in case of delinquency.

The Pacific States Telephone & Telegraph Company, an Oregon corporation engaged in business in that state, made a return of its gross receipts, as required by the [223 U.S. 118, 136] statute, and was accordingly assessed 2 per cent upon the amount of such return.

The suit which is now before us was commenced by the state to enforce payment of this assessment and the statutory penalties for delinquency. The petition alleged the passage of the taxing law by resort to the initiative, the return made by the corporation, the assessment, the duty to pay, and the failure to make such payment.

The answer of the corporation contained twenty-nine paragraphs. Four of these challenged the validity of the tax because of defects inhering in the nature or operation of the tax. The defenses stated in these four paragraphs, however, may be put out of view, as the defendant corporation, on its own motion, was allowed by the court to strike these propositions from its answer. We may also put out of view the defenses raised by the remaining paragraphs based upon the operation and effect of the state Constitution, as they are concluded by the judgment of the state court. Coming to consider these paragraphs of the answer thus disembarrassed, it is true to say that they all, in so far as they relied upon the Constitution of the United States, rested exclusively upon an alleged infirmity of the powers of government of the state, begotten by the incorporation into the state Constitution of the amendment concerning the initiative and the referendum. The answer was demurred to as stating no defense. The demurrer was sustained, and the defendant electing not to plead further, judgment went against it, and that judgment was affirmed by the supreme court of Oregon. (53 Or. 163, 99 Pac. 427.) The court sustained the conclusion by it reached, not only for the reasons expressed in its opinion, but by reference to the opinion in a prior case (Kadderly v. Portland, 44 Or. 118, 146, 74 Pac. 710, 75 Pac. 222), where a like controversy had been determined.

The assignments of error filed on the allowance of the writ of error are numerous. The entire matters covered [223 U.S. 118, 137] by each and all of them in the argument, however, are reduced to six propositions, which really amount to but one, since they are all based upon the single contention that the creation by a state of the power to legislate by the initiative and referendum causes the prior lawful state government to be bereft of its lawful character as the result of the provisions of 4 of article 4 of the Constitution, that **'the United States shall guarantee to every state in this Union a republican form of government,** and shall protect each of them against invasion; and on application of the legislature, or of the executive (when the legislature cannot be convened), **against domestic violence.'**

This being the basis of all the contentions, the case comes to the single issue whether the enforcement of that provision, because of its political character, is exclusively committed to Congress, or is judicial in its character. Because of their absolute unity we consider all the propositions together, and therefore at once copy them.

We observe, however, that in the argument the second, fourth, and fifth paragraphs, for the purposes of discussion, were subordinately classified, and these subordinate classifications we omit from our text, reproducing them, however, by a marginal reference.

I.

'The initiative and the tax measure in question are repugnant to the provisions of 1 of the 14th Amendment to the Constitution of the United States, which forbids a state to deny to any person within its jurisdiction the equal protection of the law.

II.

'The initiative amendment and the tax in question, levied pursuant to a measure passed by authority of the initiative amendment, violates the right to a republican [223 U.S. 118, 138] form of government which is guaranteed by 4, article 4, of the Federal Constitution.

III.

'Taxation by the initiative method violates fundamental rights, and is not in accordance with 'the law of the land.'
(U. S. Const. art. 6.)

IV.

'The initiative is in contravention of a republican form of government. Government by the people directly is the attribute of a pure democracy, and is subversive of the principles upon which the Republic is founded. Direct legislation is therefore repugnant to that form of government with which alone Congress could admit a state to the Union, and which the state is bound to maintain.

1. **The guaranty of article 4, section 4, of the Federal Constitution, is to the people of the states, and to each citizen, as well as to the states as political entities.**

2. **Section 4 of article 4 therefore prohibits the majority in any state from adopting an unrepublican Constitution.**

1. Difference between a republic and democracy.
2. In ascertaining the meaning of the phrase 'republican form of government,' the debates of the constitutional conventions and the federalist papers are of great importance, if not conclusive.

3. **The framers of the Constitution recognized the distinction between the republican and democratic form of government, and carefully avoided the latter.**

4. **The extent of territory of the states alone sufficed, in** the judgment of the framers of the Constitution, to **condemn the establishment of a democratic form of government.**

5. The form of state government perpetuated by the Constitution was the republican form, with the three departments of government, in force in all the states at the time of the adoption of the Constitution.

6. The history of other nations does not furnish the definition of the phrase 'republican form of government,' as those words were used by the framers of the Constitution. They distinguish the American from all other republics by the introduction of the principle of representation.

7. **Initiative legislation is invalid because government by the people directly is inconsistent with our form of government.**

8. The well-known practices of (a) adopting state Constitutions by popular vote, and of (b) local legislation in 'town meetings,' furnish no precedent for the lodgment of legislative power in the ballot box. [223 U.S. 118, 139] V.

'The Federal Constitution presupposes in each state the maintenance of a republican form of government and the existence of state legislatures, to wit: Representative assemblies having the power to make the laws; and that in each state the powers of government will be divided into three departments: a legislature, an executive, and a judiciary. **One of these, the legislature, is destroyed by the initiative.**1

VI.

'The provision in the Oregon Constitution for direct legislation violates the provisions of the act of Congress admitting Oregon to the Union.'

Our forefathers conferred, "as against a tyrannical government"! Therefore, would they approve of the recent Supreme Court rulings, "granting their/this government" eminent domain rights over our private property, with "IMMUNITY"! Those types of rulings embrace and define, "a tyrannical government"!

"The preservation of the sacred fire of Liberty and the Republican model of government is entrusted to the hands of the American People".

George Washington

"They that can give up essential liberty to obtain a little temporary safety deserve neither liberty nor safety."

Benjamin Franklin

"If we American people ever allow monopoly banking to control the issue of currency, first by inflation and then by deflation, these banks and bureaucracies that will grow up around them will deprive we, the people of all our property, until our children will wake up homeless on the continent which God gave us for stewardship."

Thomas Jefferson

"The bold efforts that the present bank has made to control the government, the distress it has wantonly caused, are but premonitions of the fate which awaits the American people should they be deluded into a perpetuation of this institution. If the people only understood the rank injustice of the money and banking system there would be a revolution before morning. You are a den of vipers and thieves."

Andrew Jackson

The Dream Of General McClellan
George Washington's Promise

"But her mission will not then be finished; for ere another century shall have gone by, the oppressors of the whole earth, hating and envying her exaltation, shall join themselves together to raise up their hands against her. But if she still be found worthy of her high calling they shall surely be discomforted, and then will be ended her third and last great struggle for existence. Thence-forth shall the Republic go on, increasing in power and goodness, until her borders shall end only in the remotest corners of the earth, and the whole earth shall beneath her shadowing wing become a Universal Republic. Let her in her prosperity, however remember the Lord her God, her trust be always in Him, and she shall never be confounded.

Chapter 8

When the candidate, who received the "most votes", does/did "not win" the election, is there any question remaining, that the winner was selected! In this case, by five Republican judges, beyond the will of the Florida Supreme Court, and its' desire to have the ballots counted. Were privacy rights actually protected, by ignoring the will of the national totals? Were privacy rights actually protected, by delaying their ruling long enough, to effectively stop the counting of voter ballots? Were privacy rights actually protected in the Senate chamber, when "NO" Senator questioned the legitimacy of the Florida electoral ballots, even though twelve congresspersons filed official protests, against recognizing their legitimacy?

Protests, by twelve disheartened, disenfranchised, and rightfully objecting Congressmen, were submitted to public record, then, "dismissed", promptly, and completely! "ALL" dismissed, due to the lack of a single Senators' signature. No Senator questioned the discovery of an official ballot box, found on the beach, and "known to be part of" the Florida "selection"! No congressional objections were ever recognized, by any Senator! Therefore, we are to assume that, an official ballot box, found on a Florida beach, is "not" an incident for consideration by our "elite" Senators, while turning over the Presidency, to a candidate with a smaller "national" vote total?

Why is it, that the "National" vote total, (all of the votes) of our countrymen, did "not" matter. Why is it that no senator, "not even one", within our government, questioned or objected to the blatant election irregularities that took place in Florida? Even though twelve colleagues (congressmen) had filed official objections, to the validity of the Electoral vote? Knowing that without a Senators signature, no objections would be recognized, the charade of objections, and summary dismissals was endured, and the blinded, senseless, silly Senators, prevailed! Where were these elite Senators, during the Florida selection?

Oh, they "were" the selectors!

How, a few legislators in Florida, were able to thwart the will of "our" national vote total, (and no Senator noticed) through the use of an archaic system of ballot counting, known as the Electoral College, is beyond my imagination, understanding and belief. I still don't believe it. I'm sickened daily by the "ambush on the beach" and the unscrupulous policies used by the Republicans, to secure an office.

I am sickened by a silly two party system, where differing viewpoints overrule all sanity. The undemocratic and unjustifiable affects of the methods, dictated by the Electoral College, were clearly exemplified after the closeness of the Florida election, and the many questionable partisan procedures that followed.

Point of order, make yourself honestly face the fact, that George Bush Jr. received fewer votes, than Al Gore. Therefore, We the People, were denied, ignored, and unquestionably treasoned by the archaic balloting laws of "The Electoral College"!

The fact that the previous sentence is true and accepted unquestionably by "Federal Authorities" (The Senate) has revealed "their" willing acceptance, of an archaic system, that "has" twice overturned "our" vote! Senators, remove your heads from the sand, and "see the ballot box", which was part of the election, (objected to by twelve Congressmen), discarded on that Florida beach. Why did no Senator observe, or display any concern about, that "selection", and the official ballot box found on the beach? Who is <u>lobbying</u> "our" Congressman and Senators?

That so-called election, was an abomination of the true mandate of the people! The national majority was clearly established, and mandated that Mr. Al Gore shall enter the duties of president. Yet, in the face of a clear national majority, five "public servant", (five Republican Supreme Court Justices), sought to over rule the will of the people (national totals), by their simple majority of one. And they did so!

Their "vote" decided the 2,000 presidency! Made by five, Republican Supreme Court Justices, whom, willfully and wantonly ignored the fact that the national vote total, clearly revealed, a majority of people had chosen Al Gore. By what right, by what authority, could five "public servants" possibly assume, that their votes counted more, than the People they had sworn to serve and protect?

A most revolting part of our history has been revisited, and few of our modern legislators, "very few", seem to be concerned. I question, how few? Is America a true Republic of states, or Not?

A true Republican form of government is ruled by a majority vote, not an Electoral vote. Under the current "archaic" rules of the Electoral College, "our right to appoint representatives", (the mandate established by the national vote total), has proven to be dreadfully insignificant, to "our" electorate, once again!

It could be reasonably assumed that all Supreme Court Judges had personal knowledge of the fact, that, the majority of voters, desired that Al Gore should enter into the duties of president in 2000A.D., Yet, they inaugurated another!

Thereby, the Electoral College system has twice, proven itself to be corruptible, undemocratic, and thus, unacceptable. It is an antiquated, "governmental ballot" counting process, still on the books, blatantly undermining, true and complete acknowledgment, of each vote. Repeal the Electoral College, or continue to visit the past, while modern legislators, count only, their votes!

The first step in solving any problem is realizing the problem exists. The problem is that "our" representatives embrace an archaic system of ballot counting, which has twice overturned the true will, of an "authorizing?" populace.

Ask yourself, why have our politicians reformed everything, except, the archaic election laws, and campaign finance laws? If they continue to insist on using that archaic form of ballot counting, "initiated in the 1770s", we should insist that they campaign from a horse and buggy.

The Electoral College and Campaign Finance Laws are the two most detrimental laws, still on the books, undermining our Republic, through balloting counting techniques, of automatic incumbents, with undisclosed sources, of unlimited funds.

Why are public servants, financed by undisclosed sources, paying a million dollars a second for airtime, while public airwaves are free? Obviously, our politicians have and will, continue to systematically hinder public access of qualified candidates, through exorbitant campaign costs, and "their" ballot counting techniques, within the Electoral College, "if", we continue to allow them!

Chapter 9

There is an obvious and prudent way, to eliminate the need for multi-million dollar campaign coffers, for "our candidates", and the (undefined influences), of donor and corporate interests, incurred by allowing unrestricted contributions. Airtime is the key to a successful candidacy, and is also the greatest expense. Corporate airtime costs approximately one million dollars a second, yet public airtime is free! Yet, our elite candidates patronize the corporate giants, as if they were the only show in town. They are not! They are simply the most imbedded in political affairs, and certainly the most expensive.

Ask yourself, what were the initial actions of/by corporate America, after witnessing the rampant hysteria, suicides, and the "state of panic" exemplified by millions, of unsuspecting Americans, upon hearing that "fateful" radio broadcast, by the infamous Orson Wells "hypothetically" describing an "invasion from Mars"? Millions fled to the country, went into hiding, or leaped to their deaths! Revealing to corporate America, the actual power of that, "broadcasting" media!

Certainly, and obviously, corporate America has since turned its' attention, to controlling all images and all information, "presented" to the American public. What is presented to the public today, is that, and "only that", which they have filtered, legitimized, propagandized, spun, and sold as an "honorable", and "patriotic", recourse!

The actual cost of projecting video over "public" airwaves is quite affordable. Evidenced by the many "public service" channels, now in existence. The problem is that our "public service" channels, and their dynamic potential, for informing, and uniting our people, have not been realized! And thereby, not "utilized"!

We can eliminate the need for, and all of the negative effects of, campaign funding, by allowing all eligible candidates to debate on public channels. We then, select the candidate with the better perspectives and ideas.

Or, we can continue to watch, as "corporate candidates" pay millions of dollars, for a thirty-second smear ad, alleging the usual "smear tactics"!

Which, supply nothing of substantive worth, concerning the true priorities, or prerogative of the candidate, nor their plans, and/or prospective methods.

Therefore, I emphatically suggest that, we, the People, demand, of each and every candidate, a ten-point list, defining what he or she considers to be the top ten problems plaguing our humanity. And, how he or she intends to solve them!

Free and open debates, aired freely on public television, is "our" best option!

Chapter 10

When a single corporation owns three of the largest American newspapers, namely the New York Times, the Chicago Tribune and the L.A. Times, realize, what you are reading, is corporate propaganda! Why, did so few news sources, cover the recent human rights atrocities of West Timar? West where? What? You've never heard of West Timar? Imagine that! But, most inquiring readers know who Gary Condit is!

Do we really care more about a celebrity's, and/or public officials' promiscuity's, than about the life and death situations, facing innocent people worldwide? Corporate news does! Scholars such as Noam Chomsky and Colman McCarthy are absolutely right, when describing the American media, as a coordinated propaganda machine, concerned simply with making or breaking a particular political entity.

Should not our corporate media moguls concern themselves more, with revealing the true and relevant facts concerning humanities problems, than they do, about covering a sporting event, or a consenting adult's sexual indiscretion. The corporate message does not necessarily promote public interests, quite the contrary!

The most glaring example of a controlled media, that I can recall, came in 1964. Why was the Warren commission so "pre-determined" to recognize only, the evidence that incriminated only, a single shooter in Kennedys' assassination, and blatantly ignored all obvious and contradictory evidence? Why did no investigative reporters address the issue of inertia, and the laws of physics, that propelled Mr. Kennedy backward? All filmed evidence of the actual impact, (the McGruder film) and, Arlen Spectres' assertions before the Warren Commission, obviously conflict with the Laws of inertia and the physics of motion. Could someone, allegedly shot from behind, yet, be propelled backward? I think not! Yet, no investigative reporter considered that obviously perplexing and contradicting dilemma.

The Warren Report was the "corporate message" of our governing authorities! Do you believe them, now? History has proven their errors, incapability's, and culpable, purposeful neglect.

History and the laws of physics have proven that they lied about the assassination of John Fitzgerald Kennedy.

Why was it done? Why was Kennedy killed? Consider, this fact, the Federal Reserve sought to stop, executive order 11110, Kennedys' re-implementation of silver certificates into the American economy. And, to retain, in circulation, the worthless debt instruments, known as Federal Reserve notes! And, they did so!

Mr. Arlen Spectre was a young Republican Senator, and a member of the 1964 Warren commission, appointed by Lyndon Johnson, who inexplicably, ignored all obvious and relevant evidence of a conspiracy, and in fact, went out of his way to espouse "a single bullet theory". Arlen developed, espoused and "led" the Warren Commission to believe, the "Single Bullet" theory, commonly known as the "Magic Bullet" theory! Arlen that had to be the "smartest"- "Single Bullet" ever made.

A bullet that was fired from behind, yet entered the right frontal lobe of Mr. Kennedys' skull, then, expelled Mr. Kennedys' brains onto the trunk, then entered Senator Connallys' back, exited His hip, and then entered his wrist. That was the coarse of Mr. Spectres' "magical" single bullet. It does seem to have been, the single bullet that (magically) changed world history, and allowed the Warren Commission, "to recognize" a lone shooter, as fact! Arlen, analyze the Mcgruder film, for in it, "and" in the laws of physics and inertia, your theory, and the entire basis of the Warren Report, (the single bullet theory) is disproved! Therefore your lack of concern, for establishing the true facts, and your motives, for diverting a thorough investigation, remain a central concern!

PS#1- Arlen Spectre is still an "active" Pennsylvania Senator!

PS#2- John Poindexter- Convicted & Pardoned, Secretary of State under Ronald Reagan (of Iran Contra fame) is/was, our head of Homeland security! Imagine that? No! Realize that! Did any newspaper declare that Poindexter was Top Cop?

PS#3- John Poindexter was forced to resign as head of Homeland Security, after he suggested that the events in the Middle East, should somehow, be open to bidding, on the stock market, and Congress could find no sensible reason to do so. Poindexter asserted that the stock market was a "good indicator" of events to come.

That misguided assertion, that we could somehow, predict the events of the "Middle East" by selling stock, associated with real time events, brought his character and his leadership ability at Homeland security to the worlds attention. And, being unable to justify his absurd recommendation concerning the "Middle East", Congress insisted on his resignation. Therefore, he resigned! He Resigned? He RESIGNED! What the heck, was he doing there? Let me get this straight! A man initiates a covert operation, breaking numerous International Laws, conspires to suppress facts, etc. Yet, IMMUNITY is granted, and he admits his complicity. Now, he's ready to be "Top Cop"! My question is; Did you know that John Poindexter is/was your "Head of Homeland Security? Did you know that he was granted "IMMUNITY" by Congress, "before" he admitted to any involvement in the Iran/Contra missions through Oliver North? How, and why, did George Jr. decide that John Poindexter, was the right man to head "our?" Homeland Security?

THE FROG FARM CONSPIRACY

How Texas Criminal Justice Became a Street Gang

By
Randall D. Kelton
PO Box 1
Boyd, TX 76023
HM: 940.433.5070
MO: 940. 399.9922

HOW GOOD THINGS GO BAD

We all like to think we live in a land governed by rule of law, but in our hearts we know better. If you live in these United States and are accused of crime, you will not get a fair trial. That is not to say you can't get acquitted, just, nothing about the process is fair and just only incidentally. The public officials we put in place to protect our rights abuse, abridge, and abate them as a matter of course and do so with arrogance and impunity. You just try to do something about it and see what happens.

This document definitively demonstrates dastardly deeds and outrageous wrongs wrought, not by the worst, by the truest of heart, in the best of faith. It will show, with 'specificity and particularity' how, in Texas, otherwise well meaning officials regularly and routinely deny you and me in our sworn protection, basic rights, simple dignity, and common civility.

It further will further show how we have all been conned, how in criminally culpable collusion with an ongoing criminal conspiracy to deprive us all the protection of our constitutions and laws we have all been coerced into accepting the unacceptable.

It will further show how, even our public officials, acting from behind the threat of the policing powers, while extorting money from us under pretense of criminal procedure, have been seduced as well. We have all been persuaded that, what appears to be wrong and in violation of clear law is somehow a misperception and acceptable.

What is happening, is not law. It only vaguely resembles law, having nothing to do with justice.
It is a conspiracy I tell you, a low down dirty rotten out right sneaking conniving conspiracy. Oh, this is a sorry sordid business.

If you think this sounds a bit outrageous you are right; it is outrageous. If you think this is not right, you're right again, it isn't, but it is how things work in Texas.

Getting a bit incredulous are we? About this time you are probably considering this the ravings of one of those outrageous radicals who rant in the public ear and rail in righteous indignation about an unidentified 'they' who conspire to enslave us all. And then there are those who find demons under every bed and conspiracies behind every motive. But, be warned of the broad brush as it has a tendency to cover more than clarify.

Freedom, whatever else, is not free. It commands constant conscientious care and critique. Its enemies are everywhere, from inside as well as out. If we are to be responsible stewards and bequeath freedom intact to our children, we must doggedly demonstrate due diligence. We must be prepared to confront all its enemies, not just the convenient and colorful.

There is an enemy out there that needs confronting. Seductive and seditious, it lies camouflaged among the common and the everyday, lurking in the details. There is no demonic despot here against whom we can rail in indignation, dehumanize beyond all compassion then let loose the dogs of war toward righteous retribution. This enemy is filled with guile and subtlety. It prays on our distraction and self-deception. It hides behind our self-made fears we refuse to face.

While the problem is persistent and pervasive, it is not inevitable. While the problem is complex in its manifestation the solution is simple, and we don't need new legislation. This problem exists from no lack of law; this problem exists from failure to follow law. Read the book, do what it says and the problem will go away. For all its complex manifestations, it will simply go away.

Our Constitutional Framers and subsequent Legislators put together a comprehensive Corpus Juris, a body of law, a homogeneous whole; it all works together. When picked apart and partitioned into disparate pieces, it can be squed and squeezed to give the appearance of supporting most any notion.

If you read the Texas Code of Criminal Procedure and Penal Code then examine the current practice of criminal justice, you will, get the impression you have stepped through the looking glass. You will find yourself in a wonderland where nothing is as it seems, where one thing is said and another done.

The problems I present stem from a simple perceptional aberration, the ill-conceived notion that our statutory construction is somehow capricious and arbitrary, that our Legislators and Constitutional Framers didn't really mean what they said. The solution is, therefore, simple. Go back to the basics. Follow the law as written even if it is not administratively convenient or adjudicated expediently.
This is not only a good strategy, it is the only strategy, as the problem exists not from lack of law, but deference to variance from law.

The first hurdle to overcome is the inherent fear of our own. There is this common notion that our police and public officials are to be feared.

"You better watch out. They will get you if you buck the system."

"You can't fight city hall."

"Bla bla, bla; yada, yada, yada."

We have all hear it, many even used it, but it is a dodge. It is simply not true. They will not get you. You don't have to fight city hall, they are your employees, your public servants. To assert our public officials are somehow adversaries is simply irresponsible and unacceptable. We, as mature responsible adults, simply cannot allow ourselves to become terrified of the governmental instruments we have created.

Our government is made up of people just like you and me; they are our neighbors, our countrymen and women. For the most part, they go into government service to serve and support us. To then dishonor them by doubting their good faith is adolescent; it is betrayal.

We look to our police and courts to protect us from our own distraction, to keep us focused and careful so we don't wind up a statistic. Our public officials deserve the same protection we ask from them. It is our duty, yours and mine, to demand and insure our public officials stay well within the limits we set for them, but we have failed them in this and we have failed our selves and our children.

The second hurdle is an illusion, a mental momentum we perpetuate out of our need to believe we are free and protected by our laws. We know things seem unfair, but we assume there is something important we simply don't know. We figure judges, prosecutors, and defense counsel are legal professionals, and they know something we don't, that explains the apparent contradictions.

When demonstrated with specifics, how the law is being subverted and perverted by our trusted public officials, people tend to feel threatened and vulnerable, as well they should. They also tend to feel helpless to address or alter the practices of the powers that be, and defend by denial. We simply refuse to see what we cannot accept.

What are you talking about? I simply refuse to accept that I am in denial.

How can any true American accept that there is no law, that we are not free from the capricious and arbitrary exercise of power to our detriment? How does one admit that everything is a lie?

Recognizing the fact, that we are not protected by our Constitution, means accepting our vulnerability, and we can't do that.

We all know how things are, but it is an unspoken rule, we don't say it out loud. Consequently, the first response I generally get is, "No way. There is no way things ca be as bad as you say, after all, we have rights."

We certainly like to think that. We were told that and taught that, but even as children we knew better. While in school, while being indoctrinated into the benefits of the American form of government and our inalienable rights under it, the reality was being demonstrated otherwise. As we were being instructed in the immutable nature of our sovereignty and rights there under, it was made clear; any attempt to claim or exercise those rights would be considered insubordination and swiftly bring the full weight of the system on our heads.

Yes, I have heard all the reasonable rationale from our educators about how a single chink in their authoritarian armor will cascade inevitably into chaos. I understand how treating the children with dignity and respect for their rights would be administratively inconvenient but consider the consequences.

From our children's first experience with government, the difference between the rhetoric and reality is stark. While they have rights somewhere, school is not somewhere. School is the reality they have to live in. They are compelled by law to rehearse the words and talk the talk, while toeing a totally different line. When these children become adults, how could you expect them to miraculously transform into empowered citizens when any attempt at empowerment for the last twelve years was met with overwhelming retribution?

People don't vote, because they feel powerless to affect the system. People don't scream in righteous indignation, when wronged by the governmental instruments they have empowered. They have been indoctrinated into powerlessness.

This is not an indictment of the school systems. I have the utmost respect for our educators and accept them as consummate professionals doing the best they can, given their circumstance. Blaming the schools would be as over simplistic as blaming the public for not policing their police. The problem with the problem is more complex. For all that is wrong, there are no bad guys to blame. Well, there may be one or two, but they are not the problem. The problem is that the good guys, doing the best they know how, have been compromised, coerced and conditioned to blindly follow a false and self-serving authority.

I only mention the schools above and the judges below in order to draw a line from the cause to the outcome of a basic, underlying problem in this country. This background is not intended to imply justification for the Frog Farm Conspiracy I will demonstrate later, but only as a way to demonstrate how something so outrageous can creep up on us.

The hardest hurdle I will have to handle is mental momentum. I understand the difficulty of stepping through the looking glass as our concocted reflection or our own expectations and need for a safe protective system is too comfortable to cast aside easily.

Our Constitutional framers and subsequent Legislators laid down a very sophisticated and well-structured body of law. Like any body, when we change parts around, even apparently small and insignificant ones, consequences inevitably evolve we never contemplated.

Therefore, it is short sighted and irresponsible to blame individuals when a problem is pervasive across the system. This is not a problem with individuals. It is a problem with ideals, expediency, and focus. We naturally tend to focus on immediate concerns, bend toward expediency, and often lose sight of basic guiding principals.

When we betray basic principals, problems radiate out, often with no clear and obvious connection. When problems accrue across a system, you must always look to the basics and the legal system is no exception. Judicial integrity is decaying across the board, from the top to the bottom, so where do we look for answers?

Our Capricious Courts

The ultimate and most basic problem with our legal system stems from the Supreme Court. We can point back to 1872 when the Justices ruled on a matter directly affecting their individual financial liability. In an asserted effort to protect the honor and sanctity of the courts, they created a condition insuring the opposite. They ruled the Legislature did not mean exactly what it clearly stated when it intended to make judges subject to civil suit for acts in violation of a citizens rights from the bench and rendered themselves above and beyond rule of law.

Consequently, in this country, the only ones who trust the courts have never been before them. All who have been there know, Judges are essentially above the law. They can do whatever they please and there is little or nothing you can do about it. When you or I stand before a Judge we are bound to the letter of law. If we have counsel s/he is similarly bound to law and the appropriate bar association standards and we are both bound to the caprice of the judge. The judges, in their turn are bound to nothing but their individual personal passions and convictions, or lack thereof.

What reasonable person of ordinary prudence would consider such a circumstance, anything but inherently unfair? In such a situation, a fair trial is simply not possible. That is not to say you can't prevail in court; one party or the other inevitably does; only that nothing about the process is fair.

Attorneys spend years in school coming out ready to change the world only to find the holy-grail of rights and freedom, was all smoke and mirrors. They quickly find, in the real world, rule of law has been supplanted by judicial personalities.
All that matters is rather or not you appeal to the personal passions of the judge, you are before. If an attorney can't sufficiently coddle and conjoal the judge, they will never get to anything even resembling law, and a successful career before the bar simply will not happen.

How we got from where we were intended, to where we are, is a classic example of the best of intentions.

During the reconstruction of the nation after the Civil War, the governmental structures in the south were left in place. The police, judges, mayors and other officials, who needed to maintain order and civil administration were retained, but under direction of the North. The Yankee interference however, was much detested and mostly disregarded. It was difficult to ensure compliance at a local level and appeals to the courts for justice went unheeded, so the Congress enacted legislation that would, first, make a public official subject to civil suit for violating a citizens rights, and second, make it a criminal act.

On January 29, 1866, Senator Trumbull took to the Senate floor to describe S. 61 to his colleagues. Trumbull indicated that "the first section will amount to nothing more than the declaration in the Constitution itself, unless we have the machinery to carry it into effect." Id., at 475. The Senator then alluded to the second section of the bill that provided:

In the Legislative hearings, it was made clear:

That any person who under color of any law, statute, ordinance, regulation, or custom shall subject, or cause to be subjected, any inhabitant of any State or Territory to the deprivation of any right secured or protected by this act, or to different punishment, pains, or penalties on account of such person having at any time been held in a condition of slavery or involuntary servitude, . . . or by reason of his color or race, than is prescribed for the punishment of white persons, shall be deemed guilty of a misdemeanor, and, on conviction, shall be punished by fine not exceeding $1,000, or imprisonment not exceeding one year, or both, in the discretion of the court." Ibid.
This ultimately became the Ku Klux Klan Act of 1871 and was eventually codified into Federal law as 42USC1983 and 18USC242   43USC1983

18 USC 1983. - Civil action for deprivation of rights
Every person who, under color of any statute, ordinance, regulation, custom, or usage, of any State or Territory or the District of Columbia, subjects, or causes to be subjected, any citizen of the United States or other person within the jurisdiction thereof to the deprivation of any rights, privileges, or immunities secured by the Constitution and laws,

shall be liable to the party injured in an action at law, suit in equity, or other proper proceeding for redress, except that in any action brought against a judicial officer for an act or omission taken in such officer's judicial capacity, injunctive relief shall not be granted unless a declaratory decree was violated or declaratory relief was unavailable. For the purposes of this section, any Act of Congress applicable exclusively to the District of Columbia shall be considered to be a statute of the District of Columbia.

This would make every public official subject to civil suit if they violated a citizen's rights.

18USC242 made the above a criminal act.

§ 242. Deprivation of rights under color of law

Release date: 2004-08-06

Whoever, under color of any law, statute, ordinance, regulation, or custom, willfully subjects any person in any State, Territory, Commonwealth, Possession, or District to the deprivation of any rights, privileges, or immunities secured or protected by the Constitution or laws of the United States, or to different punishments, pains, or penalties, on account of such person being an alien, or by reason of his color, or race, than are prescribed for the punishment of citizens, shall be fined under this title or imprisoned not more than one year, or both; and if bodily injury results from the acts committed in violation of this section or if such acts include the use, attempted use, or threatened use of a dangerous weapon, explosives, or fire, shall be fined under this title or imprisoned not more than ten years, or both; and if death results from the acts committed in violation of this section or if such acts include kidnapping or an attempt to kidnap, aggravated sexual abuse, or an attempt to commit aggravated sexual abuse, or an attempt to kill, shall be fined under this title, or imprisoned for any term of years or for life, or both, or may be sentenced to death.

Judges considered this a direct threat to their autonomy and potential personal liability. They knew full well that this would require them to act within the limits of law, or suffer consequences.

This is how the Court dealt with it.

"Title 42 U.S.C. s 1983 is written in broad terms. It purports to subject "[e]very person: acting under color of state law to liability for depriving any other person in the unite States of "rights, privileges, or immunities secured by the Constitution and law." The Court has consistently recognized, however, that s 1983 was not intended "to abolish wholesale all common-law immunities."

"As early as 1872, the Court recognized that it was "a general principle of the highest importance to the proper administration of justice that a judicial officer, in exercising the authority vested in him, [should] be free to act upon his own convictions, without apprehension of personal consequences to himself." Bradley v. Fisher, supra, at 347. For that reason the Court held that "judges of courts of superior or general jurisdiction are not liable to civil actions for their judicial acts, even when such acts are in excess of their jurisdiction, and are alleged to have been done maliciously or corruptly." 13 Wall., at 351. Later we held that this doctrine of judicial immunity was applicable in suits under § 1 of the Civil Rights Act of 1871, 42 U.S.C. § 1983, for the legislative record gave no indication that Congress intended to abolish this long-established principle. " Pierson v. Ray, 386 U.S. 547 (1967).

Nonsense, of course the Legislative debates gave indication it intended this to apply to the courts. It is clear the bill was specifically intended to create a new remedy that would protect citizens from the improper rulings of judges.

Representative Wilson of Iowa, Chairman of the House Judiciary Committee, introduced S. 61 in the House on March 1, 1866. Of 1 of the bill, he said:

"Mr. Speaker, I think I may safely affirm that this bill, so far as it declares the equality of all citizens in the enjoyment of civil rights and immunities merely affirms existing law. We are following the Constitution. . . . It is not the object of this bill to establish new rights, but to protect and enforce those which already belong to every citizen." Id., at 1117.

That the Legislatures' intent to abolish the prior common law protecting recalcitrant judges, was made even clearer when President Johnson vetoed the bill, claiming it would allow Legislators to be sued:

Trumbull took issue with both statements. As to the charge that it would result in the criminal prosecution of state legislators, Trumbull replied

"Who is to be punished? Is the law to be punished? Are the men who make the law to be punished? Is that the language of the bill? Not at all! If any person, 'under color of any law,' shall subject another to the deprivation of a right to which he is entitled, he is to be punished. Who? The person who, under the color of the law, does the act, not the men who made the law. In some communities in the South a custom prevails by which different punishment is inflicted upon the blacks from that meted out to whites for the same offense. Does this section propose to punish the community where the custom prevails? Or is it to punish the person who, under color of the custom, deprives the party of his right? It is a manifest perversion of the meaning of the section to assert anything else." Id., at 1758.

To assert that this act was meant other than to punish judges is a "manifest perversion of the meaning of the section." As to the nonsense about creating a new remedy, they were very cognizant that, that was exactly what they were doing.

Representative Shellabarger added that 1 provided a civil remedy "on the same state of facts" as 2 of the Civil Rights Act of 1866. Ibid. Obviously Representative Shellabarger's introduction of 1 of the bill to his colleagues would have been altogether different if he had been of the view that the 39th Congress, of which he had been a Member, had already created a broader federal damages remedy against state actors in 1866. The view that 1 of the 1871 Acts was an amendment of or supplement to the 1866 Act designed to create a new civil remedy against state actors, was echoed throughout the debates in the House. See id., at 461 (Rep. Coburn); id., at App. 312-313 (Rep. Burchard). Opponents of 1 operated on this same understanding. See id., at 429 (Rep. McHenry) ("The first section of the bill is intended as an amendment of the civil rights act"); id., at 365 (Rep. Arthur). [62]

Both proponents and opponents in the House viewed 1 as working an expansion of federal jurisdiction.

Supporters continually referred to the failure of the state courts to enforce federal law designed for the protection of the freedman, and saw 1 as remedying this situation by interposing the federal courts between the State, and citizens of the United States. See id., at 376 (Rep. Lowe) ("The case has arisen . . . when the Federal Government must resort to its own agencies to carry its own authority into execution. Hence this bill throws open the doors of the United States courts to those whose rights under the Constitution are denied or impaired"). Opponents recognized the expansion of original jurisdiction and railed against it on policy and constitutional grounds. See id., at 429 (Rep. McHenry) ("The first section of the bill . . . vests in the Federal courts jurisdiction to determine the individual rights of citizens of the same State; a jurisdiction which of right belongs only to the State tribunals"); id., at App. 50 (Rep. Kerr); id., at 365-366 (Rep. Authur); id., at 373 (Rep. Archer). JETT v. DALLAS INDEPENDENT SCHOOL DISTRICT 1989

Bradley v. Fisher and its' progeny is so blatant a contradiction to the Legislative intent, it cannot be construed these experienced learned men were somehow ignorant of exactly what they were doing. This act was in clear defiance of the clear intent of the law.

A fundamental canon of statutory construction is that, unless otherwise defined, words will be interpreted as taking their ordinary, contemporary common meaning. rns v. Alcala, 420 U.S. 575, 580-581 (1975). See Perrin v State (1979).

What worse betrayal can a people suffer than that of the most revered and trusted. How great the wrong, was stipulated by an earlier court in 1821.

It is most true that this Court will not take jurisdiction if it should not: but it is equally true, that it must take jurisdiction if it should. The judiciary cannot, as the legislature may, avoid a measure because it approaches the confines of the constitution. We cannot pass it by because it is doubtful. With whatever doubts, with whatever difficulties, a case may be attended, we must decide it, if it be brought before us.

We have no more right to decline the exercise of jurisdiction when it is given, than to usurp that, which is not given. The one or the other would be treason to the constitution. Questions may occur which we would gladly avoid; but we cannot avoid them.

All we can do is, to exercise our best judgment, and conscientiously to perform our duty. Cohens v. Virginia, 19 U.S. (6 Wheat) 264, 404, 5 L.Ed 257 (1821)

H.G. Wells, in his outline of history, while speaking to the corruption of the Popes during the dark ages, aptly observed:

"The giver of the law most owes the law allegiance. He of all beings should behave as if the law compels him. But, it is the universal failing of mankind that what we are given to administer, we promptly presume we own,"

No reasonable person of ordinary prudence can study this decision and not be dismayed at the audacity. The courts have ruled a police officer on the street, making decisions in the heat of the moment even at the point of a gun, can be subject to suit. In their wisdom they required a heightened pleading standard but left police at risk as they felt it necessary to prevent abuse.

But, when it came to their own acts, taken at their leisure, after careful contemplation and in possession of all the facts, ruled the public had no similar right to protection.

At best this is outrageous, at worst, Seditious Conspiracy.

Sec. 2384. - Seditious conspiracy

If two or more persons in any State or Territory, or in any place subject to the jurisdiction of the United States, conspire to overthrow, put down, or to destroy by force the Government of the United States, or to levy war against them, or to oppose by force the authority thereof, or by force to prevent, hinder, or delay the execution of any law of the United States, or by force to seize, take, or possess any property of the United States contrary to the authority thereof, they shall each be fined under this title or imprisoned not more than twenty years, or both.

By this breach of the public trust, the clearly stated letter of law, and the body of their own decisions they created a situation whereby every person within the jurisdiction of any American Court must necessarily be denied the equal protection of the laws guaranteed by the Constitution.

So, when the highest court, the remedy of last resort so abuses the rule of law to their own personal benefit as to shock the conscious of any reasonable neutral observer, what recourse remains?

I suggest two. The first is a matter of jurisdiction. The Justices who made these rulings had a personal stake in the outcome of their rulings and that points to a well-established remedy.

As we held in Aetna life Ins. Co. v. Lavoie, 475 U.S. 813 (1986), this concern has constitutional dimensions. In that case we wrote:

"We conclude that Justice Embry's participation in this case violated appellant's due process rights as explicated in Tumey, Murchison, and Ward. We make clear that we are not required to decide whether in fact Justice Embry was influenced, but only whether sitting on the case then before the Supreme Court of Alabama '"would offer a possible temptation to the average [judge] . . . [to] lead him not to hold the balance nice, clear and true.'" The Due Process Clause 'may sometimes bar trial by judges who have no actual bias and who would do their very best to weigh the scales of justice equally between contending parties. But to perform its high function in the best way, "justice must satisfy the appearance of justice."'" Id., at 825

The Court would have it that "when all are disqualified, none are disqualified." They would have us accept that judges may make decisions affecting judges with impunity. I suggest, when a matter affects all, judges must either follow the strict letter of the law or defer to the Legislature for direction. But to say, if none of us should rule on a subject, it is perfectly fine for any of us to rule is utter nonsense.

(Look up All are Disqualified)

This matter involved much more than the appearance of bias; it involved a situation where the Justices stood to be personally liable in their individual capacities if they violated a person's rights under color of their authority. So long as the court stayed within the limits of law they were at no risk, so what was the problem?

One meaning of "impartiality" in the judicial context -- and of course its root meaning -- is the lack of bias for or against either party to the proceeding. Impartiality in this sense assures equal application of the law. That is, it guarantees a party that the judge who hears his case will apply the law to him in the same way he applies it to any other party.

This is the traditional sense in which the term is used. See Webster's New International Dictionary 1247 (2d ed. 1950) (defining "impartial" as "[n]ot partial; esp., not favoring one more than another; treating all alike; unbiased; equitable; fair; just"). It is also the sense in which it is used in the cases cited by respondents and amici for the proposition that an impartial judge is essential to due process. Tumey v. Ohio, 273 U. S. 510, 523, 531-534 (1927) (judge violated due process by sitting in a case in which it would be in his financial interest to find against one of the parties); Aetna Life Ins. Co. v. Lavoie, 475 U. S. 813, 822-825 (1986) (same); Ward v. Monroeville, 409 U. S. 57, 58-62 (1972) Republican Party of Minnesota v. White, 122 S.Ct. 2528, 153 L.Ed.2d 694 (U.S. 06/27/2002)

Failing disqualification of the Justices, we might consider the potential criminal aspect of their actions. By denying every citizen in the United States in their right to a fair trial, how do the Justices avoid culpability under criminal law?

Whenever a judge acts where he/she does not have jurisdiction to act, the judge is engaged in an act or acts of treason. U.S. v. Will, 449 U.S. 200, 216, 101 S.Ct. 471, 66 L.Ed.2d 392, 406 (1980); Cohens v. Virginia, 19 U.S. (6 Wheat) 264, 404, 5 L.Ed 257 (1821)

When the Judges threw down the gauntlet to the Legislature and simply refused to enforce the law as passed, they assured the public there were other avenues of redress.

As concerns that other avenue, while they provided themselves immunity from civil litigation, I find nothing absolving them of criminal responsibility. They didn't have the audacity to go quite that far. However, what they couldn't do directly, they did on the sly. In order to protect themselves from criminal prosecution they extended immunity to those individuals who could potentially prosecute them, prosecutors.

There was a time when a citizen could pursue prosecution of a judge or other lawbreaker as a private prosecutor. That made for a very effective check to the balance of judicial power, but no longer. The right of the citizen to police our police has been usurped. If you read the law, it gives the appearance of a Grand Jury standing as a check to the balance of powers wielded by the courts.
That is the appearance, but not the reality. In the real world, it is all smoke and mirrors, as Grand Juries have been rendered mute by the illegal practices promoted by Prosecutors and condoned by Judges.

Contrary to the rule of law, by clearly stipulated statutory direction, a complaint against public official should be, yet are not, presented to "some magistrate" thereby commencing a prosecution, but rather, they are always sent to prosecutors. Prosecutors then exercise discretion as to whether or not to present the complaints to the Grand Jury.

In Texas, this is done even though it is expressly forbidden (see Article 32.02 Code of Criminal Procedure. In the case of federal prosecutors, however, the courts have gone farther and given them the authority to usurp the Judiciary and make judicial decisions concerning the sufficiency of allegations. They have given federal prosecutors the authority to dismiss prosecutions. Since Federal Prosecutors are members of the Executive Branch of government, this works an outrageous violation of the separation of powers and virtually insures no judge will be prosecuted for criminal acts unless the President finds it politically expedient.

If a judge does not fully comply with the Constitution, then his orders are void, In re Sawyer, 124 U.S. 200 (1888), he/she is without jurisdiction, and he/she has engaged in an act or acts of treason.

By creating an immunity, specifically denied by clear legislation, and granting judicial powers to prosecutors, the Supreme Court has acted well beyond any jurisdiction, so, what is to be done when the highest court in our land, stoops to the lowest of levels?

In the current climate, when a judge acts in violation of law and denies a citizen in one of his/her rights there is nothing a citizen can do about it? When those, whom are put in place to enforce law, become the violators, who is left to raise a red flag?

In such a situation, no lawyer in his/her right professional mind would do anything to incur the ire of any judge or prosecutor, not if s/he ever wants to win another case. So don't expect your defense counsel to raise much ruckus. And the Legislature will tell you real quick they just make the laws, they have nothing to do with enforcement, besides Legislators are as frightened of Judges as anyone else.

Maybe the FBI or Federal Prosecutors could be counted on to protect our rights. Not in this life! They are members of the Executive branch of government. They work for the President who appoints the Federal Judges. As must be clear to even a casual observer, those aspects of law enforcement who work for the President of this country are little more than political arms if the incumbent administrations. You can't expect them to do anything that is not politically expedient in the short term.

When the only Constitutional Court in the land abolishes the Constitution at its whim, who would risk raising a threatening issue?
American Legal System Is Corrupt Beyond Recognition
...Judge Tells Harvard Law School
By Geraldine Hawkins   3-9-3

The American legal system has been corrupted almost beyond recognition, Judge Edith Jones of the U.S. Court of Appeals for the Fifth Circuit, told the Federalist Society of Harvard Law School on February 28.

She said that the question of what is morally right is routinely sacrificed to what is politically expedient. The change has come about, because legal philosophy has descended to nihilism.

Reading the Court's reasoning in support of setting themselves apart from the rule of law, they present a logical case, but remember,

"Logic is not truth; it merely has the ring of truth and, therefore, is the first refuge of the scoundrel."

In this case the logic is specious at best, if not deliberately malicious. At the least the reasoning is without rational foundation.

If you want the real reason for their betrayal look to Imbler v Patchman:
"it is better to leave unredressed the wrongs done by dishonest officers, than to subject those who try to do their duty to the constant dread of retaliation." Imbler v Patchman 424 U.S. 409 @ 428.

It seems the Court totally missed the point. The dread of consequences of criminal behavior on the bench to which they speak was exactly the legislative point. The only reason they would have for dread, would be when they were guilty of a culpable violation of law, and it was the precise intent of our Legislators to instill just such a dread in the courts.

How could honorable judges have a problem with being subject to the same rule of law, upon which, they rule? In a decision relevant to legislation that was only two years old, if the Justices had any question as to the intent of the Legislature, asking them if they really meant "every" when they said, "every person," would have sufficed to clarify any confusion on their part.

Since the court's job is to interpret the intent of the Legislature, a few statements of intent from the Legislature when passing laws would do a world of good.

As it is, the Supreme Court gave the appearance that their judgement was clouded by personal interest, and instead of heightened standards, they opted for no standards.

Now we have courts without honor, that no one trusts or respects. We have truly capricious courts before which, citizens and attorneys alike must bow and scrape, if they expect to win cases. Just ask any attorney, if a Judge will screw their clients in retaliation for any slight or annoyance.

When I ask attorneys to take cases wherein I have made criminal allegations against judges and other public officials, they all tell me the same thing:

"Are you out of your mind? I can't take your case. I have to represent clients in this county."

"What's the matter Jerry, are you afraid the Judge will screw your next client, to get back at you?"

"You're damn right they will." (Jerry Cobb, past District Attorney for Denton County).

The Supreme Court, in rendering that horrendous ruling in Bradley v. Fisher, stated; there were other avenues of redress. From the record it appears they were referring to higher courts of appeal. They can't be serious. Could they really consider one capricious court as a remedy for another? If, I get screwed by one Court! Then, I'm to expect another, to attack the professional credibility of one of their cronies for my benefit. They can't be serious.

Surely they weren't referring to the fallacy of the ballot box, Federal judges aren't elected, and local Judges are protected by a ring of incredible secrecy. Complaints against Judges are secret, and Judges aren't allowed to point out the poor record of other judges when running against them.

This brings us to the Bar. Whereby, truly capricious courts have set themselves outside the law. What protections do we as citizens have?

Well, there is always the Bar. We have attorneys, whose duty is to protect our rights, regardless of what the judges think or prefer. It is the duty of our attorney to vigorously represent us, and to insure that all of our rights are scrupulously guarded. But, what is an attorney to do? If s/he raises a red flag and tries to take the courts to task, s/he will be committing professional suicide.

The Bar Association is supposedly there to hold all attorneys (judges, prosecutors, and defense counsel) to the highest standards of professional ethics; to insure that all act with honor and integrity. So what happened? You can find the answer in any book of lawyer jokes? Considering, what other profession inspires such universal distrust and derision?

Electricians, plumbers, doctors, engineers, stockbrokers, and most every other profession is held to high standards of professional ethics by governmental agencies, set up for the purpose of regulating them. You don't see books of doctor jokes or electrician jokes. Outside oversight is a tried and true method of maintaining a relatively high degree of professionalism in an industry. So, my question is, why not the Bar?
The Bar, unlike every other licensed professional oversight organization, is regulated by itself. The one profession, in that, we depend on to protect us, we are denied the protection of outside oversight. What attorney is going to be impartial when critiquing a crony? Who is going to risk strict adherence when they could wind up on the other end of their stern decisions?
In such a circumstance, what else could you expect? Do you really expect an association of attorneys to police itself, especially when they face member judges, who can ruin any one of them at the drop of a hat?

The Frog Farm Conspiracy below demonstrates how, most every step from arrest to trial, as presently practiced by the Criminal Justice System in Texas, is not only wrong, but very specifically against particular law. Not only is every step, at variance to law, it is at variance toward very specific purpose. It is set up and maintained by our esteemed members of the Bar.

Judges, prosecutors, and defense counsel all benefit from those practices. High ethical and moral standards would only cost them money, so who is there, to step up and (if you will excuse the pun) risk their career by raising the bar? If not for the Bar, we would still live in a land of law governed with honor and dignity. But, through the Bar, with its peer cooperation and collaboration, this is not the case. But for the Bar, lawyers and courts would still be held in the high esteem, that our Constitutional Framers enjoyed and intended to preserve.

THE PROBLEM WITH THE PROBLEM

I realize this may sound as though I have some axe to grind or personal a vendetta. If that were all, this would be much easier; but such is not the case. The problem with this problem is there is no apparent demonic inspired malignant calculus, at which to point an indignant finger, in righteous condemnation.

Once the Supreme Court, by their injudicious act toward self-preservation, managed to crack our judicial egg, a bad outcome was inevitable. The Legislature, in its turn drove a defining wedge, while acting in apparent best of faith, toward the noblest of intents, which virtually assured the system would decay to just the circumstance, we now experience.

The Legislature, in its wisdom, opted for the expedience of exploiting learned counsel, already in public employ, and directed prosecutors to provide legal advice to the police and lower courts. On cursory consideration, this appeared an efficient allocation of resources, even though it violated a basic principal of law.

Texas Disciplinary Rules of Professional Conduct

I CLIENT-LAWYER RELATIONSHIP

2. A fundamental principle recognized by paragraph (a) is that a lawyer may not represent opposing parties in litigation. The term opposing parties as used in this Rule contemplates a situation where a judgment favorable to one of the parties will directly impact unfavorably upon the other party. Moreover, as a general proposition loyalty to a client prohibits undertaking representation directly adverse to the representation of that client in a substantially related matter unless that clients fully informed consent is obtained and unless the lawyer reasonably believes that the lawyers representation will be reasonably protective of that clients interests. Paragraphs (b) and (c) express that general concept.

In the real world, the prosecutor is necessarily compromised when advising the police and lower courts on matters before which s/he will represent the State. One would expect a harried and overworked prosecutor to render advice that would tend to serve the professional agenda and prosecutors' purpose and that is exactly what has happened.

13 Am Jru Proof of Facts 3d, 21

"Without having been directly authorized, tacitly encouraged, or even adequately trained, police officers, like other public employees, may fall into patterns of unconstitutional conduct. This can result from a variety of factors, not sufficiently traceable in origin to any fault of "municipal policy" in the Monell sense (Monell v Dept. of Social Services (1978) 436 US 658, and Soell v McDaniel (1987 CA4 NC) 824 F2d 1380). If these unconstitutional practices become sufficiently widespread, however, they may assume the quality of "custom or usage" which has the force of law…"

Each impropriety I will indicate, when given cursory consideration in isolation, appear only minor adjustments toward administrative convenience and adjudicative expediency. If that were all it is, this would be much simpler.

Unfortunately, when considered in concert, they point to something much more insidious, something downright seditious. It points to a set of practices and procedures, designed and intended to put a person accused of crime, into a position such that s/he has no viable alternative, to taking what sounds like a perfectly reasonable sounding deal. Guilt or innocence is simply not a relevant issue in the current system.

In spite of the righteous rhetoric, and clear directives to prosecutors contained in Article 2.01 Code of Criminal Procedure which states:

Art. 2.01. Duties of district attorneys.
Each district attorney shall represent the State in all criminal cases in the district courts of his district, and in appeals therefrom, except in cases where he has been, before his election, employed adversely.

When any criminal proceeding is had before an examining court in his district or before a judge upon habeas corpus, and he is notified of the same, and is at the time within his district, he shall represent the State therein, unless prevented by other official duties.

It shall be the primary duty of all prosecuting attorneys, including any special prosecutors, not to convict, but to see that justice is done.

They shall not suppress facts or secrete witnesses capable of establishing the innocence of the accused.

Prosecutors routinely ignore this specific mandate of law, and deny citizens of their rights, as a matter of course. They also direct the police and lower courts toward complicit cooperation, in the subversion of well-established principals of the due course of law.

When questioned, most will readily admit things appear different than the written statutory mandates, but they assure me, that this is the way things are done and have been done. When I cite a specific statute, they start talking about "legal fiction," with the implicit presumption that, "what the law says is not really what it means." Besides, this is how they have been doing it; how they have been trained and directed to do it; and how they are going to continue to do it. It is clear, public officials trust learned counsel in the form or prosecutors, more than they trust their instincts, their personal judgement, and their ability to read and understand what is clearly written.

When I start pointing out chapter and verse and how it all fits neatly together, their eyes start darting from side to side as if looking for a rational way out. High School all over again; the book says one thing, while reality demonstrates another. When you see this same discomfort over and over, it becomes clear, we are putting otherwise well-intended officials in a position to where they have to defend a system they know is unjust. We thereby, deprive them of their dignity, their honor, and their will to do the right thing, and this is unacceptable.

On the other hand, while we put our public officials in a rather untenable position, at the end of the day, the individual must make a decision. They can either do what they know is right, and the law commands risking retribution from their superiors, or go along to get along, and in the process, become criminals themselves in the worst kind of betrayal, that of personal and public trust.

We cannot assume that any of the officials indicated are ignorant of the laws controlling their official duties.

Take the case of a local officer who persists in enforcing a type of ordinance that the Court has held invalid, as violating the guarantees of free speech or freedom of worship.

Or a local official continues to select juries in a manner that flies in the teeth of decisions of the Court. If those acts were done willfully, how can the officer possibly claim that he had no fair warning that his actions were prohibited by statute? He violated the statute, not merely because he had no cause, but because he acted in defiance of announced rules of law. He who defies a [*105] decision interpreting the Constitution knows precisely what he is doing. If sane, he hardly may be heard to say that he knew not what he did. Of course, willful conduct cannot make definite that which is undefined. But willful violators of constitutional requirements, which have been defined, certainly are in no position to say that they had no adequate advance notice that they would be visited with punishment. When they act willfully, in the sense in which we use the word, they act in open defiance or in reckless disregard of constitutional requirements that are specific and definite. When they are convicted for so acting, they are not punished for violating an unknowable something. Screws v US 325 U.S. 91 1945

So, when I demonstrate how prosecutors, police, and court officials are acting in particular violation of specific law, it must be assumed they act with culpable intent and full knowledge of the nature of their behavior.

In all of this, everything revolves around the prosecutor. Law students pass into a professional field ready to change the world, only to be faced with the reality of life before the bar. In the real world, just adjudication is not the standard by which success is measured; winning cases is.

While prosecutors may intently care about justice, they are faced with cases they have to win. From a professional perspective, while guilt or innocence may be a consideration, it not a criteria. Article 2.01 Texas Code of Criminal Procedure not withstanding, prosecutors don't get re-elected by seeking justice; they get re-elected by getting convictions and collecting money for the State.

Please forgive the length of this introduction, but the problem is complex, made more so because of an apparent lack of malicious intent. The lengthy introduction was necessary to put in perspective the horrendous wrongs and dastardly deeds demonstrated below perpetrated by otherwise well-meaning public officials.

It is my intent to indict the system, not personalities. Unfortunately the only path to the problem is though the people who populate and perpetrate it. That they have been put in a difficult position is certainly a concern, but cannot become a criteria. Failure to act from concern for personalities only serves to perpetuate the problem. Instead of taking our public officials to legal task at the first infraction, we were compassionate and understanding, winking at first one incursion onto hallowed constitutional grounds then another until the system became so distorted, it would no longer be recognizable by our founders. They would roll over in their graves.

THE FROG FARM CONSPIRACY

I call what follows The Frog Farm Conspiracy in consideration of Samuel Clemens who once said:

"You can throw a frog in a pot of hot water and it will jump out. But if you put that same frog in a pot of cold water and gradually raise the heat, it will sit there until it scalds to death."

Texas is a frog farm and we are all the beneficiaries. Over a period of years, prosecutors, advising the police and lower courts have directed them in practices and procedures, one adding to the other in a slow progression of transgressions, until the system no longer resembles anything originally envisioned.

Defense counsel knows full well, that things are not according to Vernon's, but what are they to do. As it is, if an attorney appointed to represent an indigent client puts on a vigorous defense, s/he will be paid about $350(varies by jurisdiction). If s/he gets the client to take a deal s/he gets paid, you guessed it, about $350. That is how it works in the real world, they practice in. How could you expect any attorney in his/her right professional mind to take money out of his/her pocket and in the process incur the wrath of judges and prosecutors to protect your rights?

This is how things work in the real world you and I live in.

When a person is accused of crime, the charging officer will either write out a ticket or swear out a complaint along with a statement of probable cause (it is common practice to use the Statement of Probable Cause as the complaint). For the purpose of this discussion, I will deal with those times when a person is arrested, as it covers elements not covered when a complaint is simply presented by an officer.

When an officer arrests a person, Article 14.06 Code of Criminal Procedure directs the officer to take the person arrested directly to the nearest magistrate:

Art. 14.06. Must take offender before magistrate.
(a)   Except as provided by Subsection (b), in each case enumerated in this Code, the person making the arrest shall take the person arrested or have him taken without unnecessary delay before the magistrate who may have ordered the arrest, before some magistrate of the county where the arrest was made without an order, or, if necessary to provide more expeditiously to the person arrested the warnings described by Article 15.17 of this Code, before a magistrate in a county bordering the county in which the arrest was made. The magistrate shall immediately perform the duties described in Article 15.17 of this Code.

(b) A peace officer who is charging a person, including a child, with committing an offense that is a Class C misdemeanor, other than an offense under Section 49.02, Penal Code, may, instead of taking the person before a magistrate, issue a citation to the person that contains written notice of the time and place the person must appear before a magistrate, the name and address of the person charged, and the offense charged.

The Supreme Court has held, a police officer has the authority and duty to arrest a person when that person commits a crime in the officer's sight or hearing, or if the officer has knowledge of a warrant for the person's arrest. They have further held that while the officer has the authority to arrest, s/he has no authority to imprison.

Harris v Steele, 64 NE 875,

But the power of detaining the person so arrested, or restraining him of his liberty, in such a case is not a matter within the discretion of the officer making the arrest. He cannot legally hold the person arrested in custody for a longer period of time than is reasonably necessary, considering the circumstances of the case. He must obtain a proper warrant or order for his further detention, from some tribunal or officer authorized under the law to issue such a warrant or order. If the person arrested is detained or held by the officer, for a longer period of time than is required, under the circumstances, without such warrant authority. He will have a cause of action for false imprisonment against the officer, and all others by whom he had been unlawfully detained or held."

The police and prosecutors are quick to point out, the Courts have ruled a 24 or even 48 hour delay in bringing before a magistrate is not necessarily an unreasonable delay. What they ignore is the 'necessarily' part. The courts made it clear there shall be no set time limit and any delay must be justified by a showing of due diligence in an effort to locate a magistrate.

As a case illustration, consider Hall v State, 52 NE2d 370:

At the time of plaintiff's arrest, there was a duly qualified and acting justice of the peace in the town where she was arrested. The town marshal nonetheless transported the plaintiff 25 miles to the county seat, where she was imprisoned in the county jail for 30 minutes before release. In affirming a jury verdict for the plaintiff, in her action for assault and battery and false imprisonment. The court held that, in light of the presence of a justice of the peace in the town where she was arrested, her transportation and incarceration in jail in another town was not necessary.

An officer's only defense against an allegation of false imprisonment is a showing of due diligence in an effort to locate a magistrate.

Roberts v Bohac, 574 F2d 1232, The appellate court stated:

"Although the failure to take the plaintiff before a magistrate would have been excused if good grounds had existed for the belief that a magistrate was not available. Such was not the case, since the defendant officers made no attempt to determine whether the magistrate was or would make himself available."

Prosecutors routinely advise police to arrest and imprison without concern for a magistrate. They make the argument that a magistrate has scheduled times when s/he does examinations. Magistrates are busy people, what with all the tickets they have to prosecute and all the revenue they have to collect for the State and local governments. However, they should all be reminded about their primary duty as Magistrates. They were not empowered by our founders, to collect ticket revenue. They were put in place in order that a citizen, restricted at his/her liberty, would have access to a neutral person, who could intercede to insure that all the rights of the citizen were upheld. When the Magistrate finds himself too busy to bother with this primary duty, the Magistrate forgets himself and his duty.

In all fairness, it doesn't work this way. Prosecutors have advised police to take the accused to jail where they can better be contained and to have the Magistrate come to the jail to do the examination.
This is not what the law commands. It commands the arresting officer to take the person arrested directly to the nearest Magistrate, by the most direct route. I have yet to talk to a Magistrate who has not indicated that they would readily hold an examination, if a person were brought to them.

Prosecutors have orchestrated the current practices, not to serve the convenience of the police and courts, but rather, to serve the prosecutors' purpose.

Screws v State, 325 U.S. 91 to know that.

The general rule was stated in Ellis v. United States, 206 U.S. 246, 257, as follows: "If a man intentionally adopts certain conduct in certain circumstances known to him, and that conduct is forbidden by the law under those circumstances, he intentionally breaks the law in the only sense in which the law ever considers intent." And see Horning v. District of Columbia, 254 U.S. 135, 137; Nash v. United States, 229 U.S. 373, 377.

The police, by taking a person they have arrested, to jail instead of to the nearest Magistrate are breaking the law.

The case law is clear, the officer has no authority to imprison and must seek the authority to hold the individual from some Magistrate. In order for the Magistrate to provide that authority, s/he must be presented with an evidentiary document accusing the individual of violating a specific statute. This document is called "a criminal complaint." When a Magistrate is presented with a criminal complaint and holds a hearing for the purpose of examining the sufficiency of the complaint, to determine if sufficient grounds exist to continue to hold the individual in custody. That is defined as an examination hearing by Article 2.10 Texas Code of Criminal Procedure.

Art. 2.11. [35] [62] [63] Examining court

When the magistrate sits for the purpose of inquiring into a criminal accusation against any person, this is called an examining court.
This is what the law clearly states, but somehow our prosecutors, police, and Magistrates have gotten things all confused. If you talk to the police or prosecutor about this process, you will hear the term, "magistration." My spell checker just put a red line under that one. For some reason it doesn't recognize the spelling; well join the club. My spell checker doesn't recognize it as prosecutors made it up.

What they do at the morning magistration is a corrupted combination of acts, cloaked in the color of law, but are in fact, a carefully crafted conspiratorial concoction intended to serve the prosecutors purpose.

It denies due process to the accused, and reduces the Magistrate from the position of honor as a neutral judge of the sufficiency of facts and protector of the citizen's rights, to nothing more than a rubberstamp member of the prosecutions' team. Helping the prosecutor, perfect his/her case and assure "the deal."

It is a pretty sharp prosecutor maneuver, but sharp practice, no matter how carefully couched in fluff and bluster is still criminal when it wreaks havoc on the due course of the law, at the expense of the police, the magistrates, and the public.

I can't overemphasize how important a proper examination hearing is. Our founders did not want the public to fear police. They envisioned a trust and cooperation between the police and the public. Who empower, and employ them. To ensure this, they put magistrates, elected from the local community, in place, to stand squarely between the police officer and the jailhouse door. It was the neutral magistrate who was to decide if a person arrested was to answer for crime or be set to his liberty, not the arresting officer and certainly not a prosecuting attorney.

This was not because our founders didn't trust our police. It was about posture. If the public have the perception a police officer can arrest at his whim and toss anyone in jail, they become a threat. You will feel subject to the individual personal passions of the officer, consequently responding to police with hostility and distrust, and that was never intended. It was intended, if an officer arrest you for any reason, with or without a warrant, s/he was to take you directly to the nearest magistrate and explain him/herself.

Prosecutors found this administratively inconvenient, as will become clear shortly, and advised the police to ignore 14.06 Code of Criminal Procedure as well as the Supreme Court, and toss the arrested person in jail, usually overnight. It would appear this was for the administrative convenience of the Magistrate, but such is not the case. Magistrates I have talked to assured me, they have no problem doing their jobs.

158

They complain that police simply do not bring persons arrested to them. They fail to do this as a matter of policy on advice of prosecutors.

The police, for their part, have no problem with taking people they arrest directly to the nearest magistrate. Most recognize the demoralizing effect current practice has on the public and how it undermines trust. But the State has trained and directed them otherwise and they feel bound to follow policy.

So, why would a proper examination hearing be a problem for a prosecutor?

There are two problems, first: the magistrate may actually determine there is not sufficient evidence to bind the individual over for trial and set the accused at their liberty, in which case the prosecutor will have no opportunity to work "the deal." At the end of the day, the prosecutor is not so interested in guilt or innocence, as convictions culminating in dollar flow for the state.

Second: if the magistrate holds a proper examination hearing, s/he will have to send a copy of the complaint to the court of jurisdiction, and that would never do as it would start the speedy trial clock.

Art. 32.01. [576] [642] [629] Defendant in Custody and No Indictment Presented

When a defendant has been detained in custody or held to bail for his appearance to answer any criminal accusation before the district court, the prosecution, unless otherwise ordered by the court, for good cause shown, supported by affidavit, shall be dismissed and the bail discharged, if indictment or information be not presented against such defendant on or before the last day of the next term of the court, which is held after his commitment or admission to bail or on or before the 180th day after the date of commitment or admission to bail, whichever date is later.

Yes I know the statute has been overturned, but not the right it defines. Only the directed verdict was found offending, not the Constitutional underpinnings. When a magistrate issues authority to bind a person over for trial, the citizen is restricted at their liberty, and therefore, a prosecution commences at that point in time, starting the speedy trial clock. The problem with this is that it doesn't give the prosecutor time to work the long practiced procedures that will inevitably get him "the deal." As it takes time to ripen the accused for the final offer, the prosecutor cannot have the speedy trial clock ticking.

If the compliant were sent to the protection of the Clerk of the Court of jurisdiction as Article 17.30 clearly commands, the speedy trial would start on the day of the arrest, leaving the prosecutor with too little time to work "the deal." So, rather cognizant of that purpose or just from the constant pressure of time and ill-considered reliance on past practice, prosecutors have advised the Magistrates to take some extraordinarily improper steps.

What justice and law require is easy to understand. The courts directed the arresting officer to take the person arrested before the nearest Magistrate, so the judge could hold an examination into the sufficiency of the claim against the accused. Often, in the heat of a moment, just and honest professional police officers can miss details or even miss-interpret what they see or hear.

The liberty of a free citizen was taken very serious by our founders and they did not intend it to be breached lightly, so they put a magistrate in place to measure all the evidence and weigh, with an equal hand, both sides.

By directing officers to ignore the necessity of an immediate examination, prosecutors put police at jeopardy of civil and even criminal prosecution.

Leger v Warren 57 NE 506 states:

"To afford protection to the officer or person making the arrest, the authority must be strictly pursued; and no unreasonable delay in procuring a proper warrant for the prisoner's detention can be excused or tolerated. Any other rule would leave the power open to great abuse and oppression."

Being that the arrest was made without a warrant, it was necessary that proper steps be taken, to prevent the further detention of the prisoner from becoming unlawful. Unless those steps were taken, all legal protection for such arrest ceases, and the arresting officers became wrongdoers from the beginning, liable, as such, equally with those by whom the unlawful imprisonment was continued.
Therefore, if the arresting officers choose to rely on some other person to perform that required duty, they take upon themselves, the risk of it being performed, and unless it was done in a proper time, their liability to the person imprisoned is not lessened or affected.

It cannot be presumed police are ignorant, and fail to recognize the injustice they are directed to perform. How could we expect an officer to act with honor and dignity when he is taught by leaders to serve a separate agenda?

If that were all there is, it would be bad enough, but these practices subject the officer to potential allegations of false imprisonment, which is a crime in the State of Texas.

Not only do police become criminals, they also become subject to civil litigation. Most officers think they have immunity. Yet, consequent to an improper act by the magistrate, and in concert and collusion with the jailer and prosecutor, all are stripped of any immunity they may have had, leaving the officer on the street, subject to civil litigation for every arrest s/he makes or has made.

As is practiced, people arrested, with or without a warrant, are eventually brought before a magistrate. The Magistrate must be presented with a document accusing the person of some crime in order to have jurisdiction to determine if the person is to be held or released. When this happens, an "Examination Hearing" commences in accordance with Article 2.11

Code of Criminal Procedure. Well, that is the idea anyway, but in Texas they do a "Magistration."

When the Magistrate convenes a hearing and accepts evidence against a citizen from the arresting officer, certain rights are triggered and the rules of evidence apply. Calling the hearing a "Magistration," or a "PIA" does not render it right under law. Well, in theory anyway if not in current practice.

The free citizen must, by Constitution, be presumed innocent, and that an arrest without a warrant, to be improper.
(Dillard V Syracuse (4th Dept) 51 App Div 2d 432, 381NYS2d913), The burden is on the arresting officer to present sufficient evidence to overcome that presumption, before a person can be further restricted in their liberty. How is it that a person, restricted at his liberty and brought before a Magistrate for the purpose of examining into the sufficiency of the evidence against the accused in order for a determination of probable cause to be made and this not meet the definition of and "examination hearing?"

 What the courts and prosecutors have attempted to do here is to take practices applicable to allegations against people who have not been restricted at their liberty and apply those procedures to people who have been restricted.
If a person has been accused of a crime, but has not been taken into custody, there is no automatic right to an examination hearing, as is written into law. However, when the person is actually arrested, all that changes, and an examination is now mandatory, in order to provide proper jurisdiction to the courts.

When a complaint is brought to a Magistrate and the accused has not been arrested, as a matter of fact. The accused may yet have no knowledge of the existence of the complaint and can in no way be construed to be restricted at his or her liberty. The Magistrate can examine into the sufficiency of the allegation on its face, and an examination hearing as defined by Chapter 16 Texas Code of Criminal Procedure need not be held. However, if the person is subsequently arrested, that person must be brought before the nearest Magistrate, so that a proper examination may be had, insuring that all of the rights of the accused are protected and upheld.

This raises a problem for prosecutors working "the deal." When evidence is presented in court against a citizen it triggers certain rights by Constitution which include:

The Texas Constitution -- Article 1 - BILL OF RIGHTS
Section 10 - RIGHTS OF ACCUSED IN CRIMINAL PROSECUTIONS

In all criminal prosecutions the accused shall have a speedy public trial by an impartial jury.
He shall have the right to demand the nature and cause of the accusation against him, and to have a copy thereof. He shall not be compelled to give evidence against himself, and shall have the right of being heard by himself or counsel, or both, shall be confronted by the witnesses against him and shall have compulsory process for obtaining witnesses in his favor, except that when the witness resides out of the State and the offense charged is a violation of any of the anti-trust laws of this State, the defendant and the State shall have the right to produce and have the evidence admitted by deposition, under such rules and laws as the Legislature may hereafter provide; and no person shall be held to answer for a criminal offense, unless on an indictment of a grand jury, except in cases in which the punishment is by fine or imprisonment, otherwise than in the penitentiary, in cases of impeachment, and in cases arising in the army or navy, or in the militia, when in actual service in time of war or public danger. (Amended Nov. 5, 1918.)

Magistrations and "PIA's" do not provide these rights and protections, and that is why prosecutors have made up these catchy names. They are legal fiction. They do not exist in law.

Before the Magistrate can make a determination of probable cause, there must be an examination into the sufficiency of the allegation.

Art. 2.11. [35] [62] [63] Examining court
When the magistrate sits for the purpose of inquiring into a criminal accusation against any person, this is called an examining court.

An examination hearing is governed by Chapter 16 Code of Criminal Procedure. It is a whole chapter, and is completely ignored and usurped by Magistrates at the direction and advisement of prosecuting attorneys.

In Texas, without regard to the rule of law, Magistrates have been trained and directed to completely ignore all that stuff you read about in the Constitution and laws, and accept whatever a police officer alleges without question. Prosecutors have trained Magistrates to act as assistants to his staff. Rather than perform a proper examination hearing, the Magistrate has been instructed to insure all the proper paperwork is in order, thereby perfecting the case for the prosecutor.

The Magistrate is also instructed not to prepare a warrant, as that would clearly mark the initiation of a prosecution. So, they do this thing they call a "Magistration."

If a proper examination were held, the prosecutor, or an assistant would have to perfect all the paperwork before presenting it to the Magistrate and that would be so inconvenient.

The first specious argument that comes to mind is that, prosecutors are busy and simply don't have time to be at every examination hearing. The problem is that, the Constitution and our laws demand it, and if prosecutors and magistrates deny it, they run foul of the laws they are sworn to, and are bound to uphold.

Citizens may not be compelled to forgo their constitutional rights because officials fear public hostility or desire to save money. Buchanan v. Warley, 245 U.S. 60 (1917); Cooper v. Aaron, 358 U.S. 1 (1958); Watson v. City of Memphis, 373 U.S. 526 (1963). As quoted from PALMER ET AL. v. THOMPSON, MAYOR OF THE CITY OF JACKSON ET AL. 403 U.S. 217, 91 S. Ct. 1940, 29 L. Ed. 2d 438

We could argue that other States provide just such representation, but convenience is not the motivation here.

Other States have special assistant prosecutors appointed for the purpose of the examination hearing to assure all due process rights are observed. They also have counsel appointed for the specific purpose of representing the accused for the examination hearing. Remember the comedy show Night Court? While a comedy, it was dead on the Constitution

You will hear the whining and crying about how prosecutors don't have the time or staff to be at every hearing before a magistrate, but that is nothing but blowing smoke. It is not that prosecutors don't want to be at the hearing, it is about "the deal." A proper examination hearing would ruin everything. The prosecutor can't have the accused trusting to justice, he needs him/her terrified of the possibilities and convinced he has no reasonable alternative to the perfectly reasonable deal the prosecutor is prepared to offer.

Prosecutors don't care if you are guilty or innocent. Yes, I have read all the high minded rhetoric, but in the real world, prosecutors care about conviction rate; they care about negotiating a deal in lieu of a lengthy court case. They, therefore, direct police to put a person arrested in jail in order to soften them up.
They direct magistrates to forgo their duty in order to demonstrate the power of the prosecutor, and the helplessness of the citizen before the system, so they will be inclined to take "the deal," when offered.

There are those who are habitual criminals and know the ropes. They know they can work the system and get a good deal. But, for the most of us, we never have any experience with the law except in minor matters, mostly traffic. If one of us gets arrested, we expect to be treated as if we are innocent until the courts have determined otherwise. With this expectation, we are quick to assert our rights and expect them to be honored. The first thing the prosecutor wants to do is quash that notion. They want our dignity taken away; they want us in that orange jail uniform, after spending a night on the drunk-tank floor, and having been treated like all the other riffraff, rabble, drunks and mother-rapers, before we are marched in undignified fashion before the magistrate, deep inside the jail.

You see, the prosecutor knows what we are thinking,

"When the Judge hears my side, s/he will let me go and rebuke that no good arresting officer."

The Judge will do part of an examination hearing. S/he will take a written statement from the arresting officer into evidence. The problem is, the magistrate will do this ex parte, outside a proper hearing where the accused has no opportunity to object or challenge the evidence presented against him/her.

The evidence presented is usually always in written form, the officer, if present, is not brought before the court in this process. If the paperwork presented to the Judge is incomplete or insufficient in some way, the magistrate will return it to the jailer so that it can be fixed before the magistrate continues. (If you were a law student you would be screaming foul about now, but it gets much worse.)

After the magistrate accepts and reads all evidence against the accused, s/he will start the hearing. The Judge will read the accused their rights, advise them they have the right to counsel (which under law they should have at this hearing). S/he will tell them they have a right to an examination hearing (which by law this should be). Then the Judge will rule that the evidence is sufficient to bind the individual over for trial as a matter of course, set bail, give the records to the jailer and leave.

There are a few telling things the Magistrate will not do. The Magistrate will not provide the accused counsel, or the opportunity to secure counsel. The Magistrate will not allow the accused to be faced by his/her accuser or to confront the witness against him/her. The Magistrate will not allow the accused to act in his/her own behalf at all. The Magistrate will not even allow the accused to enter a plea; neither will the Magistrate make an order binding the accused to the court. (Referred to in law, as a warrant).

Article 16.17 Decision of the Judge

After the examining trial has been had, the judge shall make an order committing the defendant to the jail of the proper county, discharging him or admitting him to bail, as the law and facts of the case may require. Failure of the judge to make or enter an order within 48 hours, after the examining trial has been completed, operates as a finding of no probable cause and the accused shall be discharged.

This is not just wrong, it is horribly wrong and it gets worse. These hearings are usually held deep in the jail, or the accused is publicly marched before the court in their jail uniforms, often shackled. This is to let the accused know s/he is at the mercy of the system and can forget his/her rights. Whatever they're previous expectations concerning justice and due course, they now know they are at the mercy and whim of the system. Thus, when the prosecutor finally comes along, s/he is the epitome of professionalism and when s/he makes this most reasonable offer, what is the accused to do but take "the deal?" Besides, the accused will have been warned, take it or spend up to a year in jail waiting for trial.

The higher the expectation of justice when the person goes up before the magistrate, the greater the devastation of the realization it was all smoke and mirrors. It will take the wind out of your ideals in a hurry. You will feel devastated and betrayed, and want little more than a way out.

The deal works. I went through the court records. Almost 99% of all people accused of crime take the deal. It is well established that about 4% of the people do some 90% of the crime. Those who stay in the system know the system. They know if the prosecutor doesn't have a really great case s/he will not want it to go to trial, so they hold out and when the prosecutor can't make a deal, s/he will almost always drop the case.

If you think this doesn't drive the police up the wall, just ask them.

The citizens who suffer most by this are the falsely accused, law-abiding citizens who cherish the unrealistic notion that we live in a land of law. They discover how guilt or innocence is simply not a consideration. Those people, they thought were out there protecting them, become the enemy. They find all the writing and righteous rhetoric we were exposed to in school was a bunch of crap.
A consideration the prosecutor sometimes has is, often the innocent, at first, react indignantly, become angry, and resistant. In order for the deal

to work, s/he needs time for the anger, through fear and anticipation, to transform into dread. Well, it takes time and time doesn't jibe well with the notion of a speedy trial, so the prosecutor needs a workaround, and he has it figured out.

There is another thing the Magistrate will not do. The magistrate will not seal all the documents, of the hearing in an envelope, cause his name to be written across the seal, and forward it to the Clerk of the Court, who will try the case. The Magistrate, after holding the abomination called a "magistration," will give the file to the Jailer, who will forward it to the prosecuting attorney.

I have looked in law and can find nothing directing a complaint to a prosecuting attorney. Except in cases of violations of 552 Government Code. Complaints directed to either "some magistrate," or the clerk of the court of jurisdiction. The only circumstance that a complaint might be sent to a prosecuting attorney is when an official needs to secure legal advice.

Now, if an officer has reason to believe a crime has been committed and is seeking legal advice about pursuing criminal allegations, this is probably a good idea, and the prosecutor could certainly give legal advice, but this is not what happens. The prosecutor could advise the official of the propriety of pursuit and legal positions. However, this is not what is happening. After a person has been arrested and the arresting officer has presented a complaint to "some magistrate," a prosecution had commenced. The prosecutor can give advice, but not take possession of the court records.

Further, under Bivens, the prosecutor is laid open for civil action if s/he is giving legal advice that amounts to an ongoing criminal enterprise.

The problem with forwarding the records to the prosecuting attorney is 17.30 Code of Criminal Procedure:
Art. 17.30. [296] [347] [335] Shall certify proceedings

The magistrate, before whom an examination has taken place upon a criminal accusation, shall certify to all the proceedings had before him, as well as where he discharges, holds to bail or commits, and transmit them, sealed up, to the court before which the defendant may be tried, writing his name across the seals of the envelope.

The voluntary statement of the defendant, the testimony, bail bonds, and every other proceeding in the case, shall be thus delivered to the proper clerk of the court, without delay.

This preserves all the evidence the Magistrate used in order to make the determination to bind the individual over for trial. This also gets a cause number set, so the accused can file motions and other papers in his/her defense. Also, by forwarding the charging instrument (the complaint) to the Clerk of the Court that will try the case, jurisdiction is properly transferred to the proper court.

The problem this causes for the prosecutor is that, a prosecution commences when a magistrate is presented with a complaint.

In fact, it has been held, long ago and recently, that the filing of a complaint, accusing one of a felony offense, with a justice of the peace, is the initial step in the commencement of a prosecution under Texas law. Baskins v. State, 75 Tex. Crim. 537, 171 S.W. 723, 725 (1914); Ex parte Clear, 573 S.W.2d 224, 228 (Tex.Cr.App. 1978). The above cited by the court in Rios v State 688 S.W.2d 642

This creates a couple problems for the prosecutor:
1. He cannot legally dismiss a prosecution once it has commenced, if he is unable to get "the Deal" and doesn't want to bother with a trial;
2. The speedy trial clock starts and he doesn't have time to work the deal;

To create time, prosecutors bury those records in the prosecutors' files. The complaint and statement of probable cause used by the magistrate, to provide jurisdiction, will never reach the court record. Not only that, after the person has been arrested, restricted at his/her liberty, and bound to the court, there is no record of the arrest. The accused is in a sort of legal limbo, as the Court Clerk doesn't know he has been arrested or accused of anything. He has no rights, whereas, he has been deprived of a court, to pursue them.

Magistrates are being trained and directed to ignore Article 17.30 and leave the file with the jailer, who may or may not keep copies, but apparently sends a copy to the prosecuting attorney. This way there is no pesky complaint in the court record, and the prosecutor has all the time s/he wants to work "the deal."

Our law consists of numerous interlacing checks and balances, which must always be maintained in order to preserve our constitutional form of government.

It is apparent that the procedure, which authorizes prosecutions by information presented by the prosecuting attorney, is bottomed upon the proposition that there must be a supporting affidavit, without which an information cannot be lawfully presented. WILMA HAZEL KENNEDY v. STATE (02/09/55) 276 S.W.2d 291, 161 Tex. Crim. 303

The Court went on to say:

The rule was so well established by the former court of appeals that opinions after 1891 routinely followed it without further explication. But there are strong public policy considerations dictating the rule.

An information is a "primary pleading in a criminal action on the part of the State," Article 27.01, V.A.C.C.P., a written pleading in behalf of the State drawn, filed and presented by a prosecuting attorney, charging an accused with an offense that may be prosecuted under the law. Article 21.20, V.A.C.C.P. in order to "protect its citizens from the inherent dangers arising from the concentration of power in any one individual," Kennedy v. State, <!--REF-->161 Tex. Crim. 303,<!--/REF--> <!--REF-->276 S.W.2d 291<!--/REF--> (1955) (Opinion on Motion for Rehearing, at 664), the Legislature precluded a prosecutor from presenting an information "until affidavit has been made by some credible person charging the defendant with an offense," and also mandated, "The affidavit shall be filed with the information." Article 21.22, supra. Such an affidavit is, of course, a complaint within the meaning of Article 15.04, V.A.C.C.P. "In other words, a prosecuting attorney is not authorized to institute prosecutions in the county court upon his independent act or of his own volition." Kennedy v. State, supra, at 294. One may not be "both the accuser and the prosecutor is misdemeanor cases." Wells v. State, 516 S.W.2d 663, at 664 (Tex.Cr.App. 1974). Compare Glass v. State, 162 Tex. Crim. 598, 288 S.W.2d 522 (1956); Catchings v. State, 162 Tex. Crim. 342, 285 S.W.2d 233, at 234 (1955).

Jailers will argue they must have the complaint in their records as required by the jail standards commission. Either the State intended the Jailers to keep a copy, or ordered jailers to act in concert and collusion with the magistrate, in clear and direct violation of the specific mandate of particular law (Article 17.30 CCP).

In the end, I suppose it wouldn't matter who had copies of the complaint, so long as the original has been properly placed in the protection of the Clerk of the Court. Without a proper complaint in the Court record, the Court is without jurisdiction. If the complaint is not sealed up, and forwarded to the clerk of the court and kept in the clerk's protection, the affidavit becomes compromised and fatally defective.

While intercepting the complaint may be a slick prosecutors maneuver, nothing is perfect, and neither is this. There are those necessary documents that sometimes are needed by others. Records of bonds and court appointed counsel sometimes show up in the files. Bondsmen and attorneys often need them, so the prosecutor can't always hide them. Also, the information must reflect the date of offense and this gives the whole game away.

So, if you look in the criminal records of most any District Court, you will find an indictment, and, "the deal", sometimes a bond form or a request for court appointed counsel, but no original complaint, or statement of probable cause.

The presence of a bond or request for court appointed counsel, begs the question:

"How did the magistrate make a determination of probable cause against a person who had been arrested, when no complaint has been filed against the individual? How can a person be bound over to the court and restricted at their liberty, either in jail or out on bond, with restricted options, without someone accusing the person of a crime? And, how can the magistrate defend against a claim of false imprisonment, for binding a citizen to the court, when there is no criminal complaint?"

The law is simple and straightforward, no complaint, no jurisdiction.

It's a slippery slope on the way to the Frog Farm.

The magistrate, by failing to abide by Article 17.30, has violated a law relating to his/her office,

37.10 Texas Penal Code, Tampering With A Government Document:

(a) A person commits an offense if he:

(1) knowingly makes a false entry in, or false alteration of, a government record:

(2) Makes, presents, or uses any record, document, or thing with knowledge of its falsity and with intent that it be taken as a genuine government record...

(3) intentionally destroys, conceals, removes, or otherwise impairs the verity, legibility, or availability of a governmental record;

(b) (Exception)

(c) Except as provided in Subsection (d), an offense under this section is a Class A misdemeanor unless the actor's intent is to defraud or harm another, in which event the offense is a state jail felony.

Thereby, entering into a criminal conspiracy with the jailer and prosecuting attorney, to deny the citizen in the due course of the laws. Normally you can't sue a judge. As indicated earlier, judges have granted themselves immunity from civil litigation. They left only one door open to civil remedy against a judge. The only time you can sue a judge is when the judge is without any jurisdiction.

The first criminal act of the conspiracy is committed by the arresting officer when he, acting in accordance with accepted policy, failed to make a due diligent effort to locate a magistrate, before tossing the accused in jail:

§ 20.02. Unlawful Restraint

(a) A person commits an offense if he intentionally or knowingly restrains another person.

(b) It is an affirmative defense to prosecution under this section that:

(1) the person restrained was a child younger than 14 years of age;

(2) the actor was a relative of the child; and

(3) the actor's sole intent was to assume lawful control of the child.

(c) An offense under this section is a Class A misdemeanor, except that the offense is:

It cannot be construed, that the arresting officer is ignorant, as to the effect of the arrest s/he makes (see Screws v State above), and is therefore, criminally culpable and civilly liable for the consequences.

Roberts v Bohac, 574 F2d 1232, The appellate court stated:

"Although the failure to take the plaintiff before a magistrate would have been excused, if good grounds had existed for the belief, that a magistrate was not available. Such was not the case, since the defendant officers made no attempt to determine whether the magistrate was, or would make himself available."

Hall v State, 52 NE2d 370:

At the time of plaintiff's arrest, there was a duly qualified and acting justice of the peace in the town where she was arrested. The town marshal nonetheless transported the plaintiff 25 miles to the county seat, where she was imprisoned in the county jail for 30 minutes before release. In affirming a jury verdict, for the plaintiff in her action for assault and battery, and false imprisonment. The court held that, in light of the presence of a justice of the peace in the town where she was arrested, her transportation, and incarceration in jail, in another town, was not necessary.

The officers will rightfully argue they were acting in accordance with accepted policy, and I would certainly agree with that.

98 ALR 2d 13, 36

Where someone, other than the arresting officer, is partially or wholly responsible for the unnecessary delay, questions arise as to the liability of the arresting officer. Generally, an arresting officer is not excused from liability for an unreasonable delay in taking a detainee before a magistrate, by reason of the fact, that the officer was following a superior's orders.

He may even believe he was acting in good faith reliance, on what he considered to be competent authority.

Manos, 16 Clev-Mar L. Rev 415, 416;Note, 19Hast L.J 974, 982

Actual malice on the part of the arresting officer, is not a necessary element of false imprisonment, and the arresting officers' state of mind, is generally irrelevant to the issue of whether a false imprisonment did occur. Neither the officer's good or bad faith, nor his motivation in making the detention and arrest, has any bearing on the lawfulness of the detention.

The problem the officer has, is ignorance. In the case of a public official, acting in his official capacity, he cannot claim ignorance, any more than

I could for any violation of any law. The only defense he would have, is a claim that he was insane, as stipulated in Screws V State above.

The problem is, when accepted policy, conflicts with specific statute! Which, should the officer be more concerned with? Should he be more worried about violating policy and possibly jeopardizing his job, or violating law and risking prosecution?

The question is mute, as the officer does not risk prosecution, as will be demonstrated later. By ignoring the law, he risks nothing! He is protected by the same conspiracy, of which he is an intricate part.

By arresting and imprisoning a person, in order to facilitate the improper actions of the magistrate, the officer becomes culpable in the act the magistrate commits.

§ 20.04. Aggravated Kidnapping

(a) A person commits an offense if he intentionally or knowingly abducts another person with the intent to:

(1) hold him for ransom or reward;

(2) use him as a shield or hostage;

(3) facilitate the commission of a felony or the flight after the attempt or commission of a felony;

(4) inflict bodily injury on him or violate or abuse him sexually;

(5) terrorize him or a third person; or

(6) interfere with the performance of any governmental or political function.

(b) A person commits an offense if the person intentionally or knowingly abducts another person and uses or exhibits a deadly weapon during the commission of the offense.

(c) Except as provided by Subsection (d), an offense under this section is a felony of the first degree.

(d) At the punishment stage of a trial, the defendant may raise the issue as to whether he voluntarily released the victim in a safe place. If the defendant proves the issue in the affirmative, by a preponderance of the evidence, the offense is a felony of the second degree.

In this case, the police officer commits false imprisonment, for the purpose of the facilitation of other criminal acts, and does so while displaying a deadly weapon. Yes, I realize the officer is a certified police officer and is allowed to carry a loaded weapon, however, he is not allowed to commit a crime while displaying that deadly weapon.

Now we get to the magistrate, who was directed to seal everything in an envelope and forward it to the Clerk of the Court, but did not. By that failure, the jurisdiction of the court, too prosecute the accused, never existed.
Without the original complaint, giving jurisdiction from the time of arrest, in the protection of the Clerk of the Court, there is no jurisdiction! And, all that participate are potentially subject to civil litigation as well as criminal prosecution. (see In Re Saywer above)

This practice is directed and condoned by prosecutors who profit by circumventing the speedy trial clock.

". . . if the pleading, on its face, shows that the offense charged is barred by limitations. The complaint, information, or indictment, is so fundamentally defective, that the trial court does not have jurisdiction, and habeas corpus relief should be granted." EX PARTE SCOTTIE GENE WARD (01/18/78) 560 S.W.2d 660

By the above practices, the stage is set for "the deal."

The prosecutor, when s/he gets the file from the jailer, will start working on the accused. S/he will first force the accused to an arraignment hearing, for the alleged purpose of taking the plea, the magistrate refused to take. See how slick this works.

Magistrates have been directed by prosecutors to deny evidentiary hearings. Or, to hear any testimony from the accused that might refute or mitigate the claims of the arresting officer. Not because they don't have jurisdiction and authority, as clearly they do:

Article 15.03, V.A.C.C.P., authorizes a magistrate to receive a complaint and issue a warrant of arrest. And Article 2.09, V.A.C.C.P., provides that the justices of the peace are magistrates within the meaning of the statute. Thus, it is beyond dispute, that the complaint in the justice court in the present case, charging appellant with rape, empowered and authorized the court to act on the matter before it. Although, it had no power to determine the issues of law and facts in the case, or to render a judgment based upon such a determination. EX PARTE SCOTTIE GENE WARD (01/18/78) 560 S.W.2d 660

By directing magistrates to refuse to hear any rebuttal of evidence from the accused, and especially, to deny a plea, the prosecutor gets the court to compel the individual back to court, for a pre-trial hearing.

Art. 28.01. [522] [587] [576] Pre-trial

Sec. 1. The court may set any criminal case for a pre-trial hearing, before it is set for trial upon its merits. And, direct the defendant and his attorney, if any of record, and the State's attorney, to appear before the court at the time and place stated in the court's order for a conference and hearing. The defendant must be present at the arraignment, and his presence is required during any pre-trial proceeding. The pre-trial hearing shall be to determine any of the following matters:

(1) Arraignment of the defendant, if such be necessary; and appointment of counsel to represent the defendant, if such be necessary;

(2) Pleadings of the defendant;

(3) Special pleas, if any;

(4) Exceptions to the form or substance of the indictment or information;

(5) Motions for continuance either by the State or defendant; provided that grounds for continuance not existing or not known at the time may be presented and considered at any time before the defendant announces ready for trial;

(6) Motions to suppress evidence—When a hearing on the motion to suppress evidence is granted, the court may determine the merits of said motion on the motions themselves, or upon opposing affidavits, or upon oral testimony, subject to the discretion of the court;

(7) Motions for change of venue by the State or the defendant; provided, however, that such motions for change of venue, if overruled at the pre-trial hearing, may be renewed by the State or the defendant during the voir dire examination of the jury;

(8) Discovery;

(9) Entrapment; and

(10) Motion for appointment of interpreter.

Sec. 2. When a criminal case is set for such pre-trial hearing, any such preliminary matters not raised or filed seven days before the hearing will not thereafter be allowed to be raised or filed, except by permission of the court for good cause shown; provided that the defendant shall have sufficient notice of such hearing to allow him not less than 10 days in which to raise or file such preliminary matters. The record made at such pre-trial hearing, the rulings of the court and the exceptions and objections thereto shall become a part of the trial record of the case upon its merits.

Sec. 3. The notice mentioned in Section 2 above shall be sufficient if given in any one of the following ways:

(1) By announcement made by the court in open court in the presence of the defendant or his attorney of record;

(2) By personal service upon the defendant or his attorney of record;

(3) By mail to either the defendant or his attorney of record, deposited by the clerk in the mail at least six days prior to the date set for hearing. If the defendant has no attorney of record such notice shall be addressed to defendant at the address shown on his bond, if the bond shows such an address, and if not, it may be addressed to one of the sureties on his bond. If the envelope containing the notice is properly addressed, stamped and mailed, the state will not be required to show that it was received.

This is the standard excuse, but I assure you, most Judges simply compel everyone accused of a crime to one of these hearings, whether there is any cause for it or not. Often, especially in misdemeanor cases, the Judge doesn't even bother to show up, as these hearings are usually not actually hearings in the legal sense. A local Justice of Peace, who happens to be a personal friend, and someone I hold in the highest esteem, calls these hearings "barter sessions." Usually there is no judge present, just the prosecutor, bailiff, and a court clerk to lend authority on the one hand, and the appearance of judicial credence on the other. The bailiff will escort you up to the clerk who will direct you to the waiting prosecutor, who will offer you this great deal, then threaten you with all the stuff he will do, if you don't take it.

Now, if you are poor or indigent and have been accused of something more serious than a class C Misdemeanor, and arrested, you will be told that you have a right to an attorney and one will be appointed for you if you can't afford one. You will be told you have a right to bail, but if you exercise your right to bail, the court will not appoint you an attorney. The Judge will tell you that since you could afford bail, they will not appoint you counsel.

Article 26.04

(l) Procedures adopted under Subsection (a) must include procedures and financial standards for determining whether a defendant is indigent. The procedures and standards shall apply to each defendant in the county equally, regardless of whether the defendant is in custody or has been released on bail.

(m) In determining whether a defendant is indigent, the court or the courts' designee may consider the defendant's income, source of income, assets, property owned, outstanding obligations, necessary expenses, the number and ages of dependents, and spousal income that is available to the defendant. The court or the courts' designee may not consider whether the defendant has posted or is capable of posting bail, except to the extent that it reflects the defendant's financial circumstances as measured by the considerations listed in this subsection.

Prior to the last change, Article 26.04 specifically forbids a judge to refuse to appoint counsel, solely because the defendant "has or may secure bail."

This puts the poor or indigent in a position of either, getting out on bail, and appearing in court without counsel. Or, sitting in jail until time of trial, which they are told could take up to a year. With or without counsel, in the end, it makes little difference; they will take the deal.
The uninitiated, usually take the deal. The first thing they get is, out of jail, and a deferred adjudication (it doesn't go on their record). The catch is, they get to pay the courts a substantial portion of their salary for a very long time. Considering the alternative, what else, could a reasonable person, of ordinary prudence, be expected to do? The chronic offender however recognizes this as a bargaining session and depending on how solid the case, knows s/he can deal a bit. The innocent law abiding citizen, falsely accused, doesn't have a clue or a chance.

Sometimes, the truly innocent, at this first hearing, become enraged and indignant and send the prosecutor packing, but that is no problem. S/he knows this anger response by the innocent will, given time, melt into fear and desperation and, since there is no pesky complaint hanging around, the prosecutor has plenty of time.

I know what you are thinking, "You need an attorney." Yeah, we all like to think we are protected by our defense counsel, but, not in this life. Eventually, an attorney will show up at the jail. Now the accused feels the wheels of justice are finally turning in their favor; wrong.
Your attorney will take you into a room and tell you, "Here is the deal, take it or spend up to a year in jail waiting for trial."

I know, most people expect their attorney to be like Perry Mason, and want them to ferret out every detail, then put on a vigorous and righteous defense. Not in this life, s/he won't! In this life, defense counsel doesn't profit by putting on a vigorous defense for a poor client. In this life, if s/he puts on a vigorous defense, the courts will pay about $350.00. If the client takes a deal, you guessed it; the courts will pay about $350.00.

All this current hub-bub about paying court appointed attorneys more to defend indigent clients will do nothing to improve defense. It will only increase the amount the attorney can get, for getting you to take a deal.

If you are truly innocent and incredibly stubborn or courageous and refuse the deal again, the prosecutor will look at your case and exercise his "prosecutors' discretion". The prosecutor is not interested in whether or not you are innocent, but in whether or not he has enough leverage to turn up the screws. If not, the case will be dropped, because it will cost too much to fight it. Unless it is a high profile case, and it is politically expedient to put on a show. In the end, it is not about justice, it is political. Everything is political.

In the professional practice of prosecution, there is much more the prosecutor will do to coerce a deal from the accused. The fact that there is no complaint recorded with the Clerk of the Court allows him ample time to hold the accusation over the accused. If the accused is especially difficult, the best strategy is to simply let things lie. With a bit of luck, the accused will get charged with something else, then the prosecutor can pull out both complaints and really turn up the screws.

There is no need to belabor this point further, other than to say that it doesn't get better. However, after doing the math, if the dollars don't add up to good sense, the prosecutor will simply refuse to prosecute and the case will just go into limbo, only to be dropped when the accused or their bondsman screams to high heaven.

The problem with this is, the prosecutor is forbidden to drop a case in Texas.

Art. 32.02. [577] [37,643] [37,630] Dismissal by state's attorney

The attorney representing the State may, by permission of the court, dismiss a criminal action at any time, upon filing a written statement with the papers in the case, setting out his reasons for such dismissal, which shall be incorporated in the judgment of dismissal. No case shall be dismissed without the consent of the presiding judge.

The language of this law is not hard to understand. A Prosecutors' Discretion is specifically forbidden in Texas. This is one reason the prosecutor makes the original complaint disappear. If he can't get a deal and the case is not politically expedient for the prosecutor, s/he will want to just drop it. But, when a complaint is filed with the Clerk of the Court, s/he can't just do that. With no complaint recorded with the court, the prosecution does not, actually exist. Even though the accused is bound to the court on bail, s/he has not really been charged with a crime, and is sort of stuck in between. The prosecutor can simply let them dangle, as long as s/he wants, or until someone raises a ruckus. Then, all s/he has to do is drop the case.

Generally, the guilty don't mind the wait and it puts off punishment. The problem is with the rights of the innocent defendants, that are bound to the courts, and who suffer. When time wears on and they complain about their right to a speedy trial, the prosecutor is very quick to let them know the speedy trial act has been overturned. What s/he won't tell them is that only the act has been overturned, not the right. But, then it is perfectly legal for prosecutors to lie to citizens. They are even protected by the courts, when they knowingly present perjured testimony to the courts.

When the prosecutor gets a deal, or decides to pursue prosecution, s/he has the original complainant come in and sign a new complaint, dated the date it is signed. This way the complaint, if requested, will reflect a current date, not the date of the original, and thus, this starts the speedy trial clock at a much later date. The courts have held that, the complaint and information can have the same date. Prosecutors perverted that to mean they could hide or destroy the original complaint, by which the accused has been bound to the court for months, and start the prosecution all over again. The problem with this is, it is a fraud on the court. By secreting the original complaint from the court, the prosecutors behavior has the effect of dismissing the original prosecution that commenced when the original complaint was presented to the magistrate, and is now, re-initiating the prosecution with a new one.

The problem is that, this second complaint is a fraud on the court and will be demonstrated as such by the other documents that will necessarily appear in the court file. The bond form and request for court appointed counsel in particular. They will reflect the date, or approximate time of arrest. So, the prosecutor fails to include this incriminating document with the information, as specifically mandated by particular law, and by that act, deprives the court of proper jurisdiction.

This is not simply a minor adjustment toward administrative convenience, or adjudicative expedience. It is the elephant in the corner. It is major bad, as it puts everyone involved in the process, in criminal and civil jeopardy. It also puts the State in a position of having to release every person convicted under these badly flawed practices, and subjects the State to suit for actual and punitive damages.

You have to give the prosecutors credit. This is a smooth operation. Even defense counsel shows up to represent their clients, and follows this ritual without question or objection. Being learned counsel, they know full well, it is improper and at variance with law, but since they get to shake out their deals, collect their fees and go home, no problem.

Well, one problem, that pesky complaint, the magistrate had to look into, in order to bind the person arrested over for trial. It keeps leaving all these telltale clues. Like the indictment, it must show the date of the offense or it is fatally defective, so the date of offense will be much different than the date of the indictment.

That will reflect the date of arrest, but nothing else in the criminal file will, except maybe a bond form or request for court appointed counsel. I am sure the prosecutor would like these to disappear, but bondsmen and court appointed counsel would notice they were missing, as they often need them.

The irony of all this would be funny if not so serious.

That is how it works on the Frog Farm. I know what you are thinking.

"If things are so bad, why hasn't someone done something about it?"

Now we get to the really good part. In the above, I demonstrated an ongoing criminal conspiracy perpetrated by the State of Texas against its own citizens, for the purpose of converting the Criminal System into an unauthorized taxing authority in the truest sense of a street gang.

Now I will demonstrate a second conspiracy intended to protect the first.

When you think it got bad, it gets worse.

SEE NO EVIL

Prosecutors have one minor problem with the above; it is illegal. Everything is illegal. So what happens if someone starts making waves? What if someone realizes these practices are criminal, and starts filing criminal complaints to correct it? In a word, "nothing."

A private citizen cannot file a criminal complaint against a public official in Texas. Well, that isn't exactly true. A citizen can file a complaint; s/he can file all the complaints s/he wants to, but it is a futile effort. They will, as a matter of course and accepted practice, be forwarded to the prosecutor, who will simply trash them. That's right, s/he will trash them. Well, that may not be right, but that is how things work down here on the Frog Farm, we call Texas Criminal Justice.

Police officers, by policy and accepted practice, are routinely directed to present complaints to prosecutors. If an officer has reason to believe a crime has been committed s/he is commanded to, what? Article 2.13 Texas Code of Criminal Procedure commands as follows:

Art. 2.13. [37] [44] [45] Duties and powers

    (a) It is the duty of every peace officer to preserve the peace within the officer's jurisdiction. To effect this purpose, the officer shall use all lawful means.

    (b) The officer shall:

    (1) in every case authorized by the provisions of this Code, interfere without warrant to prevent or suppress crime;

    (2) execute all lawful process issued to the officer by any magistrate or court;

    (3) give notice to some magistrate, of all offenses committed within the officer's jurisdiction, where the officer has good reason to believe there has been a violation of the penal law; and

    (4) arrest offenders without warrant in every case where the officer is authorized by law, in order that they may be taken before the proper magistrate or court and be tried.

    (c) It is the duty of every officer to take possession of a child under Article 62.009(g).

O.K. so, when is a complaint a complaint? If a citizen comes in complaining and fills out a voluntary statement alleging facts which amount to an accusation of a specific person violating a particular law, is that a complaint, or is the citizen simply complaining?

What if the citizen presents the police officer with a verified affidavit, complete in accordance with Article 15.04 Texas Code of Criminal Procedure, is that a complaint, as the term is used in Article 2.13?

What about, when the officer fills out a statement of probable cause, and uses that statement of probable cause as grounds to arrest a citizen. Then, presents it to some magistrate for the purpose of giving the magistrate jurisdiction to rule on the sufficiency of the arrest and further incarceration. Is that a complaint?

The courts have held that a complaint is sufficient, if it clearly states that a specific person had violated a particular crime. What about verification? When a voluntary statement is taken by a police officer, is that statement considered, taken under oath? We know the one given to the magistrate, is done so, whether sworn to directly or not.

In all the cases illustrated below, when I mention complaints I have filed, those complaints will have been duly verified criminal affidavits, complete in accordance with Article 15.04 Texas Code of Criminal Procedure.

So, if an officer receives a complaint against someone that they did not see or hear committing a crime. Are they bound to present the complaint to some magistrate, or can they simply forward it to the prosecutor for legal advice? This is standard procedure when the officer believes he has evidence of a criminal act.

When the person in question has not been restricted at his/her liberty, this may be a perfectly proper and legal practice, as prosecutors have been directed to provide legal advice to the police and lower courts. However, when the officer has made an arrest and the complaint must be used to provide jurisdiction to the court, can he still have the original and only complaint forwarded to the prosecuting attorney? Or, is s/he bound by Article 2.13?

In the case where the complaint is forwarded to the prosecutor, does the prosecutor have the authority to dismiss the prosecution by exercising his/her discretion? And if so, precisely where does the prosecutor obtain this power to render judicial decisions? The Legislature certainly can't do it, as the overturning of the Speedy Trial Act clearly demonstrates. So, where does the prosecuting attorney get that authority?

The answer is simple, the prosecutor does not have the authority. As a matter of fact, the prosecutor has been specifically forbidden by particular statute to dismiss a prosecution.

It is not legal, but is standard procedure.

This is not hard to understand. Nowhere in law, is a complaint directed to a prosecuting attorney, except 552 Government Code, which will never stand constitutional muster. The only excuse for such an action is to seek legal advice from the prosecutor. The problem is, the prosecutor does not give legal advice.

Prosecutors have criminal complaints directed to them, not so they can render legal advice to the police, but so they can exercise judicial discretion. They don't want magistrates ruling on the sufficiency of complaints, after all, they are learned counsel, and it is they who will have to ultimately prosecute the cause, so it is logical to have them make the determination.

While that may be logical, it is certainly not legal. Our Constitutional Framers and subsequent Legislators knew well the great potential for abuse when power is concentrated in a single individual. So, they forbid prosecutors from making those determinations, and put neutral magistrates in place, to do just that. But prosecutors found neutral intervention inconvenient and potentially disastrous to "the deal." They advised police and magistrates toward practices and procedures that are horrendously illegal. But, those pesky citizens have a way of interfering with the best-laid plans of mice and men. They even have the audacity to complain about it, sometimes even in writing. So, what to do? What are prosecutors to do when they have complaints against public officials forwarded to them?

Sure, the prosecutor is going to prosecute a public official, for following advice, the prosecutor has given them. Not in this life. In this life the prosecutor has commandeered the complaint, and all s/he needs to do is simply throw it in the trash.

Art. 2.03. [27] [33] [34] Neglect of duty

(a) It shall be the duty of the attorney representing the State to present by information to the court having jurisdiction, any officer for neglect or failure of any duty enjoined upon such officer, when such neglect or failure can be presented by information, whenever it shall come to the knowledge of said attorney that there has been a neglect or failure of duty upon the part of said officer; and he shall bring to the notice of the grand jury any act of violation of law or neglect or failure of duty upon the part of any officer, when such violation, neglect or failure is not presented by information, and whenever the same may come to his knowledge.

(b) It is the duty of the trial court, the attorney representing the accused, the attorney representing the state and all peace officers to so conduct themselves as to insure a fair trial for both the state and the defendant, not to impair the presumption of innocence, and at the same time, afford the public the benefits of a free press.

Under the Screws v State doctrine, it cannot be construed that prosecutors are somehow unaware of the impropriety of this practice. If they are sane, they must know exactly the legal ramifications of their actions. I assure you, they know. They know because I have told them. I have crammed it down their throats with multiple and continuous complaints against them for just these behaviors, but they are not impressed.

The more I file the more they trash. I file on the trashers, for trashing, and the complaints go to the very individuals, I alleged against, and they trash them, all with absolute impunity.

We like to think the law matters. We need to believe there is some teeth in the authority of the individual to express and exert his/her individual rights. Unfortunately, at least in Texas, it is not so.

I have filed a great number of complaints against public officials, mostly felony complaints and all dead-bang. They are dead-bang because I set them up with opportunity, and they have never failed to be most accommodating, all the way up to the Attorney General (not Greg, but his predecessor General). I have filed with or on them all, and all trashed my complaints.

When I file a criminal complaint it is complete in accordance with Article 15.05 CCP, affirmed and verified along with an affirmed and verified statement of probable cause. When I give them to police officers, they follow policy and give them to the prosecuting attorney instead of following law, which directs them to 'some magistrate.' Prosecutors then simply trash them, exercising 'prosecutorial discretion,' even though it is expressly forbidden in Texas.

Art. 32.02. [577] [37,643] [37,630] Dismissal by state's attorney

The attorney representing the State may, by permission of the court, dismiss a criminal action at any time, upon filing a written statement with the papers in the case setting out his reasons for such dismissal, which shall be incorporated in the judgment of dismissal. No case shall be dismissed without the consent of the presiding judge.

By failing to present the complaint to the Grand Jury, along with an information, the prosecutor violates a law relating to his office, specifically Article 2.03 Texas Code of Criminal Procedure (see above). His actions have the effect of secreting the compliant from "some magistrate," and the information and complaint from the Grand Jury.

37.10 Texas Penal Code:

§ 37.10. Tampering With Governmental Record

   (a) A person commits an offense if he:

(1) knowingly makes a false entry in, or false alteration of, a governmental record;

(2) makes, presents, or uses any record, document, or thing with knowledge of its falsity and with intent that it be taken as a genuine governmental record;

(3) intentionally destroys, conceals, removes, or otherwise impairs the verity, legibility, or availability of a governmental record;

(4) possesses, sells, or offers to sell a governmental record or a blank governmental record form with intent that it be used unlawfully;

(5) makes, presents, or uses a governmental record with knowledge of its falsity; or

(6) possesses, sells, or offers to sell a governmental record or a blank governmental record form with knowledge that it was obtained unlawfully.

(b) It is an exception to the application of Subsection (a)(3) that the governmental record is destroyed pursuant to legal authorization or transferred under Section 441.204, Government Code. With regard to the destruction of a local government record, legal authorization includes compliance with the provisions of Subtitle C, Title 6, Local Government Code.

(c)(1) Except as provided by Subdivision (2) and by Subsection (d), an offense under this section is a Class A misdemeanor unless the actor's intent is to defraud or harm another, in which event the offense is a state jail felony.

(2) An offense under this section is a felony of the third degree if it is shown on the trial of the offense, that the governmental record was a public school record, report, or assessment instrument required under Chapter 39, Education Code. Or, was a license, certificate, permit, seal, title, letter of patent, or similar document issued by

government, by another state, or by the United States, unless the actor's intent is to defraud or harm another, in which event the offense is a felony of the second degree.

(d) An offense under this section, if it is shown on the trial of the offense that the governmental record is described by Section 37.01(2)(D), is:

(1) a Class B misdemeanor if the offense is committed under Subsection (a)(2) or Subsection (a)(5) and the defendant is convicted of presenting or using the record;

(2) a felony of the third degree if the offense is committed under:

(A) Subsection (a)(1), (3), (4), or (6); or

(B) Subsection (a)(2) or (5) and the defendant is convicted of making the record; and

(3) a felony of the second degree, notwithstanding Subdivisions (1) and (2), if the actor's intent in committing the offense was to defraud or harm another.

(e) It is an affirmative defense to prosecution for possession under Subsection (a)(6) that the possession occurred in the actual discharge of official duties as a public servant.

(f) It is a defense to prosecution under Subsection (a)(1), (a)(2), or (a)(5) that the false entry or false information could have no effect on the government's purpose for requiring the governmental record.

(g) A person is presumed to intend to defraud or harm another if the person acts with respect to two or more of the same type of governmental records, or blank governmental record forms. And if, each governmental record or blank governmental record form is a license, certificate, permit, seal, title, or similar document issued by government.

(h) If conduct that constitutes an offense under this section also constitutes an offense under Section 32.48 or 37.13, the actor may be prosecuted under any of those sections.

Art. 2.04. [28] [34] [35] Shall draw complaints

Upon complaint being made before a district or county attorney that an offense has been committed in his district or county, he shall reduce the complaint to writing and cause the same to be signed and sworn to by the complainant, and it shall be duly attested by said attorney.

Acts 1965, 59th Leg., vol. 2, p. 317, ch. 722.

Art. 2.05. [29] [35] [36] When complaint is made

If the offense be a misdemeanor, the attorney shall forthwith prepare an information based upon such complaint and file the same in the court having jurisdiction; provided, that in counties having no county attorney, misdemeanor cases may be tried upon complaint alone, without an information, provided, however, in counties having one or more criminal district courts an information must be filed in each misdemeanor case. If the offense is a felony, he shall forthwith file the complaint with a magistrate of the county.

It doesn't take a legal genius to figure this out. The Prosecutor has a clearly defined duty, by failing this duty, the prosecutor has the effect of dismissing a prosecution in impersonation of a judicial officer, in violation of 37.11 Texas Penal Code:

§ 37.11. Impersonating Public Servant

(a) A person commits an offense if he:

(1) impersonates a public servant with intent to induce another to submit to his pretended official authority, or to rely on his pretended official acts; or

(2) knowingly purports to exercise any function of a public servant or of a public office, including that of a judge and court, and the position or office through which he purports to exercise a function of a public servant or public office, has no lawful existence under the constitution or laws of this state or of the United States.

(b) An offense under this section is a felony of the third degree.

I have filed a number of these complaints in a number of counties and they trash them. When I file criminal complaints charging prosecutors with felonies for failing to present criminal complaints against public officials to the Grand Jury, the complaints are forwarded to the accused prosecutors who simply trash them. When I bushwhack a judge and drop the complaints on him/her and they are sent to the Grand Jury, the prosecutor intercedes and there is never a hearing. I even had a prosecutor in Tarrant County, Tom Bellows, (I contend) forge a letter of dismissal of 30 felony complaints against Tarrant County Prosecutors, including some against himself.

In Wise County, the prosecutor actually gave the complaints to District Judge John Fostel, who forwarded them to Assistant District Attorney Tim Cole in Montage County, for, as the Judge personally told me, legal advice, and Tim Cole simply trashed them. When I tried to take them directly to the Grand Jury, I was drug down the stairs by the District Court Baliff, Dick Woods, and the investigator for the District Attorney, Mark Petterson, against whom I was attempting to file criminal complaints at the time. I was forced out the door and knocked to the ground, causing a chipped elbow, which still smarts if I touch it just right.

In Denton County, I was arrested by the court bailiff in order to keep me from presenting criminal complaints to an assistant District Attorney who was there for one of those pretrial hearing. That day I got to spend the whole day in a stinking stifling drunk tank so full of people there was no place to sit and I had to stand on my bad leg all day.

Combat was tough, but at least I was fighting an identifiable enemy. When the enemy is all around you, when it is your own public officials, it is far more difficult.

You might call it a Catch 22, but I call it a deliberate and ongoing criminal conspiracy perpetrated for the specific purpose of shielding criminal wrong-doers from prosecution in violation of 38.05 Texas Penal Code:

38.05. Hindering Apprehension or Prosecution

(a) A person commits an offense if, with intent to hinder the arrest, prosecution, conviction, or punishment of another for an offense, or with intent to hinder the arrest, detention, adjudication, or disposition of a child for engaging in delinquent conduct that violates a penal law of the grade of felony, he:

(1) harbors or conceals the other;

(2) provides or aids in providing the other with any means of avoiding arrest or effecting escape; or

(3) warns the other of impending discovery or apprehension.

(b) It is a defense to prosecution under Subsection (a)(3) that the warning was given in connection with an effort to bring another into compliance with the law.

(c) An offense under this section is a Class A misdemeanor, except that the offense is a felony of the third degree if the person who is harbored, concealed, provided with a means of avoiding arrest or effecting escape, or warned of discovery or apprehension is under arrest for, charged with, or convicted of a felony, or is in custody or detention for, is alleged in a petition to have engaged in, or has been adjudicated as having engaged in delinquent conduct that violates a penal law of the grade of felony, and the person charged under this section knew that the person they harbored, concealed, provided with a means of avoiding arrest or effecting escape, or warned of discovery or apprehension is under arrest for, charged with, or convicted of a felony, or is in custody or detention for, is alleged in a petition to have engaged in, or has been adjudicated as having engaged in delinquent conduct that violates a penal law of the grade of felony.

I further contend, this conspiracy on the part of prosecutors is perpetrated in order to facilitate the commission of other crimes, those demonstrated above and below.

In the current condition, the legal system in Texas is out of control. You can't sue the judges and you certainly can't get one prosecuted. You can't get a fair trial and you certainly can't expect to exert your rights as a sovereign citizen.

It is a conspiracy I tell you, a low down dirty rotten sneaking conniving conspiracy. I am mad as hell and am not going to take it any more. When I think of the chimp with the stick, banging it on the ground, I can't help but empathize with him his frustration.

POSTURE AND POSITION

That is a pretty depressing story. What is a law abiding citizen to do in the face of such overwhelming corruption, dishonor, and disregard? How is a simple lowly individual supposed to buck such an overwhelming system?

Actually, it is simple, not easy maybe, but simple. First, we must remember this is a republic, not a democracy. It is a democratic republic, but a republic first. In a republic the individual is sovereign, when we forget that, we abdicate our authority and responsibility. When we take it to heart, the answer is obvious.

I may appear an outrageous radical and many would like to paint me as such, but I am not. I am a father of two well grown children, a fat papa to three well spoiled grandsons, a husband these last 31 years and business owner for almost that long, a voter, and a combat veteran. I stand squarely on the backbone of this proud nation, bound under my personal oath to protect this country from all enemies, foreign and domestic.

The oath I swore a long time ago, in what now seems another life, still binds me as if a lifetime oath. Consequent to that oath I went half way around the world and in a stinking stifling jungle I paid heavy for my rights and freedoms. In the petulance of my youth, toward false motives and misdirected patriotism, these hands accrued wrongful blood on them, but no more. More tragically, others paid a far greater price than I for the rights and freedoms I now see trampled for convenience and expedience.

These rights and freedoms I tout are mine. As a sovereign citizen I claim them as my personal property. And, as a sovereign citizen it is my responsibility to ensure the rights, in my stewardship, are passed to my children intact and unfettered. To that end, I pursue the following.

THE FIX IS IN

The solution is simple if seemingly daunting. When public officials violate laws they are as culpable as any criminal. While judges and prosecutors have carved out a nice little set of immunities for themselves from civil litigation, there is no immunity from criminal behavior. At least, there is no legal immunity from criminal behavior.

Therefore, the solution follows from the problem. If you have it made known to you that a person (public official or otherwise) has violated a law, you have a civil duty to report the crime and the duty of officials receiving notice is clear. If you report a crime and make no untrue statement and anyone takes any threatening posture toward you, you should consider it an act of felony retaliation.

Taking my own advise, I have had it made known to me that police officers, in Texas, have been arresting citizens and taking them directly to jail, making no effort to ascertain the availability of a magistrate for the purpose of securing authority to continue to hold the individual. The Supreme Court has said, in such a case the arrested individual has a cause of action for unlawful detention, which is a crime in Texas.
Further, the officer leaves the arrested person in the custody of a jailer, trusting the jailer to perform the duties required by law to insure proper authority to hold and protect all of the detainees' constitutional rights. The problem the officer has is s/he is responsible for the actions of the jailer. If the proper authority is not promptly procured, if the jailer fails in that duty, all are culpable.

Well, sure enough, the jailer routinely fails miserably in that duty. The jailer will eventually bring the detainee before a magistrate, who will have already helped the jailer perfect the allegations against the accused in ex parte fashion.

Then the magistrate will refuse to perform a proper hearing, deny the accused the presumption of innocence, and take evidence from the accuser, while denying the accused his/her right to rebut, or to enter exculpatory evidence.

S/he will bind him/her over for trial and set bail as a matter of policy and practice. The magistrate will then give the file back to the jailer, who will secret it from the Clerk of the Court of jurisdiction, thereby denying the accused the right to access to the courts, and contaminating the evidence used at the hearing.

The arresting officer, by committing the act of improper detention of the citizen, for the purpose of the facilitation of a felony, becomes guilty of Aggravated Kidnapping as are all who participate in the crime.

The potential ramifications of this type of criminal behavior, is enormous. Therefore, if there is no complaint in the court record, or the complaint is fatally defective, which it must be, if not sealed and put in the protection of the Clerk of the Court, the trial judge has no jurisdiction. With no jurisdiction, there is no authority to act, and any act committed is treason to the Constitution, and it gets worse.

Judges have absolute immunity from civil litigation for their acts committed on the bench, except in one circumstance. You guessed it, when they have no jurisdiction.

So, by conspiring to deny the detainee in his/her rights, the magistrate, along with the arresting officer and jailer, set up the judge having jurisdiction in the cause, to be sued personally. If a judge acts with no jurisdiction, he has no immunity, and can be prosecuted criminally.

Rather they realize it or not, they set themselves up, as well as all who participate in the above, are trespassers from the beginning.

I have looked in the court records of several counties and you probably won't believe this, but there is something glaring by its absence. In the records, there is no complaint, or if one exists, it is not the one the magistrate was directed to forward to the clerk of the court. The ones that occasionally show up in the court records are frauds on the court. They have been made up, long after the person has been bound to the authority of the court and set to bail. They have been drawn up by the prosecutor and signed by the original complainant, and dated at a date much later than the original, in order to hide the fact that the detainee has been illegally bound to the court. This is done in order to bypass the Constitutional right to a speedy trial.

It is a slippery slope on the way to the Frog Farm.

On point of fact, criminal prosecutions in Texas are indeed criminal. They commit nothing less than acts in furtherance of an ongoing criminal enterprise, perpetrated and perpetuated by the State itself, through training and enforcement of public policies and practices, in incredible violation of most every Constitutional right, we citizens have. All this is being done in order to extort an unauthorized tax from the public, in the form of fines and fees, collected in violation of the due course of the laws of the State.

Under Texas law, a street gang is a group of people acting in concert and collusion toward on ongoing criminal enterprise with a recognizable leadership. Texas Criminal Justice is, by this definition, a street gang.

Rulings by judges without jurisdiction, are not voidable, they are void. Under law, it is as if they never happened, so what happens to all those people now in jail, consequent to the current practice?

No jurisdiction means no immunity from personal civil suit, for all who participated in the prosecution, and more. If a governmental agency collects a fine or fee in violation of the due course of the laws, that fine must be paid back, in triplicate.

It's a fine mess we have gotten ourselves into here on the Frog Farm, a fine mess indeed.

198

DUE NOTICE AS FAIR WARNING

Please don't misinterpret this as a call for aid and assistance. In point of fact, I don't need the succor and support of the masses. It is the point of this republican form of government that, as a sovereign citizen, I have all the authority I need to get this fixed. It is the point of being an American that we are individual free men and women with the power to take our government to task, and I intend to do just that.

This is fair warning. When the sky falls in on Texas as a result of these improper practices, none may say they did not know as, to quote Fox Mulder, "The truth is out there."

When I ask for the arrest, of all those involved in these dastardly deeds and horrendous wrongs, none may be seen to cry foul. The Supreme Court has held, "If a public official violates a ruling of this court and he is sane, he may not say he knows not what he does."

I have been chasing this donkey for fifteen years, and now I have it by the tail, and do not intend to let go.

It is a common practice for governmental officials, when taken to task, to use their authority as a weapon against the challenger. I have certainly seen that first hand. I have been banged up, beat up, pushed around, threatened, jailed and in all, discounted and disrespected. But they have only broken a couple of bones and dislocated a couple of others. I have only spent a few nights in jail, and as to all the threats, they are mostly fluff and bluster.

I have been considered crazy and a crackpot, a lunatic and pariah, but I am none of those. Richard Roper, head U S Attorney in Fort Worth called me a man on a mission. Well, I suppose I am.

I am also a father of two well grown children, a fat papa to three well spoiled grandsons, a husband of these last 31 years, and business owner almost that long. I am a citizen, a voter, a taxpayer, and a veteran.

Long ago, in what now seems another life, I swore on my oath, I would protect this country from all enemies, foreign and domestic. At the time, it was made clear, it was a lifetime oath and I took it to heart. Consequent to the petulance of my youth, I went half way around the world and paid heavy for the rights and freedoms I now claim.

Because I listened without critique, accepted without challenge, and acted without cause, these hand have wrongful blood on them, but no more. I paid for my impetuousness heavily, but in deference to those who paid much more, I stand on my duty. I am repeatedly warned by concerned friends, including and mostly police officers, of what could happen to me, but what threat can my own government pose that does not pale into insignificance, before the price I watched others pay for the rights I now enjoy?
We recently watched our sons and daughters topple a sovereign nation, loosing many and killing more. Who could stand by and fade from duty for petty and unfounded fear in the face of our children's demonstrated courage?

Benjamin Desraile once said:

"Nothing can resist the human will that will stake its very existence on the extent of its purpose."

I am throwing down the gauntlet. Let any who will take it up with me do so with honor and dignity. For those who would deny my fellow Americans in their rights and freedoms, take care as, to quote one of our Iraq liberators, "I am no kidding coming." I am coming in the form of candidate for Wise County Sheriff.

As Sheriff I will begin to implement changes that will put an end to the problems I present. The problems with the criminal justice system are complex and convoluted. It has taken 56 pages to get here, but the solution is as simple as the problem is complex.

The crux of our problem is a lack of leadership.

WE NEED LEADERSHIP

The Sheriff's we have been electing have been well indoctrinated into the status quo. After years of operating under a system, they have to know does not follow law, they just don't have it in them to change it.

The practices I have been trying to change these last 15 years, have set the police at odds with the public. They have undermined the public trust and denied police the honor and dignity they deserve. I see police becoming more and more isolated and antagonistic and that has to stop.

We have been waiting for our police, or defense attorneys or someone to make sure our rights are protected. Well, that isn't going to happen. The root of the problem lies at the feet or our judges and prosecutors, and they are not about to change anything.
The practices and procedures that cause the police and public so much grief serve the professional interest of the courts, and they are not about to change them. They don't have to change, as long as they have the Sheriff subdued.

When the Sheriff refuses to enforce laws relating to judges and prosecutors, they become totally immune from all law, as you cannot sue a judge or prosecutor. With no check to the balance of official abuse, they don't have to follow law; they can do what is convenient for them with impunity.

The police are as terrified of prosecutors and judges as everyone else. And defense counsel can be put out of business by judges who can rule against a client on a whim, or to get back at an attorney for any slight. So, do you really expect your attorney to risk his career to protect your rights? Not in this life; not in Texas.

The fear officials have, of the absolute power of the judge to do as he pleases, I assert, this is a false fear, as judges are, for the most part, just and reasonable people. They tend to be the best of the best, but fear seldom knows logic, and the imagined threat seems always more tangible than the reality.

The solution to this problem is simple. If the Sheriff simply enforces the law equally toward all, even judges and prosecutors, the problem will go away. When the public can be assured, if any public official denies a citizen in the full and free access to, or the enjoyment of any right, that is a crime in the State of Texas, even if a judge does it, and the Sheriff will arrest the offender. As Sheriff, I will make it clear, I will hold all officials to the same rule of law as citizens.

This is not about arresting judges as that will not be necessary. The problem has never been with the judges; it has been with the irrational fear of judges. Most people in law enforcement know the law as laid down by our Constitutional Framers is not being followed, and we are all paying the price for it. On the one hand, remove our fear of judges, refusing to follow law, and on the other give them confidence that the judges will enforce the laws as written, and most of the problems we are having with law enforcement will simply go away.

The permutations of the problem are far to complex to properly explain in this short statement. However, the solution is as simple as the problem is complex; just follow the law. Do as our Constitutional Framers and subsequent Legislators commanded and intended.

Police can talk about fighting crime all they want, but if they continue alienating their most potent weapon, a trusting and cooperative public, they will do no better than they have. When the people no longer have need to fear their public officials, when they can with confidence cooperate and participate, the effectiveness of our law enforcement efforts will increase dramatically.

There are a number of steps I intend to institute, but they take too much explaining to include here. On my web site, SherifWise.com you will find detailed information.
There is a document I call The Frog Farm Conspiracy in which I demonstrate, with what attorneys call "specificity and particularity" what is being done wrong. In the part titled "The Fix," I detail what I intend to do to fix it.

Don't be surprised if the solution sounds too simple and straightforward. In fact it is simple and straightforward and taken directly from law.

BAILIFFS AS PEACE OFFICERS

Few people who have stood before a judge in this country will tell you they trust the judge. We are all only too well aware that the judge can pretty well do as he pleases, with little or no regard to law. We know full well, we are subject to the whim and caprice of the judge, so we had better watch our step. We simply don't trust someone who can act with impunity. We trust rule of law and forbade royalty in this country, then came judicial immunity.

In order to insure the integrity and sanctity of the courts, as Sheriff I will call in all the bailiffs in the county and remind them, they are certified police officers and as such have a duty to keep the peace and enforce law. If, in the course of the performance of their duties, they have it made known to them that a law has been broken, they have a duty to act in accordance with their sworn oath and the laws of the State of Texas.

If they observe a public official, acting under the color (pretence) of any authority, denying a citizen in the full and free access to or enjoyment of any right, they have a duty to arrest the offender as such is a violation of Section 39.03 Penal Code. It is an act of Official Oppression and is a class A misdemeanor in Texas.
If I am made known that such a thing has happened in the presence of a bailiff, and the bailiff failed to perform his duty, I will arrest that bailiff myself for violating Section 38.05 Penal Code, Shielding from Prosecution.

This is not a difficult concept. Judges made themselves immune from civil suit, but even judges didn't trust judges enough to give them complete immunity. The Supreme Court, though willing to protect their personal assets from civil litigation, didn't trust their fellow judges enough to give them complete immunity criminal prosecution as well. That came later. It came because judges had the power to assert it rather than declare it.

What public official would dare risk angering other judges by lodging allegations against one of their cronies? In fact, that fear is most likely unfounded, as judges are people like everyone else and more likely to be of the highest moral standards. But, like a tame tiger, they must be treated with ever diligent care and suspicion.

When the public can be assured their judges will be held to the same rule of law as everyone else, there will be no more reason to fear and distrust them. If you know, they must act in accordance with their oath and honor, you will be in a position to begin to trust and respect that honor.

TAKE BEFORE MAGISTRATE

My children fear my police. The public, for the most part, fear and distrust the police, and it is the fault of neither. People in positions of power and public trust, have directed and advised the police and lower courts in practices and procedures, which act in clear and direct violation of the law, while serving the personal and professional agenda of those officials, and it must stop.

It is my contention and will be my position, that no police officer has the power to arrest and imprison. Those powers were never authorized by our Founding Fathers. When I am Sheriff, no person arrested in this county will be taken to jail. When an arrest is made, the officer will act in accordance with Article 14.06 Code of Criminal Procedure and take the person arrested directly to the nearest magistrate and explain himself.

Quote 14.06

This is from no lack of trust in our peace officers. It is a very specific statutory requirement put in place by our Founders to insure trust and cooperation between the pubic and the police. When a policing agent is granted the power to arrest and imprison on their individual authority, the officer becomes a threat, and people rightfully come to fear the potential personal passion of the officer. Even when the officer acts in the best of faith in strict accordance with law and justice, people tend to interpret their actions, through the filter of their personal fears.

Our Founders understood the nature of the human animal and in order to insure public trust, they created the position of Magistrate. They deliberately made it a position, not an office. Magistrates are not judges, though judges can act as magistrates along with mayors and reporters (don't ask what reporters are; it is in the law, but no one seems to know exactly who they are).
The position of Magistrate was created to act as a go-between, to stand squarely between the peace officer and the jailhouse door.

When any citizen is arrested for any reason, s/he is to be taken directly to the nearest magistrate by the most direct route. The Magistrate must then examine into the sufficiency of the allegation and decide whether to bind the citizen to the authority of the court, or release that person at his/her liberty.

There is a whole chapter devoted to the examination, the magistrate must perform which serves to protect the rights of the citizen. This is not a difficult concept, so why is it not being done?

Well, the Legislature, in its wisdom, decided, since we already have learned counsel in government employ, in the form of prosecuting attorneys, we may as well take advantage of their knowledge, toward advising the police and lower courts. That may have seemed like a good idea at the time, but prosecutors are necessarily compromised, and nationally accepted bar standards would normally forbid such a thing.

You would expect prosecutors to be influenced by the pressures of their conflicting position, and that is exactly what has happened. Prosecutors have swayed the police and lower courts, into practices and polices, that only serve the prosecutors' purpose, at the expense of law and the right of things.

It is all about the deal. Prosecutors have neither the time, nor resources to vigorously prosecute every case that comes before them. They had to do something, so they came up with "the deal." The difficulty with the deal is it takes time. Sometimes, you have people, who have the gall to consider themselves innocent. For prosecutors, this is a time consuming problem, but they got that fixed.

"The Deal" has become so effective that the statistical conviction rate in Texas, according to the Criminal Justice Oversight Counsel is virtually 100%. Everybody takes the deal. Why would everyone take the deal? They take he deal because the system has been set up so that no rational person can have a reasonable alternative, and it starts with the magistrate.

Prosecutors can't effectively work "the deal", if Magistrates start protecting all the rights of the accused. If the accused feels empowered before the law, if they have faith in the system, they will fight for their rights, forcing the prosecutor to either petition the court to dismiss or put on a vigorous prosecution.

To avoid this and facilitate "the deal," prosecutors advise police, they could wait 24 hours before seeking a magistrate. This is simply not true. Well, I suppose it is when public officials can do as they please, but in a land of law, this is against it.

The prosecutor wants you to go through the humiliation of the booking procedure, the fingerprints, the mug shots, and then a night on the drunk-tank floor. He then wants you to be brought before a magistrate in your orange jail uniform and to have the magistrate remand you to the authority of the court, without regard to the sufficiency of the allegations against you.

This is a humiliating and debilitating experience. I once spent the night in the Wise County Jail for driving with a headlight out. I did and it was an eye opening experience. By the next morning my ideals weren't as important as getting out of there, especially when the Magistrate made it clear she was not interested in anything I might have to say. And, all those rights, I thought were protecting me, were just so much high-minded rhetoric.

We spend our lives living in arrogant assurance of the surety of our rights. It only takes a minor bout with the criminal justice system to knock that naïve notion out of a person. Once you realize you are naked before the law and all this righteous rhetoric was only that, rhetoric, you are ready for most any deal the prosecutor throws at you.

The Supreme Court held a 24 hour delay is not necessarily unreasonable considering all the circumstances; however, there shall be no set time limit. An officer's only defense against an allegation of false imprisonment for failure to timely take before a magistrate is a showing of due diligence in trying to locate a magistrate.

Prosecutors lied to the police. But the police need have no fear of violating law. The prosecutor will insure they are not taken to account for following their improper instructions, as it serves the prosecutions' purpose, and any complaint made, will promptly be trashed by prosecutors.

As Sheriff, I will hold all police in the county to law. If any police officer, local, county, state, or federal brings someone they have arrested to the county jail, without first securing an order from some magistrate, and cannot show a due diligent effort to locate a magistrate, I will arrest that officer myself.

Mark Autry, Justice of Peace for Precinct 4 told me, if an officer brings someone to him at 2:00 in the morning for a hearing, there is nothing that tells him he has to hear the complaint. I agreed but assured him, if the magistrates don't make some arrangements, so that they have a magistrate available anytime a peace officer is authorized to restrict a citizen at his/her liberty, then he will have to tell the deputies that, as they would be waking him up. And, if the judge does or says anything, that would tend to chill the officers' access to them, I will arrest the judge myself.

I only mention Judge Autry as he is not only a personal friend of mine, but a man I consider to be the most honest and forthright judge in the county.

In all fairness, after talking to several magistrates, none of then had a problem with handling this situation. The main complaint I heard was that the police simply do not bring people to them. And the police, they indicated they have no problem with this either, they are just following policy.

As much as I rag on the prosecutors, they really didn't. This is something that evolved over time and the current administration inherited what others were doing. In fact, I have talked with the present prosecutors and I doubt either will have any problem with things being done according to law.

PROPER EXAMINATIONS

When in the military, I was trained to work with nuclear weapons. With something so potentially lethal, there can simply be no mistakes. We were continually being warned about the details. The real danger always lurked in the details. Familiarity breeds contempt was drummed into us constantly.

Our police and courts deal with the same issues over and over, and it can get old after a while. They hear, "I'm innocent; I didn't do it; its not how it looks," until they have it coming out their ears, and become somewhat insensitive. Liberty, from their perspective looses its luster.

Liberty, we fought a revolution for it, established a nation dedicated to it, and often take it so for granted, we forget to protect it at every turn. When challenged by law enforcement, we often waive our right to it, for fear, or for convenience. When we hold our liberty in such low regard, we refuse to fight for it, what can we expect but that our public officials would loose respect for it.

This is not what our Founders intended. They intended out liberty be taken very serious. It was there intent that the liberty of a free citizen be held sacred and restricted only as a last and extreme resort.

It was intended, before a person could be restricted at their liberty, certain and very definite steps were taken, to insure their rights were scrupulously protected. They went so far as to dedicate an entire chapter in the Code of Criminal Procedure to this end.

As it stands, chapter 16 of the Code of Criminal Procedure may as well not be there, as it is totally ignored by magistrates, per instructions from prosecutors. When a person is arrested, it is commanded that he is brought before a magistrate for an examination hearing, but that doesn't happen. Instead of an examination, magistrates have been directed to perform a magistration.

Don't bother to look for that in law; you won't find it. It is something prosecutors made up to describe an abomination they concocted, in order to get around all those pesky rights defined in Chapter 16.

What happens, is an act of distortion for the purpose of extortion. Prosecutors, regardless of their duty to seek justice, are more interested in getting guilty pleas, and go to great lengths toward that end, even to points well beyond those allowed by law, and this is one of them.

Prosecutors have advised magistrates to make no inquiry into the sufficiency of an allegation made by an arresting officer. I am sure we have all heard the phrase, "presumption of innocence." Well, not in Texas. In Texas, a police officer can arrest you for any reason, with or without cause, throw you in jail and have you hauled in front of a magistrate the next morning. Where, the magistrate will bind you over for trial as a matter of course.

That may not be right, but it is how things work in Texas.

Don't blame the magistrates. They are, for the most part, not attorneys, but ordinary citizens just like you and I. They are elected from the public and act in accordance with their training and the advice given by prosecutors.

The position of magistrate was created to act as a neutral check to the balance of the policing powers. They are intended to decide, if there is sufficient reason, to bind a free citizen over for trial. The problem prosecutors have with this is, it interferes with the deal. If the magistrate does a proper examination into the sufficiency of the allegations, those without merit will be dismissed and the prosecutor will loose the opportunity to work "the deal." A proper hearing also tends to bolster the citizen's confidence in a just adjudication of their cause, making it much more difficult for the prosecutor to finagle a deal.

There is another problem. If the magistrate does a proper hearing in accordance with the law, he will seal all instruments had in the hearing, cause his name to be written across the seal, and forward it to the court of jurisdiction, and prosecutors can't have that.
If that happens, the speedy trial clock will start when the prosecution starts and that won't leave enough time to work on "the deal".

Prosecutors pretty well know most people arrested feel they are innocent and will react indignantly if approached too soon with the deal. They need a little softening up first. A night on the drunk-tank floor is a good start. Next, is a hearing where the judge finds against them, as a matter of course! People, who have never experienced the system, expect hearings to be fair. They are sure, that when the judge hears their side, they will be set free.

When the judge makes it clear, he doesn't care what the accused may have to say, he is going do what he is going to do, that is all there is to that, any expectations of justice go right out the window. This is a crushing and demoralizing experience. After that, the deal gets a lot more appealing, but prosecutors aren't ready yet.

What prosecutors do, has evolved over a long time, and is as sophisticated as it is illegal, but it couldn't happen if magistrates did their jobs.

All this begs the question, "How could prosecutors get magistrates to act in such horrendous violation of clear law.

It's called sharp practice when attorneys focus on one aspect of law out of the context the rest of law. By doing that they can make anything they want appear correct and legal.

They interpreted an inclusive statute as if it were an exclusive. They interpreted Article 15.17 to exclude all requirements, not specifically mentioned in the article. Article 15.17 came into being in order to include in the examination, the warnings required by the Miranda decision. It requires the magistrates to issue the Miranda warnings. Prior to this statute, they only did an examination hearing.

Instead of including Miranda warnings in the examination process, prosecutors directed magistrates to replace the examination with the warnings.
They told magistrates they no longer had to protect all the citizen's rights; all they had to do is advise them, that they had the rights while systematically denying the citizen in most every one of them.
The Catch 22 here would almost be funny if not so horrendous.

The result is, there is not longer any presumption of innocence in Texas. If you are accused of crime, you will be forced to stand and answer without regard to the sufficiency of the allegations, and more. The magistrate, by the current practice, has become a member of the prosecutions' team. Instead of acting as a neutral go-between, the magistrate perfects the case for the prosecutor.

Magistrates have been instructed that their duty to examine only referred to the completeness of the complaint as made by the officer. You have to admit it is a slick maneuver. The prosecutor no longer has to insure the charge is properly made, before presenting it to the judge; he gets the judge to do that for him. The magistrate will insure all the paperwork is in order when presented, if not it will be returned to the officer so it can be corrected.

The magistrate, by this, forgoes any neutrality by helping the prosecutor prepare his case. By taking advantage of the fact that most magistrates are not attorneys, but lay judges, prosecutors have twisted their advise so as to enlist the magistrates to do their job for them, and deny citizens of most every protection the Constitution and laws, were intended to insure.

I have talked to a number of magistrates and none have a problem with doing a proper examination. Their only concern is that, they have been instructed to do otherwise. In fact, they have acted in good faith accordance with advice from respected authority. That the advice was horribly illegal, is a condemnation of learned counsel who, even though they inherited the practices, have a responsibility to realize, it is improper.

Cause No. 05-04-03361-CV

Ronald-Edwin...Duncan, Sui Juris	§	IN THE 221ˢᵗ DISTRICT COURT
Plaintiff	§	
VS.	§	
Trooper Caryn Mosier McAnarney	§	_____
Emp: ORA04-0905 Individually and	§	
in her official capacity	§	MONTGOMERY COUNTY, TEXAS

And

Montgomery County Sherriffs' Officer
Valenzuela # 8211, Individually and
in his Official Capacity

And

All Responding Officers cited in video and
Feb. 24ᵗʰ, 2005A.D. Request for Information

And

Montgomery County Sherriffs' Department

And

THE CITY OF CONROE

MEMORANDUM OF LAW ON
ARREST WITHOUT WARRANT

COMES NOW THE PLAINTIFF, Ronald-Edwin...Duncan, a free sovereign of the state of Texas, respectfully presenting and submitting this memorandum as evidence and proof of the prevailing and controlling law regarding the matter now before this Court.

ARGUMENTS AND STATEMENTS OF LAW

The Defendant usurped her authority and failed to follow due process, during and after, she initiated an arrest without warrant or probable cause for alleged misdemeanor traffic violations, and for allegedly interfering with the duties of a public servant, where only speech was involved. I asked Trooper McAnarney, why was she arresting us?

She responded that, "you disobeyed a police order". I stated that, "you do not have authority to order me around". She responded that, quote;

"I have all the authority in the world". Such actions and mindset, on the part of a "public servant" is a clear violation of Art. 1, Sec. 2 of the Texas Constitution.

The facts of this case lead to the conclusion of law, that the Defendant did not have lawful authority to arrest the Plaintiff. The Defendant had no warrant for the arrest of the Plaintiff, and she alleges that she only saw the Plaintiff commit a misdemeanor, i.e., a traffic violation.

She never claimed that a felony had been committed, nor a breach of the peace. At common law, and under the provisions of Due Process of Law, such an arrest without warrant can not be made.

Whereas, the arrest deprived the Plaintiff of his God given liberty, by an act not pursuant to due process of law, the arrest is unlawful. Due Process is not determined by the legislature.

It is manifest, it was not left to the legislative power to exact any process that might be devised. The [due process] article is a restraint on the legislative as well as on the executive and judicial powers of government, and cannot be so construed as to leave congress free to make any process, "due process of law", by its' mere will. Murray's Lessee v. Hoboken Imp. Co., 18 How. (59 U.S.) 272, 276 (1855).

The Constitution of the state of Texas, Art. 1, Sec. 19 declares; No citizen of this state shall be deprived of life, liberty, property, privileges or immunities, or in any manner disfranchised, except by the due course of the law of the land.

The words "due process" does not mean anything that the legislature may see fit to declare to be "due process of law". State ex rel. v. Billings, 55 Minn. 466, 474 (1893). Due process was intended to preserve established fundamental rights by requiring that they can not be deprived except by the established modes of law, as existing under the common law. This guarantee, that government shall follow a specified and pre-existing rule of conduct, process, or procedure is in itself a right the citizen held at common law, and was claimed by the colonists in early America. Thus, "it is clear that the common law is the foundation of that which is designated as due process of law" (6 R.C.L. "Const. Law",~ 435).

The Constitution guarantees these pre-existing rights and procedures in the due process provision.

What is due process of law may be ascertained by an examination of the settled usage and modes of proceedings existing in the common and statute law of England before the emigration of our ancestors. Twining v. New Jersey, 211 U.S. 78, 100 (1908).

The expressions "due process of law" and "law of the land" have the same meaning. *** The "Law" intended by the Constitution is the <u>common law</u>, that came down to us from our forefathers, as it existed and was understood and administered when that instrument was framed and adopted. State v. Doherty, 60 Maine 504, 509 (1872).

In interpreting what due process of law is, it has been held that "none of our liberties are to be taken away except in accordance with established principles" Ekern v. McGovern, 154 Wis. 157, 142 N.W. 595, 620 (1913). Thus, the mode of arrest by which one can be deprived of his liberty is to be determined by the pre-existing common law principles and modes of procedure. A properly constituted warrant of arrest is a process at common law by which persons could lawfully be deprived of their liberty. The common law on arrest without warrant recognized only certain specific and well defined cases whereby a citizen could be deprived of his liberty. That common law process cannot be abrogated or changed by the legislature.

The common law drew a distinction between an arrest for misdemeanors, such as that which the Defendant arrested the Plaintiff, and between arrests for felonies. When a felony was committed, an arrest could be made without a warrant, but no arrest could be made for a misdemeanor without a warrant unless it constituted a "breach of the peace". The alleged misdemeanor traffic violations, cited by Caryn McAnarney On April 18th, 2003A.D., was not a breach of the peace, and therefore, the Defendant needed a warrant to make an arrest for such offense.

In determining the law surrounding arrests, the Supreme Court of South Carolina, in the case of State v. Byrd, 72 S.C. 104, 51 S.E. 542, 544 (1905), affirmed a prior decision of the Court holding that:

At <u>common law</u>, as a general rule, an arrest could not be made without warrant for an offense less than a felony, except for a breach of the peace. 3 Cyc. 880; State v. Sims, 16 S.C. 486.

In a New York case, the State Supreme Court held that a city alderman or justice of the peace could not, at common law, arrest or cause an arrest for a misdemeanor not amounting to a breach of the peace, without warrant, though happening in his presence. The Supreme Court, in the case of Butolph v. Blust, 5 Lansing's Rep. 84, 86 (1871) stated:

At common law an arrest could not be made of a person charged with a misdemeanor except on warrant of a magistrate, unless it involved a breach of the peace, in which case the offender might be arrested by any person present at its' commission. (1 Chitty, Criminal Law, 15; Carpenter v. Mills, 29 How. Pr. R. 473).

In the very reasoned and authoritative case of Ex parte Rhodes, 202 Ala. 68, 79 So. 462, 464 (1918), the Supreme Court of Alabama related the due process provision to the act of arrests. It asserted that, any seizure or arrest of a citizen is not reasonable, or "due process", merely because a Legislature has attempted to authorize it. These phrases are limitations upon the power of the Legislature, as well as upon that of the other departments of government, or their officers. In determining what was "due process" regarding arrests, the Court stated:

It must not be forgotten that there can be <u>no arrest without due process of law.</u> An arrest without warrant has never been lawful, except in those cases where the public security requires it; this has only been recognized in <u>felony</u>, and in <u>breaches of the peace</u> committed in the presence of the officer. Ex parte Rhodes, 202 Ala. 68, 79 So. 462, 465; citing, Sarah Way's Case, 41 Mich. 304, 1 N.W. 1023 (1879), et al. Also cited and affirmed in Pinkerton v. Verberg, 78 Mich. 573, 44 N.W. 579, 583 (1889); State v. Williams, 45 Ore. 314, 77 Pac. 965, 969, (1904); Adair v. Williams, 24 Ariz. 422, 210 Pac. 853, 856 (1922).

The Alabama Supreme Court in the Rhodes case went on to say that, "the phrase due process, must be determined by what it meant <u>at the common law</u>, and when the Constitution was adopted" (p. 469). The Court then cited the case of Tillman v. Beard, 121 Mich. 475, 80 N.W. 248 (1899), in stating:

Officers are justified in arresting without warrant only in cases of felony and breaches of the peace. This is elementary. It is needless to cite authorities.

At one time in the history of American Law and jurisprudence, the concept that no one could be arrested for a misdemeanor except with a proper warrant was so basic and "elementary" that it was not necessary

216

to give any authorities to prove it. Yet, this foundational concept was found to be too restrictive to the ever-growing, oppressive government that has gained power in this country.

Thus, in order for it to control the liberty of citizens, and to enforce its' oppressive laws, the corrupt, de facto government has gradually undermined a very basic principal of constitutional law.

In the Pinkerton case, supra, it was held that a police officer could not arrest a woman, without a warrant, upon mere suspicion that she was upon the street for the purpose of prostitution, even under provisions of the city ordinance allowing such arrests. The fact that she had a reputation of being a "street walker", and that the officer knew of her reputation and believed that she was plying her vocation as such, (plus the fact that she did not give her name to the officer stating, "it was none of his business" and that she dared the officer to arrest her), did not give the officer grounds to arrest her. The Court said:

If persons can be restrained of their liberty, and assaulted and imprisoned, under such circumstances, without complaint or warrant, then there is no limit to the power of a police officer.

*** Any law which would place the keeping and safe conduct of another, in the hands of even a conservator of the peace, unless for some breach of the peace committed in his presence, or upon suspicion of felony, would be most oppressive and unjust, and destroy all the rights which our Constitution guarantees.

These are rights which existed long before our Constitution, and we have taken just pride in their maintenance, making them a part of the fundamental law of the land. Pinkerton v. Verberg, 78 Mich. 573, 44 N.W. 579, 582-83 (1889); Larson v. Feeney, 196 Mich. 1, 162 N.W. 275, 276-77 (1917).

Under the topic of "arrest" as found in Vol. 2 Ruling Case Law, we find the heading, "Constitutional Requirements as to Warrants", wherein it states:

The fundamental constitutional guarantees of personal liberty protect private individuals in the right of enjoyment of personal freedom without unlawful restraint, and it is universally recognized that no one may be arrested except by due process of law. (2 R.C.L. 463, ~ 21).

Here again we find that the principle of arrest only by due process of law was once universally recognized, yet the Defendant has ignored such process in her arrest of Plaintiff.

The law regarding arrest without warrant was also declared by the Supreme Court of Wisconsin in the case of Radloff v. National Food Stores, Inc., 20 Wis.2d 224; 121 N.W.2d 865, 867 (1963) as follows:

In Stittgen v. Rundle, (1898), 99 Wis. 78, 80, 74 N.W. 536, this court established the principal that; "An arrest without a warrant has never been lawful, except in those cases where the public security requires it; and this has only been recognized in felony, and in breaches of the peace committed ion the presence of the officer". This rule was reaffirmed in Gunderson v. Stuebing (1905), 125 Wis. 173, 104 N.W. 149; 1 American Law Reports, Annotated, 585.

The Radloff case involved a shoplifter who was stopped and arrested by store employees for taking two cartons of cigarettes. The State Supreme Court said that the employees had the right to stop the shoplifter and recover the goods he had stolen from their employer, and were not negligent per se in so doing. However, since the taking of the cigarettes constituted a misdemeanor, the store employees had no right to arrest the shoplifter when they had no warrant to arrest. In the Gunderson case, the court explained that arrests without warrants were allowed at common law "only where the ends of justice would be defeated without it", and that it "must be confined to cases of strict public necessity".

Where a person was arrested without a warrant and charged with "public drunkeness" which resulted in charges of "resisting arrest", it was held by the Supreme Court of North Carolina that the arrest was illegal, as the state failed to make a prima facie case by showing that the defendants' conduct at the time of arrest amounted to either an actual or threatened breach of peace. The court said "it is manifest that mere drunkeness, unaccompanied by language or conduct which creates public disorder amounting to a breach of the peace, will not justify arrest without warrant", and that "not every misdemeanor is a breach of the peace". In a very well-reasoned decision on the subject of arrests, the Court held the following:

It has always been the general rule of the common law that ordinarily an arrest should not be made without warrant and that, subject to well-defined exceptions, an arrest without warrant is deemed unlawful. 4 Bl. Comm. 289 et seq.; 6 C. J. S., Arrest, ~ 5, p. 579. This foundational principal of the common law, designed and intended to protect the people against the abuses of arbitrary arrests, is of ancient origin.

It derives from assurances of Magna Carta, and harmonizes with the spirit of our constitutional precepts that the people should be secure in their persons.

Nevertheless, to this general rule, that no man should be taken into custody of the law, without the sanction of a warrant or other judicial authority, the processes of the early English common law, in deference to the requirements of public security, worked out a number of exceptions.

These exceptions related in the main to cases <u>involving felonies and suspected felonies and to breaches of the peace</u> (authorities cited). State v. Mobley, 240 N. C. 476, 83 S. E. 2d 100, 102 (1954).

The overall opinion of the Court stressed the principle of the common law as controlling in arrests, thus characterizing as erroneous the view that any offense in the presence of an officer is subject to arrest without warrant.

In Texas it was held that an arrest without warrant, for selling a railroad ticket in the officers' presence, in violation of a city ordinance prohibiting the selling of such tickets, was unlawful, as the offense charged was not a felony, nor an offense "against the public peace". M. K. & T. Ry. Co. v. Warner, 19 Tex. Civ. App. 463.

Sheriffs, constables and other officers under the executive branch of government have always been recognized as having authority to arrest for felonies committed and for misdemeanors amounting to a breach of the peace. But that is the extent of their power to arrest without warrant, and this constitutional principle is well-grounded in ancient common law safeguards of individual liberty.

In England, under the common law, sheriffs, justices of the peace, coroners, constables, and watchmen were entrusted with special powers as conservators of the peace, with authority to arrest felons and persons reasonably suspected of being felons. *** Conservators of the peace also had the authority to make arrests without warrants in case of a misdemeanor which involved a breach of the peace committed in the presence of the officer making the arrest. 2 Ruling Case Law, p. 446; Orick v. State, 105 So. 465, 469 (Miss., 1925); Grahm v. State, 143 Ga. 440, 85 S.E. 328, 330 (1915); Kennedy v. State, 139 Miss. 579, 104 So. 449, 450 (1925); Wilson v. Town of Mooresville, 222 N.C. 283, 22 S.W.2d 907, 911 (1942); People v. McGurn, 341 Ill. 632, 173 N.E. 754, 756 (1930).

It has been held that constitutional provisions of rights are to be interpreted according to "the common and statute law of England prior to the emigration of our ancestors", and by the law established here before the Constitution was adopted.

"Under the common law, the powers of state agents were limited and the requirements for an arrest warrant were strictly enforced". United States v. Tarlowski, 305 F. Supp. 112, 116 (1969). This procedure for arrest is part of the "due process of law" provisions of the constitution which protects citizens from the arbitrary infringement of their right to personal liberty. Thus, any specific authority for arrests must be based upon the common law procedures that allow a deprivation of one's liberty. This was so held by the Supreme Court of Michigan:

It has already been decided that no arrest can be lawfully made without warrant, except in the cases <u>existing at common law</u> before our constitution was adopted. People v. Swift, 59 Mich. 529, 26 N.W. 694, 698 (1886).

Liberty cannot be deprived, except by the law of the land or due process of law, no statute or ordinance can constitutionally be enacted which allows arrests without a warrant for any purpose the legislature decides. Due process is a limitation upon the legislature, and thus a legislative statute cannot be the due process by which one can be deprived of his liberty by arrests.

In a legal article titled, "Arrest With and Without a Warrant", written in the University of Pennsylvania Law Review, Vol. 75, No. 6, April, 1927, p. 485, numerous authorities were cited in support of the following proposition:

It is usually said that not even a peace officer is privileged to make an arrest without a warrant for a misdemeanor which does not amount to a breach of the peace, and there are many cases which expressly deny the privilege to arrest for such a misdemeanor (p. 486).

In the Annotation of the American Law Reports, vol. 1, p. 585, is found a legal study titled: "Constitutionality of statute or ordinance authorizing an arrest without a warrant", in which the following is stated:

It has been stated that in cases less than a felony an arrest could only be made without a warrant, where there was a breach of the peace in the presence of the person making the arrest. (cases cited).

"The limits to the power of arrest by a constable, without process, <u>are well defined at common law</u>. ... To prevent the escape of a felon, and to

220

arrest anyone whom he reasonably suspected of having been engaged in the perpetration of a felony. To prevent breaches of the peace, he had the right to arrest any person who was engaged in, or in his presence threatened to engage in, an affray or other breach of the peace.

Beyond this, the law does not allow him to exercise the function of determining whether there was a sufficient case, of a violation of a law, to justify an arrest. Reed, J., in Newark v. Murphy (1878) 40 N.J.L. 145.

After this excerpt the law report stated that "the foregoing statement from Newark v. Murphy is in accord with the weight of American opinion". Those cases which seemed to deviate from this proposition are those which have upheld arrests for certain acts that were unlawful at common law, such as "streetwalkers".

In Tiedemans' "Treatise on the Limitations of Police Power" (1886) ~~33 is found the requirements for a lawful arrest and the exceptions to an unwarranted arrest.

33. What constitutes a lawful arrest. – As a general proposition, no one can make a lawful arrest for a crime, except an officer who has a warrant issued by a court or magistrate having competent authority.

33a. Arrests without a warrant. – Although it is the general rule of law that there can be no arrest without a warrant of the nature just described, there are cases in which the requirement of a warrant would so obstruct the effectual enforcement of the laws, that the ends of justice would be defeated. For public reasons, therefore, in a few cases, the personal security of the citizen is subjected to the further liability of being arrested by a police officer or private individual without a warrant. But, the right to arrest without a warrant must be confined to the cases of strict public necessity. The cases are few, and stated as follows;

1. When a felony is being committed, an arrest may be made without a warrant to prevent any further violation of the law.
2. When a felony has been committed, and the officer or private individual is justified by the facts within his knowledge, in believing that the person arrested has committed the crime.
3. All breaches of the peace, by assaults and batteries, affrays, riots, etc., for the purpose of restoring order immediately.

The rule of the common law, that a police officer or a private citizen may arrest a felon without a warrant, or on view of a breach of the peace, has never been extended to any and all misdemeanors. While there have been some erroneous decisions that have recognized statutes authorizing arrests for misdemeanors that do not constitute a breach of the peace, none are based upon the meaning of due process of law.

Therefore, arrests are not lawful where only a misdemeanor occurs, unless it is in the nature of a "breach of peace".

At the common law, an officer had no authority to make an arrest for a misdemeanor, though committed in his presence, unless it involved a breach of the peace. *** The right of personal liberty is a very high prerogative right, and to deprive one of that right, without due process of law, we must find specific authority for doing so. It can not be left to inference or some strained construction of statute or ordinance. State v. Lutz, 85 W. Va. 330; 101 S.E. 434, 43 (1919).

The specific authority for arrests is grounded in the ancient settled maxims of law, which no statute can abrogate without violating the "due process of law" provisions of the Constitution. Therefore, a warrant must be obtained for a misdemeanor that is not a "breach of peace". The Supreme Court of Minnesota has stated on several occasions that even in the case of a felony an "arrest and search should not be made without a warrant unless there is a compelling necessity to do so". State v. Mastrain, 285 Minn. 51, 57 (1969). The Supreme Court of Rhode Island in declaring the requirements at common law for an arrest stated:

That law permitted an officer to arrest without a warrant on reasonable suspicion based on his knowledge that a felony had been committed. *** In all other cases, except in the case of a misdemeanor amounting to a breach of the peace committed in his presence, an officer had no authority, at common law, to arrest without a warrant. (authorities cited) Kominsky v. Durand, 64 R.I. 387, 12 Atl.2d 652,654 (1940).

In American Jurisprudence, 2d., Vol. 5, under the subject of 'Arrest", sections 26 and 28, pp. 716, 718, it states:

At common law, a peace officer cannot arrest without warrant for a misdemeanor, although committed in his presence, unless a breach of peace is involved.

At common law, the right to arrest for a misdemeanor committed in the presence of the officer is limited to those offenses that amount to a breach of the peace. The basis for the rule is that arrest without warrant is permitted, in cases less than felony, not for the apprehension of the offender, but only for the immediate preservation of the public peace;

and, accordingly, when the public peace is not menaced, a warrant is necessary. (authorities cited, see also section 22).

In Corpus Juris Secundum, Vol. 6A, under the subject of "Arrest" and under the heading of "Arrest or Detention Without Warrant" ~~ 10, p. 17 it is written:

At common law, however, it has always been the rule that, except in cases where the public security has demanded it, arrest without a warrant is unlawful.

"Due process of law", which declares that no citizen shall be deprived of any of his rights to life, liberty or property, unless by the law of the land, or the judgement of his peers, (Texas Constitution, Art. 1, Sec. 19), is the controlling factor in the matter of the arrest made by the defendant. An arrest is a deprivation of ones' God given liberty, and the due process that must be followed in an arrest, is that process which existed at common law. To prevent the exercise of arbitrary power at the discretion of government, it was deemed wise to secure the principles already settled in the common law upon this vital point of civil liberty in written constitutions (Cooley, Const. Lim. 364 and notes).

Blackstone says: "The constable hath great original and inherent authority with regard to arrests. He may, without warrant, arrest anyone for a breach of the peace committed in his view, and carry him before a justice of the peace; and in case of felony actually committed, or a dangerous wounding whereby felony is likely to ensue, he may, upon probable suspicion, arrest the felon, and, for that purpose, is authorized (as upon a justices' warrant) to break open doors, and even kill the felon, if he cannot otherwise be taken". 4 B1 Comm. 292.

In all other cases, however, the authorities are uniform, a constable or policeman has no authority to make an arrest without a warrant (authorities cited) Shanley v. Wells, 71 Ill. 78, 82 (1873).

In a case for false imprisonment, the Supreme Court of Maine examined the law regarding arrests and held: "The principle which, by the common law, regulate the right to arrest, or cause an arrest, without warrant, have been long settled both in this country and England; and, by these principles, the rights of these parties must be determined". After citing numerous cases involving the authority to arrest, the Court stated:

In many of these cases it seems to have been held that the authority of an officer to arrest for misdemeanor, without warrant, is limited to breaches of the peace or affrays, committed in his presence. Palmer v. Maine Cent. R. Co., 42 Atl. 800, 803, 92 Me. 399 (1899).

In a case involving a state liquor prohibition law, a man, while walking along a public street, was accosted by a police officer, and asked if he had any liquor on his person. He replied that he did. Thereupon the officer searched him and found a pint bottle of liquor in his inside coat pocket. He was then taken to the police station. The State Supreme Court of Wisconsin said that when the police officer stopped the man, he was illegally arrested and was illegally searched, as he had no warrant to do either. The Court said that "it is a serious thing to arrest a citizen, and it is a more serious thing to search his person" and it must be done "in conformity to the laws of the land". Regarding the law on arrests it held:

At common law, arrest for misdemeanors were not permissible without a warrant, except for acts committed in the presence of the officer, causing a breach of the peace. Allen v. State, 183 Wis. 323, 197 N.W. 808, 810, 811 (1924).

Thus, in order that the citizens' sacred right of liberty be secured and preserved, it has always been fundamental law that arrests without warrant were not deemed lawful, with only a few well-established exceptions of felonies and breaches of peace. The liberty of citizens would never be safe if such principles could be determined and thus abrogated by statute. Therefore, the principles surrounding arrests are regarded as fundamental law under our American system of government, as held by the Supreme Court of Michigan:

Under our system we have repeatedly decided, in accordance with constitutional principles as construed everywhere, that no arrest can be made without warrant except in cases of felony, or in cases of breaches of the peace committed in the presence of the arresting officer. This exception, in cases of breaches of the peace, has only been allowed by reason of the immediate danger to the safety of the community against crimes of violence. Yerkes v. Smith, 157 Mich. 557, 122 N.W. 223, 224 (1909), citing: Robinson v. Miner, 68 Mich. 549, 557-58, 37 N.W. 21, 25.

In the Yerkes case, it was held that the playing of baseball on Sunday did not necessarily involve a breach of the peace justifying an arrest, though it may cause a breach of peace. The Court said that before a summary arrest can be made for a breach of the peace, not only must overt acts be committed in the presence of the officer, yet they must be violent and dangerous acts of some sort.

In the Robison_case, the Court held that a liquor law ordinance that allowed arrests without process was unconstitutional because it was not pursuant to due process of law._

Where a man was arrested for public intoxication, the question arose whether this was an offense for which one could be arrested without a warrant. The Supreme Court of Appeals of Virginia declared the law on arrest as follows:

[T]he common law relating to arrests is the law on that subject in Virginia. At common law a peace officer may arrest without a warrant for a breach of the peace committed in his presence, but for no other misdemeanor. Galliher v. Commonwealth, 161 Va. 1014, 170 S.E. 734, 736 (1933), authorities cited.

The common law on arrest is the same in every state, as due process of law has the same meaning throughout America. The security of the citizens' liberty in this country is to be more highly regarded than it was in England under the common law. To say it is less regarded, is to make a mockery of the Revolution.

In a New Jersey case a man was arrested by two city policemen on orders of their superior to do so, alleging that he was guilty of disorderly conduct, and was taken to a police station and held overnight. This was done without any charge or complaint made against the man and without any warrant, the only authority for the arrest was that the officers were told to do so. In a suit for false imprisonment it was held by the Supreme Court of New Jersey that the arrest was without authority and gave the following opinion:

The legal principle underlying this case and the one to be applied to the facts is firmly embodied in the roots of the common law, which has been handed down to us from early times unimpaired, in its' full vigor, for the protection of personal liberty, against illegal arrests. The liberty of the person is too important a matter to the state to be interfered with, without the safeguards with which the law guards such invasions. This Court has said: The limits to the power of arrest by a constable, without process, was well defined at common law. The regard for liberty of the person was so great that the common law did not confer upon a mere conservator of the peace, the power to touch the person of the subject, of his own volition, except in those cases when the interests of the public absolutely demanded it. Collins v. Cody, 95 N.J. Law 65, 113 Atl. 709, 710 (1920).

In a Pennsylvania case a woman was arrested for causing and procuring to be made, loud and annoying sounds and noises at late hours of the night, in a certain tent near a city street, by beating on a drum. Upon indictment, her counsel moved that the indictment be quashed as she was arrested without affidavit or warrant, while she was in a tent upon private property. It was held that the arrest was unlawful, as the act was such that summary arrest was not justified, and due process required a warrant for such an arrest:

It is the undoubted right of every person in this community, not to be deprived of liberty without due process of law, and if a defendant has been arrested without due process of law, the indictment against him cannot be sustained. *** It has long been recognized that arrests without warrant are justified in cases of treason, felony or breach of peace, in which actual or threatened violence is an essential element:

1 Hales' P.C., 589; 2 Hawkins' P.C., ch. 13, sec. 8; 1 Burns, J., 287; 4 Blackstone, 292; 9 Bacon, Abrid., 468; 1 Chitty Cr. Law, 15; Clarks' Criminal Procedure, 39; Russell, Crimes, vol. 3, page 83; 4 Amer. And Eng. Ency. Of Law, 902. Commonwealth v. Krubeck, 8 Penn. Dist. Rep. 521, 522 (1899).

It must be remembered that, "Not every misdemeanor involves a breach of the peace". Commonwealth v. Gorman, 192 N.E. 618, 620. Under the common law, acts that were malum per se, that is wrong or unlawful by their nature, were often felonies or breaches of the peace, and subject to arrest without warrant. But, that is not the law for an act that was only malum prohibitum, being made unlawful only by statute, and without such enactment, were otherwise innocent acts. The law asserts that for such statutory misdemeanors, not amounting to a breach of the peace, there is no authority in an officer to arrest without a warrant.

As a general principle, no person can be arrested or taken into custody without warrant. But, if a felony or a breach of the peace, has in fact, been committed by the person arrested, the arrest may be justified. Burns v. Erben, 40 N.Y. 463, 466 (1869); see also Cunningham v. Baker, 104 Ala. 160, 16 So. 68 70 (1894).

While the "search and seizure" provision of the Constitution regulates the manner in which warrants can be issued, it is the "due process" clause that protects citizens from unlawful arrests without warrant:

"No person shall be deprived of life, liberty, or property without due process of law".

And, under like restrictions in the Constitution, it has been held in some states that arrests shall not be without warrant, except for felonies, and for breaches of the peace committed in the presence of the arresting officer. North v. People, 139 Ill. 81, 28 N.E. 966, 972 (1891).

Thus, where an arrest is made without warrant, in a case not involving a felony or breach of peace, the arrest is unlawful. "Arrest without warrant, where a warrant is required, is not due process of law, and is arbitrary or despotic power, no man possesses under our system of government". Thus, "when a police officer exceeds his powers in making an arrest he becomes a trespasser" and he is liable for false imprisonment. Muscoe v. Commonwealth, 86 Va. 443, 10 S.E. 534, 536.

For other authorities on this matter see: 1 Am. Law Rep., Anno., 585, et. seq.; Com. V. Carey, 12 Cush. 246 (Mass., 1853); 6A C.J.S., "Arrest" ~~10, p. 17; Anderson, A Treatise on the Law of Sheriffs, Vol. 1,~~ 166 (1941); Hill v. Day, 168 Kan. 604, 215 P.2d 219; Lee v. State, 45 Tex. Cr. R. 94, 74 S.W. 28 (1903); 22 Mich. Law Review 673, 703-707; Ulvestad v. Dolphin, 278 P. 681, 684 (Wash. 1929); In re Kellam, 55 Kan. 700, 41 P. 960, 961 (1895); Pavish v. Meyers, 225 Pac. 633 (Wash., 1924); Delafoile v. State, 54 N.J.L. 381, 24 Atl. 557, 558 (1892); Giroux v. The State, 40 Tex. 99, 104 (1874); (1892); Staker v. U.S.., 2 F.2d 312, 314 (1925); Porter v. State 52 S.E. 283, 285 (Ga. 1905); Cave v. Cooley, 152 P.2d 886 (N.M.)

Conclusions

It is a maxim of law that, "Liberty is more favored than all things" (Dig. 50, 17, 122). Thus the law favors liberty above all things and applies the most liberal interpretation to it. The common law rule regarding the procedure and process for arrest was established in this country in; Allor v. Wayne Co., 43 Mich. 76, 94, 4N.W. 492, 495-96 (1880), Mr. Justice Campbell says:

The Constitution has also provided that no one shall be deprived of liberty without due process of law, and has provided that no warrant shall issue except upon oath or affirmation establishing probable cause. It has been settled for centuries, and the doctrine has been recognized here, that except in cases of reasonable belief of treason or felony, or breach of the peace committed in the presence of an officer, there is no

<u>due process of law without a warrant</u>, issued by a court or magistrate upon a proper showing or finding.

It is thus fundamental that, "the due process clause of the Constitution protects the citizen from unlawful arrest". State v. Quinn, 97 S.E. 62, 64, (S.C. 1918). By the common law, which is the law, that due process guarantees, a citizen cannot be summarily arrested when he is found violating a law that is only a misdemeanor. A warrant must first be acquired to arrest such a person pursuant to due process of law. If that, which constitutes due process of law, is made to depend upon the will of the legislature, as expressed in a statute or charter, then no fundamental principles of law or rights are perpetuated, or secured against abrogation.

An arrest is a deprivation of ones' liberty. The State Constitution requires that, "No citizen of this State shall be deprived of life, liberty, property, privileges or immunities, or in any manner disfranchised, except by the due course of the law of the land". (Texas Constitution, Art. 1, Sec. 19). The procedure for arrest under the common law is what constitutes "due process" today. The Minnesota Supreme Court held;

What is due process of law is usually a traditional or historic question. Was it due process of law under the common law, and did it remain such up to the time of adopting the constitution. C. N. Nelson Lumber Co. v. M'Kinnon 61 Minn. 219, 222.

The Law is very jealous of the liberty of the citizen. Where the offense is less serious, the greater the formality prescribed for the exercise of the power which can deprive the citizen of his liberty. Porter v. State, 124 Ga. 297, 52 S.E. 283, 285 (1905)

The citizen cannot be summarily deprived of his liberty because of his infraction of some ordinance or statute, unless at common law, he was liable to arrest.

The misdemeanor traffic statute involved in this case is such that it does not allow the Defendant to arrest the Plaintiff without the formality of a warrant. Therefore, the Defendant is guilty of false imprisonment for arresting the Plaintiff without authority of law.

The foregoing proves that the common law surrounding arrests was always recognized in this country and is thus a requirement for "due process" in depriving the Plaintiff of his liberty. It is the "Law of the land". As such, these principles are Constitutional mandates and cannot be abrogated by mere statutes.

Appeals Court Cause No. 10-04-00270-CR
Trial Court Cause No. 03-185426

Eddie Duncan, Sui Juris	§	TENTH COURT OF APPEALS
	§	
VS.	§	MCLENNAN COUNTY
COURTHOUSE		
	§	
THE STATE OF TEXAS	§	WACO, TEXAS

Judicial Notice

Pursuant under 201(d) & (g) of the Texas and Federal Rules of Evidence

MEMORANDUM AND PETITION TO DISMISS FOR LACK OF SUBJECT MATTER JURISDICTION

COMES NOW THE ACCUSED, denying and challenging the jurisdiction of the "trial court" over the subject matter in the above-entitled cause 03-185426, for the reasons explained in the following memorandum:

MEMORANDUM OF LAW

I. The Nature of Subject Matter Jurisdiction.

The jurisdiction of a court over the subject matter has been said to be essential, necessary, indispensable and an elementary prerequisite to the exercise of judicial power. 21 C.J.S., "Courts," ~ 18, p. 25. A court cannot proceed with a trial or make a judgement without such jurisdiction existing.

It is elementary that the jurisdiction of the court over the subject matter of the action is the most critical aspect of the court's authority to act. Without it the court lacks any power to proceed; therefore, a defense based upon this lack cannot be waived and may be asserted at any time. Matter of Green, 313 S.E.2d 193 (N.C. App. 1984).

Subject matter jurisdiction cannot be conferred by waiver or consent, and may be raised at any time. Rodrigues v. State, 441 So.2d 1129 (Fla. App. 1983). The subject matter jurisdiction of a criminal case is related to the cause of action in general, and more specifically to the alleged crime or offense, which creates the action. The subject matter of a criminal offense is the crime itself. Subject-matter in it's broadest sense means the cause; the object; the thing in dispute. Stillwell v. Markham, 10 P.2d 15, 16, 135 Kan. 206 (1932).

An indictment or information in a criminal case is the main means by which a court obtains subject matter jurisdiction, and is "the jurisdictional instrument upon which the accused stands trial". State v. Chatmon, 671 P.2d 531, 538 (Kan. 1983). The complaint is the foundation of the jurisdiction of the magistrate or court. Thus, if these charging instruments are invalid, there is a lack of subject matter jurisdiction.

Without a formal and sufficient indictment or information, a court does not acquire subject matter jurisdiction and thus an accused may not be punished for a crime. Honomichl v. State, 333 N.W. 2d 797, 798 (S.D. 1983).

A formal accusation is essential for every trial of a crime. Without it, the court acquires no jurisdiction to proceed, even with the consent of the parties, and where the indictment or information is invalid, the court is without jurisdiction. Ex parte Carlson 186 N. W. 722, 725, 176 Wis. 538 (1922).

Without a valid complaint, any judgement or sentence rendered is " void ab initio". Ralph v. Police Court of El Cerrito, 190 P. 2d 632, 634, 84 Cal. App. 2d 257 (1948).

Jurisdiction to try and punish for a crime cannot be acquired by the mere assertion of it, or invoked otherwise than in the mode prescribed by law, and if it is not so acquired or invoked, any judgement is a nullity. 22 C.J.S., "Criminal Law" ~ 167, p. 202.

The charging instrument must not only be in the particular mode or form, prescribed by the constitution and statute to be valid, but it also must contain reference to valid laws. Without a valid law, the charging instrument is insufficient and no subject matter jurisdiction exists for the matter to be tried.

Where an information charges no crime, the court lacks jurisdiction to try the accused. People v. Hardiman, 347 N. W. 2d 460, 462, 132 Mich. App. 382 (1984).

[W]hether or not the complaint charges an offense, is a jurisdictional matter. Ex parte Carlson, 186 N. W. 722, 725, 176 Wis. 538 (1922).

An invalid law charged against one in a criminal matter also negates subject matter jurisdiction by the sheer fact that it fails to create a cause of action. "Subject matter is the thing in controversy". Holmes v. Mason, 115 N.W. 770, 80 Neb. 454, citing Black's Law Dictionary. Without a valid law, there is no issue or controversy for a court to decide upon. Thus, where a law does not exist or does not constitutionally exist, or where the law is invalid, and void of constitutional authority, there is no subject matter jurisdiction to try one for an offense alleged under such a law.

If a criminal statute is unconstitutional, the court lacks subject matter jurisdiction and cannot proceed to try the case. 22 C.J.S. "Criminal Law,"~ 157,p. 189; citing People v. Katrinak, 185 Cal. Rptr. 869, 136 Cal. App.3d 145 (1982).

Where the offense charged, does not exist, the trial court lacks jurisdiction. State v. Christensen, 329 N.W.2d 382, 383, 110 Wis.2d 538 (1983).

Not all statutes create a criminal offense. Thus, where a man was charged with "a statute which did not create a criminal offense", such a person was never lawfully charged with any crime, or lawfully convicted, because the trial court did not have "jurisdiction of the subject matter", State ex rel. Hansen v. Rigg, 258 Minn. 388, 104 N.W.2d 553 (1960). There must be a valid law in order for subject matter to exist.

In a case where a man was convicted of violating certain sections of some laws, he later claimed that the laws were unconstitutional, which deprived the county court of jurisdiction to try him for those alleged offenses. The Supreme Court of Oregon held:

If these sections are unconstitutional, the law is void, and an offense created by them is not a crime and a conviction under them cannot be a legal cause of imprisonment, for no court can acquire jurisdiction to try a person for acts which are made criminal only by an unconstitutional law. Kelly v. Meyers, 263 Pac. 903, 905 (Ore. 1928).

Without a valid law, there can be no crime charged under that law, and where there is no crime or offense, there is no controversy or cause of action, and without a cause of action there can be no subject matter jurisdiction to try a person accused of violating said law.

The court then has no power or right to hear and decide a particular case involving such invalid or nonexistent laws.

These authorities and others make it clear that if there are no valid laws charged against a person, there is nothing that can be deemed a crime, and without a crime there is no subject matter jurisdiction. Further, invalid or unlawful laws make the complaint fatally defective and insufficient, and without a valid complaint there is a lack of subject matter jurisdiction.

The accused asserts that the laws charged against him are not valid, or do not constitutionally exist, as they do not conform to certain constitutional prerequisites, and thus are not laws at all, thus preventing subject matter jurisdiction of the trial court.

The information in question alleges that the accused has committed 4 crimes, by the violation of certain alleged laws listed in that information, to wit:

1. Interfering With the Duties of a Public Servant
2. Expired Drivers License
3. Expired Motor Vehicle Registration
4. No liability Insurance

I have investigated these "statutes" used in the information against me, and discovered that they are located in and derived from a collection of books entitled, Vernon's "Texas Codes Annotated". Upon investigating the alleged laws in this publication, I have also discovered that they fail to adhere to several constitutional provisions of the Texas Constitution.

By Article 3 Sec. 1 of the Constitution of the State of Texas (1876), all lawmaking authority for the State is vested in the legislature of the State of Texas. This Article also prescribes certain forms, modes and procedures that must be followed in order for a valid law to exist under the Constitution. It is fundamental that nothing can be a law that is not enacted by the Legislature prescribed in the Constitution, and which fails to conform to constitutional forms, prerequisites or prohibitions. These are the grounds for challenging the subject matter jurisdiction of this court, since the validity of a law on an information or indictment goes to the jurisdiction of a court. The following explains in authoritative detail why the laws cited in the information against the Accused are not constitutionally valid laws.

II. By Constitutional Mandate, all Laws Must Have an Enacting Clause.

One of the forms that all laws are required to follow by the Texas Constitution (1876), is that they contain an enacting style or clause. This provision is stated as follows:

Article 3 Sec.29. The enacting clause of **"all laws"** shall be: "Be it enacted by the Legislature of the State of Texas".

The alleged law cited in the information against the Accused, as found in Vernon's "Texas Codes Annotated", contains no enacting clause.

The constitutional provision which prescribes an enacting clause for all laws, is not directory, it is mandatory. This provision is to be strictly adhered to, as asserted by the Supreme Court of Minnesota:

Upon both principle and authority, we hold that Article 4,~ 13, of our constitution, which provides that, "the style of all laws of this state shall be, "Be it enacted by the legislature of the state of Minnesota", **is mandatory,** and that a statute without an enacting clause **is void.** Sjoberg v. Security Savings & Loan Assn, 73 Minn. 203, 212 (1898).

III. What is the purpose of the Constitutional Provision for an Enacting Clause?

To determine the validity of using laws without an enacting clause against citizens, we need to determine the purpose and function of an enacting clause; and also to see what problems or evils were intended to be avoided by including such a provision in our state Constitution. One object of the constitutional mandate for an enacting clause is to show that the law is one enacted by the legislative body which has been given the lawmaking authority under the Constitution.

The purpose of thus prescribing an enacting clause – "the style of the acts"- is to establish it; to give it permanence, uniformity, and certainty; **to identify the act of legislation as of the general assembly ; to afford evidence of its' legislative statutory nature;** and to secure uniformity of identification, and thus prevent inadvertence, possibly mistake and fraud. State v. Patterson, 4 S.E. 350, 352, 98 N.C. 660 (1887); 82 C.J.S. "Statutes", ~ 65, p. 104; Joiner v. State, 155 S.E.2d 8, 10, 223 Ga. 367 (1967).

What is the object of the style of a bill or enacting clause? To **show the authority** by which the bill is enacted into law; to show that the act comes from a place pointed out by the Constitution as the **source of legislation.** Ferrill v. Keel, 151 S.W. 269, 272, 105 Ark. 380 (1912).

To fulfill the purpose of identifying the lawmaking authority of a law, it has been repeatedly declared by the courts of this land that an enacting clause is to appear **on the face of every law** which the people are expected to follow and obey.

The almost unbroken custom of centuries has been to preface laws with a statement in some form, **declaring the enacting authority**. The purpose of an enacting clause of a statute is to **identify** it as an act of legislation by expressing **on its' face, the authority behind the act.**73Am. Jur.2d, "Statutes", ~ 93, p. 319, 320; Preckel v. Byrne, 243 N.W. 823, 826, 62 N.D. 356 (1932)

For an enacting clause to appear on the face of a law, it must be recorded and published **with the law,** so that the public can readily identify the authority for that particular law, which they are expected to follow. The "codes" used in the information against the accused have no enacting clauses.

They thus cannot be identified as acts of legislation by the Texas Legislature, pursuant to its' lawmaking authority under Article 3 of the Constitution of the State of Texas (1876), being that, a law is mainly identified as a true and Constitutional law by way of its' enacting clause.

The Supreme Court of Georgia asserted that a statute must have an enacting clause, even though their State Constitution had no provision for the measure. The Court stated that an enacting clause establishes a law or statute as being a true and authentic law of the State.

The enacting clause is that portion of a statute, which gives it jurisdictional identity and constitutional authenticity. Joiner v. State, 155 S.E.2d 8, 10 (Ga. 1967).

The failure of a law to display on its' face an enacting clause, deprives it of essential legality, and renders a statute which omits such clause, " a nullity and of no force of law". Joiner v. State, supra. The code cited in the information has no jurisdictional identity and is not authentic law under the Constitution of the State of Texas (1876).

The Court of Appeals of Kentucky held that the constitutional provision requiring an enacting clause is a basic concept which has a direct affect upon the validity of a law.

The Court, in dealing with a law that had contained no enacting clause, stated:

The alleged act or law in question is **unnamed**; it shows **no sign of authority;** it carries with it **no evidence** that the General Assembly or any other lawmaking power is responsible or answerable for it. *** By an enacting clause, the makers of the Constitution intended that the General Assembly should make its' impress or seal, as it were, upon each enactment for the sake of identity, and to assume and show responsibility. While the Constitution makes this a necessity, it did not originate it.

The custom is in use practically everywhere, and is as old as parliamentary government, as old as kings' decrees, and even they borrowed it. The decrees of Cyrus, King of Persia, which Holy Writ records, were not the first to be prefaced with a **statement of authority**. The law was delivered to Moses in the name of The Great I Am, and the prologue to the Great Commandments is no less majestic and impelling. But, whether these edicts and commands are promulgated by the Supreme Ruler, or by petty kings, or by the sovereign people themselves, they have always begun with some such form **as evidence of power and authority.** Commonwealth v. Illinois Cent. R. Co., 170 S.W. 171, 172, 175, 160 Ky. 745 (1914).

The alleged **"laws"** used against the Accused are unnamed. They show no sign of authority on their face as mandated in the Texas Constitution. They carry with them no evidence that the Legislature of the State of Texas, pursuant to Article 3 of the Constitution of the State of Texas (1876), is responsible for these laws. Without an enacting clause, the codes cited in the information have no official evidence that they are from an authority that I am subject to, or am required to obey.

When the question of the "objects intended to be secured by the enacting clause provision" was before the Supreme Court of Minnesota, the Court held that such a clause was necessary to show the people, whom are to obey the law, the authority for their obedience. It was revealed that historically, this was a main use for an enacting clause, and thus its' use is a fundamental concept of law. The Court stated:

All written laws, in all times and in all countries, whether in the form of decrees issued by absolute monarchs, or statutes enacted by king and council, or by a representative body, have, as a rule, **expressed upon their face the authority by which they were promulgated or enacted.**

The almost unbroken custom of centuries has been to preface laws with a statement in some form **declaring the enacting authority**.

If such an enacting clause is a mere matter of form, a relic of antiquity, serving no useful purpose, why should the Constitutions of so many of our states require that **"all laws"** must have an enacting clause, and prescribe its' form? If an enacting clause is useful and important, if it is desirable that **"laws"**, **shall bear upon their face the authority by which they were enacted, so that the people who are to obey them, need not search legislative and other records to ascertain the authority,** thus it is not beneath the dignity of the framers of the Constitution, or unworthy of such an instrument, to prescribe a uniform style for each enacting clause.

The words of the Constitution, that the style of all laws of this state shall be, "Be it enacted by the legislature of the state of Minnesota", imply that **"all laws"** must be so expressed or declared, to the end that they may **express upon their face the authority by which they were enacted;** and, if they do not so declare, **they are not laws of this state.** Sjoberg v. Security Savings & Loan Assn, 73 Minn. 203, 212-214 (1898).

This case was initiated when it was discovered that the law relating to "building, loan and savings associations", had no enacting clause as it was printed in the statute book, "Laws 1897, c. 250." The Court made it clear that a law existing in that manner is **"void"**. Sjoberg, supra, p. 214.

The purported laws in the information, which the Accused is alleged to have violated, are referenced to various codes found printed in Vernon's "Texas Codes Annotated". I have examined the alleged laws charged against me in this book, and found no enacting clause for any of the alleged laws. A citizen is not expected or required to search through other records or books for the enacting authority.

If such enacting authority is not **"on the face"** of the laws, which are referenced in the information, then **"they are not laws of this state",** and thus are not laws to which I am subject. Since they are not laws of this state, the above-named Court has no subject matter jurisdiction, as there can be no crime that can exist, for failing to follow laws that do not constitutionally exist.

In speaking on the necessity and purpose, that each law be prefaced with an enacting clause, the Supreme Court of Tennessee quoted the first portion of the Sjoberg case cited above, and then stated:

The purpose of provisions of this character is that **all statutes** may **bear upon their faces, a declaration of sovereign authority** by which they are enacted and declared to be **the law of the land,** and to promote and preserve uniformity in legislation. Such clauses also import a command of obedience and clothe the statute with a certain dignity, believed in all times to command respect and aid in the enforcement of laws. State v. Burrow, 104 S.W. 526, 529, 119 Tenn. 376 (1907).

The use of an enacting clause does not merely serve as a "flag" under which bills run the course through the legislative machinery. Vaughn & Ragsdale Co. v. State Bd. of Eq., 96 P.2d 420, 424 (Mont. 1939). The enacting clause of a law goes to its' substance, and is not merely procedural. Morgan v. Murray, 328 P.2d 644, 654 (Mont. 1958).

Any purported statute which has no enacting clause **on its' face**, is not legally binding and obligatory upon the people, as it is not constitutionally a law at all. The Supreme Court of Michigan, in citing numerous authorities, said that an enacting clause was a requisite to a valid law, since the enacting provision was mandatory:

It is necessary that **every law** should show **on its' face** the authority by which it is adopted and promulgated, and that it should clearly appear that it is intended by the Constitutionally defined legislative power that enacts it, that it should take effect as a law. People v. Dettenthaler, 77 N.W. 450, 451, 118 Mich. 595 (1898); citing Swann v, Buck, 40 Miss. 270.

The alleged laws in the "Texas Penal Code" do not show on their face the authority by which they are adopted and promulgated. There is nothing on their face that declares that they should be law, or that they are of the proper legislative authority in this state.

These and other authorities, all hold that the enacting clause of a law is to be **"on its' face".** It must appear directly above the content or body of the law. To be on the face of the law, does not and cannot mean that the enacting clause can be buried away in some other volume or some book or records.

Face- The surface of anything, especially the front, upper, or outer part or surface. That which particularly offers itself to the view of a spectator.

That which is shown by the language employed, without any explanation, modification, or addition from extrinsic facts or evidence. Blacks' Law Dictionary, 5th ed., p. 530.

The enacting clause must be intrinsic to the law, and not "extrinsic" to it. Therefore, it cannot be hidden away in other records or books. Thus the enacting clause is regarded as part of the law, and has to appear directly with the law, **on its' face**, so that one charged with said law, knows the authority by which it exists.

IV. Laws Must be Published and Recorded with Enacting Clauses

Since it has been repeatedly held that an enacting clause must appear "on the face" of a law, such a requirement affects the printing and publishing of laws. The fact that the Constitution requires **"all laws"** to have an enacting clause makes it a requirement on not just bills within the legislature, but on published laws as well. If the Constitution said **"all bills"** shall have an enacting clause, it probably could be said that their use in publications would not be required.

But the historical usage and application of an enacting clause has been that it was printed and published along with the body of the law, thus appearing **"on the face"** of the law.

It is obvious, that the enacting clause must be readily visible on the face of a statute in the common mode in which it is published, so that citizens don't have to search through the legislative journals or other records and books to see the kind of clause used, or if any exists at all.

Thus a law in a statute book without an enacting clause is not a valid publication of law. In regards to the validity of a law, that was found in their statute books with a defective enacting clause, the Supreme Court of Nevada held:

Our constitution expressly provided that the enacting clause **of every law** shall be, "The people of the state of Nevada, represented in senate and assembly, do enact as follows". This language is susceptible of but one interpretation. There is no doubtful meaning as to the intention. It is, in our judgement, an imperative mandate of the people, in their sovereign capacity, to the legislature, requiring that **'all laws"**, to **be binding upon them,** shall, **upon their face,** express the authority by which they were enacted; and, since this act comes to us without such authority appearing **upon its' face, it is not a "law".**

State of Nevada v. Rogers, 10 Nev. 120, 261 (1875); approved in Caine v. Robbins, 131 P.2d 516, 518, 61 Nev. 416 (1942); Kefauver v. Spurling, 290 S.W. 14, 15 (Tenn. 1926).

The manner in which the law came to the Court was by the way it was found in the statute book, cited by the Court as "Stat. 1875,66," and that is how they judge the validity of the law.

Since they saw that the act, as it was printed in the statute book, had an insufficient enacting clause on its' face, it was deemed to be, "not a law". It is only by inspecting the publicly printed statute book that the people can determine the source, authority and constitutional authenticity of the law, they are expected to follow.

It should be noted that laws in the above cases were held to be void for having no enacting clauses, despite the fact that they were published in an official statute book of the state, and were next to other laws which had the proper enacting clauses.

The preceding examples and declarations on the use and purpose of enacting clauses shows beyond doubt that nothing can be called or regarded as a law of this state, being that it is published without an enacting clause on its' face. Nothing can exist as a state law, except in the manner prescribed by the State Constitution.

One of those provisions is that **"all laws"** must bear on their face a specific enacting style – "Be it enacted by the Legislature of the State of Texas". (Texas Const., Article 3 Sec. 29). All laws must be published with this clause, in order to be valid laws, and since the "statutes" in Vernon's "Texas Codes Annotated" are not so published, they are **not** valid laws of this state.

V. The Laws Referenced in the Information Contain no Titles. 213

The alleged laws listed in the information in question, as cited in the "Texas Penal Code" contain no titles. All laws are to have titles indicating the subject matter of the law, as required by the Constitution of the state of Texas.

Article 3 Sec. 35 (a) No bill shall contain more than one subject. (b) The rules of procedure of each house shall require that the subject of each bill be expressed in its' title in a manner that gives the legislature and the public reasonable notice of that subject. The legislature is solely responsible for determining compliance with the rule.

By this provision a title is required to be on all laws. The title is another one of the forms of a law required by the Constitution. This type of constitutional provision "makes the title an essential part of every law", thus the title "is as much a part of the act as the body itself". Leiniger v. Alger, 26 N.W.2d 348, 351, 316 Mich. 644 (1947).

The title to a legislative act is a part thereof, and must clearly express the subject of the legislation. State v. Burlington & M. R.R. Co., 60 Neb. 742, 84 N.W. 254 (1900).

Most lawful authorities have held that the title is part of the act, especially when a constitutional provision for a title exists. 37 A.L.R. Annotated, pp. 948, 949. What then can be said of a law, in which an essential part of it is missing, except that, "it is not a law under our state Constitution?

This provision of the state Constitution, providing that every law is to have a title expressing one subject, is mandatory and is to be followed in all laws, as stated by the Supreme Court of Minnesota:

We pointed out that our constitutional debates indicated that the constitutional requirements relating to enactment of statutes were intended to be remedial and mandatory, - remedial, as guarding against recognized evils arising from loose and dangerous methods of conducting legislation, and mandatory, as requiring compliance by the legislature without discretion on its part to protect the public interest against such recognized evils, and that the validity of statutes should depend on compliance with such requirements *** Bull v. King, 286 N.W. 311, 313 (Minn. 1939).

The constitutional provisions for a title have been held in many other states to be mandatory in the highest sense. State v. Beckman, 185 S.W.2d 810, 816 (Mo. 1945); Leininger v. Alger, 26 N.W.2d 384, 316 Mich. 644; 82 C.J.S. "Statutes", ~ 64, p.102. The provision for a title in the Constitution "renders a title indispensable" 73 Am. Jur. 2d, "Statutes" ~ 99, p. 325, citing People v. Monroe, 349 Ill. 270, 182 N.E. 439. Since such provisions regarding a title are mandatory and indispensable, the existance of a title is necessary, in regard to the validity of the act. If a title does not exist, then it is not a law pursuant to Article 3, Sec. 35 (a) & (b) of the Constitution of The State Of Texas (1876). In speaking of the constitutional provision requiring one subject to be embraced in the title of each law, the Supreme Court of Tennessee stated;

Requirement of the organic law is mandatory, and, unless obeyed in every instance, the legislation attempted is invalid and of no effect whatever. State v. Yardley, 32 S.W. 481, 482, 95 Tenn. 546 (1895).

To further determine the validity of citing laws in a complaint which have no titles, we must look at the purpose for this constitutional provision, and the evils and problems which it was intended to prevent or defeat. The aim and purpose for a title or caption to an act is to convey to the people whom are to obey it, the legislative intent behind the law.

The constitution has made the title, the conclusive index to the legislative intent, as to what shall have operation. Megins v, City of Duluth, 106 N.W. 89, 90, 97 Minn. 23 (1906); Hyman v. State, 9 S.W. 372, 373, 87 Tenn. 109 (1888).

In ruling as to the precise meaning of the language employed in a statute, nothing, as we have said before, is more pertinent towards ascertaining the true intention of the legislative mind in the passage of the enactment than the legislatures' own interpretation of the scope and purpose of the act, as contained in the caption. Wimberly v. Georgia S. & F.R. Co., 63 S.E. 29, 5 Ga. App. 263 (1908).

Under a constitutional provision *** requiring the subject of the legislation to be expressed in the title, that portion of an act is often the very window through which the legislative intent may be seen. State v. Clinton County, 76 N.E. 986, 166 Ind. 162 (1906).

The title of an act is necessarily a part of it, and in construing the act, the title should be taken into consideration. Glaser v. Rothchild, 120 S.W. 1, 221 Mo. 180 (1909). Without the title, the intent of the legislature is concealed or cloaked from public view. Yet, a specific purpose or function of a title, to a law, is to "protect the people against covert legislation". Brown v. Clower, 166 S.E.2d 363, 365, 225 Ga. 165 (1969). A title will reveal or give notice to the public of the general character of the legislation. However, the nature and intent of the "laws" in the "Texas Penal Code" have been concealed and made uncertain by its' nonuse of titles. The true nature of the subject matter of the laws therein, is not made clear without titles. Thus another purpose of the title is to apprise the people of the nature of the legislation. Thereby preventing fraud or deception in regard to the "laws", they are to follow. The U.S. Supreme Court, in determining the purpose of such a provision in state constitutions, said:

The purpose of the constitutional provision is to prevent the inclusion of incongruous and unrelated matters in the same measure, and to guard against inadvertence, stealth and fraud in legislation. *** Courts strictly enforce such provisions in cases that fall within the reasons on which they rest, *** and hold that, in order to warrant the setting aside an enactment for failure to comply with the rule, the violation must be substantial and plain. Posados v. Warner, B. & Co., 279 U.S. 340, 344 (1928); Internat. Shoe Co. v. Shartel, 279 U.S. 429, 434 (1928).

The complete omission of a title is about as substantial and plain a violation of this constitutional provision as can exist. The laws cited in the complaints against the Accused are of that nature. They have no titles at all, and thus are not laws under our state Constitution. The Supreme Court of Idaho, in construing the purpose for its' constitutional provision requiring a one-subject title on all laws, stated:

The object of the title is to give a general statement of the subject-matter, and such a general statement will be sufficient to include all provisions of the act having a reasonable connection with the subject-matter mentioned. *** The object or purpose of the clause in the Constitution *** is to prevent the perpetration of fraud upon the members of the Legislature, or the citizens of the state, in the enactment of laws. Ex parte Crane, 151 Pac. 1006, 1010, 1011, 27 Idaho 671 (1915).

The Supreme Court of North Dakota, in speaking on its' constitutional provision requiring titles on laws, stated that, "This provision is intended *** to prevent all surprises or misapprehensions on the part of the public". State v. McEnroe, 283 N.W. 57, 61 (N.D. 1938). The Supreme Court of Minnesota, in speaking on Article 4, ~ 27 of the state Constitution, said:

This section of the Constitution is designed to prevent deception as to the nature or subject of a legislative enactment. State v. Rigg, 109 N.W.2d 310, 314, 260 Minn. 141 (1961); LeRoy v. Special Ind. Sch. Dist., 172 N.W.2d 764, 768 (Minn. 1969).

[T]he purpose of the constitutional provision quoted is *** to prevent misleading or deceiving the public as to the nature of an act by the title given it. State v. Helmer, 211 N.W. 3, 169 Minn. 221 (1926).

The purpose of the constitutional provision requiring a one-subject title, and the mischief which it was designed to prevent, are defeated by the lack of such a title on the face of a law which a citizen is charged with violating.

After examining the laws charged in the information, from Vernon's "Texas Codes Annotated", I am left asking, what is the subject and nature of the laws used in the allegations against me. What interests or rights are these laws intended to affect? Since the particular objects of the provision requiring a one-subject title, are defeated by the publication of laws which are completely absent of a title, the use of such a publication to indict or charge citizens with violating such laws, is fraudulent and obnoxious to the Constitution.

It is to prevent surreptitious, inconsiderate, and misapprehended legislation, carelessly, inadvertently, or unintentionally enacted through <u>stealth or fraud</u>, and similar abuses, that the subject or object of a law is required to be stated in the title. 73 Am. Jur. 2d, "Statutes", ~ 100, p. 325, cases cited.

Judge Cooley says that the object of requiring a title is to "fairly apprise the people, through such publication of legislative proceedings as is usually made, of the subjects of legislation that are being considered". Cooley, Const. Lim., p. 144. The state Constitution requires one-subject titles. The particular ends to be accomplished by requiring the title of a law are not fulfilled within the codes referred to in the Vernon's "Texas Code`s Annotated". Thus the alleged laws charged against me, are not valid laws.

VI. Texas Codes Annotated, are of an Unknown and Uncertain Authority

The alleged "laws" in the Vernon's "Texas Code Annotated" are not only, absent enacting clauses, but are surrounded by other issues and facts that make their authority unknown, uncertain, and therefore questionable.

The title page of the Vernon's "Texas Codes Annotated" expresses the fact that it is a copyrighted @ 2003 material and Vernon's is a registered trademark. It does not declare that they are the official laws of the Legislature of the state of Texas.

The official "Session Laws" of this state have always been listed with the Secretary of State. The title page of all constitutionally enacted laws makes it clear as to the nature of the laws therein, to wit – ["Session Laws of the State of Minnesota passed during the forty-fourth session of the State Legislature". The Minnesota Statutes state that: Minnesota Revised Statutes must not be cited, enumerated, or otherwise treated as a session law". (M.S. 3C.07, Subd. 1).The "Session Laws" are also published by the Secretary of the State, that is historically and constitutionally in possession of the enrolled bills of the Legislature, that are constitutionally competent, to be State Law. The Texas Constitution, Article 3 Sec. 38 (1876) requires that the presiding officer of each House shall, in the presence of the House over which he presides, sign all bills and joint resolutions passed by the Legislature, after their titles have been publicly read before signing; and the fact of signing shall be entered on the journals.

The Texas Constitution, Article 4 Sec. 21 requires that the Secretary of State, authenticate the publication of the laws, and keep a fair register of all official acts and proceedings of the Governor, and shall, when required, lay the same and all papers, minutes and vouchers relative thereto, before the Legislature, or either House thereof, and shall perform such other duties as may be required of him by law. Thus, in this state, as in nearly all other states, all official laws, records, and documents are universally recognized by their being issued or published by the Secretary of State.

The Vernon's "Texas Codes Annotated" are published by WEST GROUP and are also copyrighted by that office. The "Session Laws" were never copyrighted, as they are true public documents. In fact, no true public document of this state, or any state, or of the United States, has been, **or can be**, under a copyright. Public documents are inalienable within the public domain. A copyright infers a private right over the contents of a book, suggesting that the laws in the Vernon's "Texas Code Annotated" are derived from a private source, quote; (West Group has created this publication) end quote! Thus, codes in that publication are not true public law.

The title page of Vernon's "Texas Codes Annotated" contains a disclaimer that declares; Quote - West Group has **created** this publication to provide you with accurate and authoritative information concerning the subject matter covered. However, **this publication was not necessarily prepared by persons licensed to practice law in a particular jurisdiction.** West Group is not engaged in rendering legal or other professional advice, and this publication is not a substitute for the advice of an attorney. If you require legal or other expert advice, you

244

should seek the services of a competent attorney or other professional. End Quote!

In order to understand and use statutory law, it is necessary to know the meaning of the terms used and the inclusiveness and <u>authority of the laws</u> found in the various arrangements The terms laws, acts, statutes, revisions, compilations, and codes are often used indiscriminately, but in the following discussion, each has a specific meaning. "Minnesota Statutes", vol. I, p.x.

The disclaimer on the title page points out the differences that exist between the "Laws Enacted By The Texas Legislature", and that of a compilation, revision or code. It makes it apparent that the "Session Laws" **are of a different authority,** than that of compilations, revisions and codes. Vernon's "Texas Codes Annotated" is apparently a "revision", **created** by West Group publications. Vernon's "Texas Codes Annotated" appears to be nothing more than a reference book, such as the American Digest System or Corpus Juris Secundum, which are also copyrighted. The contents of such reference books cannot be used as law in charging citizens with crimes or criminal complaints.

The title page does not say that the statutes in his book are the official laws of the state of Texas. There are many confusing and ambiguous statements made by the author, as to the nature and authority of the statutes in the "Texas Penal Code". It is not at all made certain that they are laws pursuant to Article 3 of the Texas Constitution. That which is uncertain cannot be accepted as true or valid in law.

Uncertain things are held for nothing. Maxim of Law! The law requires, not conjecture, but certainty. Coffin v. Ogden, 85 U.S. 120, 124. Where the law is uncertain, there is no law. Bouvier's Law Dictionary, vol. 2, "Maxims", 1880 edition.

The purported statutes in Vernon's "Texas Codes Annotated" do not make it clear by what authority they exist. The statutes therein have no enacting authority on their face. In fact, there is not a hint that the Legislature of Texas had anything at all to do with this so-called "Code" book. Thus, the statutes used against the Accused are just idle words, which carry no authority of any kind on their face.

VII. Established Rules of Constitutional Construction.

The issue of subject matter jurisdiction for this case squarely rests upon certain provisions of the Constitution of the state of Texas (1876), to wit:

Article 3 Sec. 29. Enacting Clause of Laws. The enacting clause of **"all laws"** shall be: "Be it enacted by the Legislature of the State of Texas".

Article 3 Sec. 35. Subjects and Titles of Bills. (a) No bill shall contain more than one subject. (b) The rules of procedure of each house shall require that the subject of each bill be expressed in its' title in a manner that gives the legislature and the public reasonable notice of that subject. The legislature is solely responsible for determining compliance with the rule.

These provisions are not in the least ambiguous or susceptible to any other interpretation than their plain and apparent meaning. The Supreme Court of Montana, in construing such provisions, said that they, "were so plainly and clearly expressed and are so entirely free from ambiguity", that "there is nothing for the court to construe". Vaughn & Ragsdale Co. v. State Bd. of Eq., 96 P.2d 420, 423, 424. The Supreme Court of Minnesota stated how these provisions are to be construed, when it was considering the meaning of another provision under the legislative department (Art. 4, ~ 9):

In treating of constitutional provisions, we believe it is the general rule among courts to regard them as mandatory, and not to leave it to the will or pleasure of a legislature to obey or disregard them.

Where the language of the Constitution is plain, we are not permitted to indulge in speculation concerning its' meaning, nor whether it is the embodiment of great wisdom. *** The rule with reference to constitutional construction is also well stated by Johnson, J., in the case Newell v. People, 7 N.Y. 9, 97, as follows: If the words embody a <u>definite meaning</u>, which involves no absurdity, and no contradiction between different parts of the same writing, then, <u>the meaning apparent upon the face of the instrument</u> is the one which, alone, we are at liberty to say was intended to be conveyed. In such a case <u>there is no room for construction</u>. That which the words declare is the meaning of the instrument; and, <u>neither courts nor legislatures have the right to add or to take away from that meaning</u>. *** It must be very plain, - nay, absolutely certain – that the people did not intend, that the language they have employed, and its'

<u>natural signification imports</u>, before a court will feel itself at liberty to depart from the <u>plain meaning</u> of a constitutional provision.

State ex rel. v. Sutton, 63 Minn. 147, 149, 150, 65 N.W. 262 (1895); affirmed, State v. Holm, 62 N.W.2d 52,55, 56 (Minn. 1954); Butler Taconite v. Roemer, 282 N.W.2d 867, 870, 871 (Minn. 1979).

It is certain that the plain and apparent language of these Constitutional provisions are **not** followed in the publication known as Vernon's "Texas Codes Annotated". It contains no titles and no enacting clauses, one the face of the alleged law, and it also contains a disclaimer stating; "this publication was not necessarily prepared by persons licensed to practice law in a particular jurisdiction". Thus, it does not reveal its' authority, and cannot be used as the **"Law"** of this state under **our** Constitution.

No language could be plainer or clearer than that used in Article 3 Sec. 29 and Sec. 35 of the Minnesota Constitution. There is no room for construction! The contents of these provisions were written in ordinary language, making their meaning self-evident, as stated by the Supreme Court of Minnesota:

In construing a provision of our constitution, however, we are governed by certain well-established rules. Foremost among these is the rule that, where the language used is clear, explicit, and unambiguous. The language of the provision itself, is the best evidence of the intention of the framers of the constitution. If the language is free from obscurity, the courts must give it the ordinary meaning of the words used. State v. Holm, 62 N.W.2d 52, 55, (Minn. 1954).

No matter how often the courts of this state have relied upon and used the publication entitled Vernon's "Texas Codes Annotated" as being law, that use can never be regarded as an exception to the states' Constitution.

To support this publication as law, it must be asserted that it is "absolutely certain" that the framers of the Constitution did not intend for titles and enacting clauses to be printed and published with all laws. But instead, that they did intend for them all to be stripped away and concealed from public view, when a compilation of statutes is made. Such an absurdity will gain the support, or respect, of no one. Nor can it be speculated that a revised statute publication, which dispenses with all titles and enacting clauses, should be allowed under the Constitution, because it is more practical and convenient than the "Session Law" publication. The use of such speculation or desired exceptions can never be used in construing such plain and unambiguous provisions.

[T]he general rule of law is, when a statute or Constitution is plain and unambiguous, the court is not permitted to indulge in speculation concerning its' meaning, nor whether it is the embodiment of great wisdom. A Constitution is intended to be framed in brief and precise language. *** It is not within the province of the court to read an exception in the Constitution, which the framers thereof did not see fit to enact therein. Baskin v. State, 232 Pac. 388, 389, 107 Okla. 272 (1925).

There is of course no need for construction or interpretation of these provisions as they have been adjudicated upon, especially those dealing with the use of an enacting clause. The Supreme Court of Minnesota has made it clear that Art. 4,~ 13 of its' Constitution "is mandatory, and, a statute without an enacting clause is void". Sjoberg v. Security Savings & Loan Assn., 73 Minn. 203, 212. Being that, the statutes used as grounds for allegations against me, are without titles and enacting clauses, and are therefore void. Therefore, there is no valid complaint, and thus, no offense, fore lack of -subject matter jurisdiction.

The provisions requiring an enacting clause and one-subject titles were not adhered to within the publication known as Vernon's "Texas Codes Annotated". Whereas, and because certain people in government thought they could devise a more convenient way of doing things, without regard for provisions of **our** state Constitution, they devised the contrivance known as the "Texas Penal Code", and then held it out to the public as being "law". This of course was **fraud**, **subversion,** and a great deception upon the people of this state, which is now revealed and exposed.

There is no justification for deviating from, or violating a written Constitution. Vernon's "Texas Codes Annotated" cannot be used as law, as the "Session Laws" were once used, solely because the circumstances have changed, or that we now have more "codes" to deal with. It cannot be asserted that the use and need of revised penal codes, without titles and enacting clauses, must be justified, due to expediency. New circumstances or needs, do not change the meaning of Constitutions, as Judge Cooley expressed:

A constitution is not to be made to mean one thing at one time, and another at some subsequent time, when the circumstances, may have, so changed as perhaps to make a different rule in the case seem desirable.

248

A principal share of the benefit expected, from written Constitutions, would be lost if the rules they established were so flexible as to bend to circumstances or be modified by public opinion. *** [A] court or legislature which should allow a change in public sentiment to influence it in giving to a written constitution, a construction not warranted by the intentions of its' founders, would be justly chargeable with reckless disregard of official oath and public duty; and if its' course become a precedent, these instruments would be of little avail. *** What a court is to do, therefore, is to declare the law as written. T. M. Cooley, A treatise on the Constitutional Limitations, 5th edition, pp. 54, 55.

There is great danger in looking beyond the Constitution itself to ascertain its' meaning and the rule for government. Looking at the Constitution alone, it is not at all possible to find support for the idea that the publication called the "Texas Penal Code" is valid law of this state. The original intent of Article 3,Sec. 29 and Sec. 35 of the Texas Constitution cannot be stretched to cover their use as such.

These provisions cannot now be regarded as antiquated, unnecessary or of little importance, since "no section of a constitution should be considered superfluous". Butler Taconite v. Roemer, 282 N. W.2d 867, 870, (Minn. 1979). The Constitution was written for all times and circumstances, because it embodies fundamental principals, which do not change with time.

Judges are not to consider the political or economic impact that might ensue from upholding the Constitution as written. They are to uphold it, without fail. Citing an ancient maxim of law: "Though the heavens may fall, let justice be done".

Petition

Based upon the above memorandum, the Accused moves that this action and cause be dismissed for lack of subject matter jurisdiction.

A court lacking jurisdiction cannot render judgement but must dismiss the cause at any stage of the proceedings in which it becomes apparent that jurisdiction is lacking. United States v. Siviglia, 686 Fed.2d 832, 835 (1981), cases cited.

Nothing can be regarded as a law in this state, which fails to conform to the Constitutional prerequisites that require an enacting clause and title. There is nothing in the information – "charging instrument"—that can Constitutionally be regarded as law, and thus, there is nothing in them, which I am answerable for, or which can be charged against me.

Whereas, there is no valid constitutional law, charged against me, no crime exists! Therefore, the trial court acted without subject matter jurisdiction. Thus, there are no lawful grounds for action against me! Therefore, petitioner moves this court to dismiss trial cause No. 03-185426.

Caveat

I regard it as just and necessary to give fair warning to this court of the consequences of its' failure to follow the clear mandates established in the Constitution of the state of Texas (1876), and to uphold their oath and duty in this matter. Failure to honor that oath and duty can result in this court committing acts of treason, usurpation, and tyranny. Such trespasses would be clearly evident to the public, especially in light of the clear and unambiguous provisions within **"our"** Constitution that are involved here. Those provisions leave no room for construction, and in light of the numerous adjudicated cases upon them, as herein stated, leave no basis for any other ruling than that of dismissal. The possible breaches of law that may result by denying this petition are enumerated as follows:

1. The failure to uphold these clear and plain provisions of our Constitution cannot be regarded as mere error in judgement, but deliberate USURPATION. Usurpation is defined as unauthorized arbitrary assumption and exercise of power. State ex rel. Danielson v. Village of Mound, 234 Minn.. 531, 543, 48 N.W.2d 855, 863 (1951). While error is only an issue judgement and due process, such usurpation is void.

   The boundary between an error in judgement, and the usurpation of judicial power is: The former is reversible by an appellate court and is, therefore, only voidable, which the latter is a nullity. State v. Mandehr, 209 N.W. 750, 752 (minn. 1926).

   To claim, or assert jurisdiction where it clearly does not exist, is usurpation. Whereas, no man is bound to follow acts of usurpation, and in fact, it is a duty of citizens to disregard and disobey them, being, they are void and unenforceable.

[N]o authority need be cited for the proposition that, when a court lacks jurisdiction, any judgement rendered by it is void and unenforceable. Hooker v. Boles, 346 Fed.2d 285, 286 (1965)

The fact that the "Texas Penal Code" has been in use for over forty years cannot be held as a justification to continue to usurp power and set aside the constitutional provisions that are contrary to such usurpation, as Judge Cooley cites:

Acquiescence for no length of time can legalize a clear usurpation of power, where the people have plainly expressed their will in the Constitution. Cooley, Constitutional Limitations, p. 71.

2. To assume jurisdiction in this case would result in TREASON. Chief Justice John Marshall once stated:

We [judges] have no more right to decline the exercise of jurisdiction, which is given, than to usurp that which is not given. The one or the other would be treason to the Constitution.

Cohens v. Virginia, 6 Wheat. (19U.S.) 264, 404 (1821).

The judge of this court has taken an oath to uphold and support the Constitution of the state of Texas, and any blatant disregard of that obligation and allegiance can only result in an act of treason.

3. If this court departs from the clear meaning of our Constitution, it will be regarded as a blatant act of TYRANNY. Any exercise of power that is done without the support of law, or beyond what the law allows, is tyranny.

It has been said, with much truth, "Where the law ends, tyranny begins". Merritt v. Welsh, 104 U.S. 694, 702 (1881).

The law, the Constitution, does not allow laws to exist without titles or enacting clauses. To go beyond that, and allow the "Texas Penal Code" to exist as "law" is nothing but tyranny.

Tyranny and despotism exists, where the will and pleasure of those in government is followed, rather than established law.

It has been repeatedly stated and affirmed as a most basic principle of our government that: "this is a government of laws and not of men: and that there is no arbitrary power located in any individual or body of individuals". Cotting v. Kansas City Stock Yards Co., 183 U.S. 79, 84 (1901).

The Constitution requires that all laws have enacting clauses and titles. If these clear and unambiguous provisions of our state Constitution can be disregarded, then we no longer have a Constitution in this state, and we no longer live under a government of laws, but a government of men. i.e., a system that is governed by the arbitrary will of those in office. The creation of Vernon's "Texas Codes Annotated" is a typical example of the arbitrary acts of government that, have become all too prevalent in this century. Its' use as law is a nullity under **"our"** Constitution.

Petition

Based upon the fact that the alleged violation called, "Interfering With The Duties of a **Public Servant**" is in association with a "code" cited from Vernon's "Texas Codes Annotated" as the charging instrument, it is void of lawful authority. That edition is, "privately copyrighted material", and **not** "Public Law", enacted by "The Legislature Of The State Of Texas".

Whereas, "Public Laws" belong to, and are within "Public Domain" and are thereby "Public Property" and therefore "they" cannot be copyrighted. The alleged laws, or "codes" cited, are lacking constitutionally mandated provisions, and are thereby void and unenforceable, for lack of subject matter jurisdiction.

I, Eddie Duncan, Sui Juris, the Accused, never waived any inherent constitutional right. Therefore, the Accused moves that this action and cause be dismissed for lack of subject-matter jurisdiction. The trial court failed in its' duty to complete the court as required by the Sixth Amendment. Therefore, jurisdiction was lost, and the only remedy for a judgement rendered, where jurisdiction did not exist, is dismissal.

Petitioner moves this court to dismiss Trial Cause No. 03-185426.

"All God Given Rights Reserved"
Without Prejudice UCC 1-207 & 1-103

Ronald – Edwin... Duncan, Sui Juris

Court of Appeals No. 10-04-00270-CR
Trial Court Case No. 03-185426

THE STATE OF TEXAS	§	TENTH COURT OF APPEALS
	§	
VS.	§	MCLENNAN COUNTY COURTHOUSE
	§	
Ronald Edwin Duncan, Sui Juris	§	WACO, TEXAS

Judicial Notice

Pursuant under 201(d) & (g) of the Texas and Federal Rules of Evidence

Writ of Error, Advancing Second Point of Error; Trial Court Failed To Assure Accuseds' Right To; "Assistance of Competent Counsel".

I, Eddie Duncan Sui Juris, the Accused, assert and declare that the trial court denied my inherent constitutional rights under the provisions of the Texas Constitution, Article 1 Sec.6. Also within the Sixth Amendment, U.S.C.A. Const. Amend.6, that, 'In all criminal prosecutions, the accused shall enjoy the right... "to have the Assistance of Counsel for his defense". Being deprived of competent counsel constitutes trial error or irregularities, which can be corrected on appeal.

The Sixth Amendment guarantees that: 'In all criminal prosecutions, the accused shall enjoy the right... to have the assistance of counsel for his defense'. It is one of the safeguards of the Sixth Amendment **deemed necessary to insure** fundamental human rights of life and liberty. This right, and mandate stands as a prerequisite to any justifiable proceeding, within any criminal cause, within any lawful tribunal.

Omitted from the Constitution as originally adopted, provisions of this and other Amendments were submitted by the first Congress convened under that Constitution, as essential barriers against arbitrary or unjust deprivation of human rights. The Sixth Amendment stands as a constant admonition that if the constitutional safeguards it provides be lost, justice will not 'still be done'.

It embodies a realistic recognition of the obvious truth that the average defendant does not have the professional legal skill to protect himself [304 U.S. 458, 463] when brought before a tribunal with power to take his life or liberty, whereas the prosecution is presented by experienced an learned counsel.

That which is simple, orderly, and necessary to the lawyer- to the untrained layman – it may appear intricate, complex, and mysterious.

Consistent with the wisdom reflected in the policy of the Sixth Amendment, and other parts of **our** fundamental charter. Courts have pointed to '... the humane policy of the modern criminal law...' which now provides that a defendant '... if he be poor... may have counsel furnished him by the state.

The '... right to be heard would be, in many cases, of little avail if it did not comprehend the right to be heard by counsel. Even the intelligent and educated layman has small and sometimes no skill in the science of law. If charged with a crime, he is incapable, generally, of determining for himself whether the indictment is good or bad. He is typically unfamiliar with due process mandates, and rules of evidence. Left without the aid of counsel, he may be put on trial without a proper charging instrument, and convicted upon incompetent evidence, or evidence that is irrelevant to the issue, or otherwise inadmissible. The layman lacks both the skill and knowledge, to adequately prepare his defense, even though he have a perfect one. He requires, and is entitled to the guiding hand of counsel, at every step in the proceedings against him. The Sixth Amendment withholds from federal courts, in all criminal proceedings, the power and authority to deprive an accused of his life or liberty, unless he has, or waives the assistance of counsel. [304 U.S. 458, 464]

Courts are to indulge every reasonable presumption against waiver of fundamental constitutional rights, and that the court does not presume acquiescence, in the accused.

The purpose of the constitutional guaranty insuring the right to counsel is to protect an accused from conviction, resulting from his own ignorance of his legal and constitutional rights. That guaranty would be nullified, by a determination by this court, that failure by an accused, to claim his rights, removes the protection of **our** Constitution.

It is stated in Mooney v. Holohan, 294 U.S. 103, 113, 55 S.Ct. 340, 342,98 A.L.R. 406- that it 'falls with the premise'.

To deprive a citizen of his only effective remedy would not only be contrary to the "rudimentary demands of justice", but destructive of a constitutional guaranty, specifically designed to prevent injustice.

Since the Sixth Amendment constitutionally entitles one charged with a crime to the assistance of counsel, and, compliance with this constitutional mandate is an essential jurisdictional prerequisite to a court's authority to deprive an accused of his life or liberty. If the accused is not represented by counsel, and has not competently and intelligently waived his constitutional right, the Sixth amendment stands as a jurisdictional bar to a valid conviction and sentence, depriving him of his life or his liberty.

A court's jurisdiction at the hearing of a trial may be lost 'in the course of the proceedings' due to failure to complete the court − as the Sixth Amendment requires − by providing counsel for an accused who is unable to obtain counsel, who has not intelligently waived this constitutional guaranty, and whose life or liberty is at stake.

If this requirement of the Sixth Amendment is not complied with, the court no longer has jurisdiction to proceed. The judgement of conviction pronounced by a court without jurisdiction is void, and one imprisoned thereunder may obtain release by habeas corpus.

The trial court, presided over by Judge Jerry Sandel, was negligent of his duty to complete the court, by fulfilling the Sixth Amendment mandate, concerning my right to competent counsel.

Even though the court appointed attorney Tay Bond to represent me on September 28th, 2003 A.D., our first consultation proved to be very disappointing. He visited me in the County jail, while I was incarcerated for an alleged traffic violation. He displayed no concern for my welfare, or the fact that I was currently incarcerated. In fact, his advice to me was; "sit it out"! His "legal advice" was, "stay in jail". Yet, after making bond, the following day, the charges were dismissed.

Therefore, he did prove, by our first consultation, and by his advice, that he was actually, unconcerned and incompetent. He displayed no concern about my loss of liberty, and no knowledge of my constitutional rights. In fact, he displayed disdain of my efforts, to secure my constitutional rights.

Being that the public record is the highest form of evidence, and that I have filed on public record, my "Constructive Legal Notice" # 027-10-0438 on February 25th, 2002 A.D., That document has never been contested, and thus, stands as fact.

Being that appointed counsel, Mr. Tay Bond displayed no interest in the public record, or in the constitutional provisions, concerning my inherent rights, I had no alternative other than to dismiss Mr. Tay Bond on grounds of incompetence. The trial court allowed the dismissal of appointed counsel, but failed in its' duty, to complete the court, as defined in the Sixth Amendment of the United States, and by Article 1, Sec. 10. of the Constitution of the State of Texas (1876).

Citing Argersinger v. Hamlin (1972) under the rule we announce today, every judge will know, when the trial of a misdemeanor states that no imprisonment may be imposed, even though local law permits it, unless the accused is represented by counsel.

Whereas, I was not represented by competent counsel in this case, and, never waived my right to competent counsel, my right thereof, was denied. In fact, I informed the trial court that, Mr. Tay Bond displayed no concern for my liberty, or my rights. His lack of concern for my well being was exemplified by his advice, Quote; "Eddie, just sit it out!" Such advice, given by appointed counsel, during our first consultation, displays a total disregard for my situation, and no concern for my liberty, thus his obvious lack of concern about my liberty, exemplifies that fact that he was "incompetent", merely by, such a blatant lack of concern.

Petition

Based upon the fact that I was not represented by competent counsel and that I never waived that inherent right, the Accused moves that this action and cause be dismissed for lack of subject matter jurisdiction. The trial court failed in its' duty to complete the court as required by the Sixth Amendment. Therefore, jurisdiction was lost, and the only remedy for a judgement rendered, where jurisdiction did not exist, is dismissal. Petitioner moves this court to dismiss Trial Cause No. 03-185426.

A court lacking jurisdiction cannot render judgement but must dismiss the cause at any stage of the proceedings in which it becomes apparent that jurisdiction is lacking. United States v. Siviglia, 686 Fed.2d 832, 835 (1981), cases cited.

"All God Given Rights Reserved"
Without Prejudice UCC 1-207 & 1-103

Ronald - Edwin...Duncan, Sui Juris
C/o 17690 Peach Creek Drive
Conroe, city
Texas, Non-Domestic

Court of Appeals No. 10-04-00270-CR
Trial Court Case No. 03-185426

THE STATE OF TEXAS	§	TENTH COURT OF APPEALS
	§	
VS.	§	MCLENNAN COUNTY COURTHOUSE
	§	
Ronald Edwin Duncan, Sui Juris	§	WACO, TEXAS

Judicial Notice

Pursuant under 201(d) & (g) of the Texas and Federal Rules of Evidence

Writ of Error, Advancing Third Error; Trial Court Failed To Uphold The Provisions of Article 1 Sec. 10 of The Texas Constitution (1876).

Appellant advances a third point of error, that error being, a blatant violation of Article 1 Section 10. – "In **all** criminal prosecutions **the accused shall have a speedy trial by an impartial jury**. He shall have **the right to demand the nature and cause of the accusations against him, and have a copy thereof.** He shall not be compelled to give evidence against himself, and shall have **the right** of being heard by **himself or counsel, or both,** shall be confronted by the witnesses against him and **shall have compulsory process for obtaining witnesses in his favor"**.

The trial court responded to my request in open court, for a speedy trial, that, a speedy trial would ensue, yet, the trial court continued to violate the speedy trial provision of Article 1 Section 10, by repeatedly resetting my case. The trial court, on its' own volition, reset the proceedings on twelve different occasions. Assistant District Attorney threatened all people in the courtroom that, Quote; "If you do not sign a court reset form, a warrant will be issued for your arrest!" End Quote!

The initial, unauthorized arrest by Caryn McAnarney occurred on April 18th, 2003A.D., yet my trial did not occur until 15 months later, on July 14th, 2004A.D.

The trial court failed to respond to my written request for a copy of the Nature and Cause of the accusations against me.

The trial court failed in its' duty to secure my Sixth Amendment rights and those expressed in Article 1 Section 10 pertaining to my right to counsel.

The trial court initially honored Article 1 Section 10, and recognized my right to subpoena witnesses in my favor, then negated that right, "the right to compulsory process for obtaining witnesses in ones' favor", when it suppressed subpoenas that were issued, summoning witnesses for my defense.

Through my indigent status, the trial court issued subpoenas for Judge Trey Spikes, and Judge Edie Conally. Yet, within sixty days, and by a "Motion to Suppress", from State Attorney Stacy Mooring, the visiting, presiding Judge Jerry Sandel granted the suppression of those subpoenas, which thereby, denied my right to compulsory process for obtaining witnesses in my favor.

The trial court, by its' suppression of issued subpoenas, did also violate Article 1 Section 5, "No person shall be disqualified to give evidence in any of the Courts of this state on account of his religious opinions, or for the want of any religious belief, but all oaths or affirmations shall be administered in the mode most binding upon the conscience, and shall be taken subject to the pains and penalties of perjury.

Art. 2.01... It shall be the primary duty of all prosecuting attorneys, including any special prosecutors, not to convict, but to see that justice is done. They shall not suppress facts or secret witnesses capable of establishing the innocence of the accused.

The trial court initially fulfilled my right to counsel, yet, after appointed counsel divulged to me, many negative sentiments, regarding my rights, and his passive acceptance of my incarceration. His advice concerning my incarceration was; quote- "just sit it out" end quote! His lack of concern for my well being, and by the detrimental nature of his advice, reasonably affirmed to me, his incompetence.

After my initial consultation with appointed counsel Tey Bond, I objected to his appointment as counsel of record, for reason of his obvious lack of concern for my well being, and for his lack of concern for the fact that I was unjustly incarcerated, and therefore, his incompetence.

He was relieved of his "appointed counsel" capacity, yet, no subsequent counsel was appointed, and further, I never waived my right to competent counsel.

Therefore, the trial court violated numerous provisions of Article 1, Section 10 of The Texas Constitution, and thereby failed to complete the court, and thus failed to gain subject matter jurisdiction. Therefore, this third writ of error, citing the trial courts' numerous violations of provisions within Article 1 Section 10 is presented as just reason for the Tenth Court Of Appeals, to grant this petition to dismiss.

Court of Appeals No. 10-04-00270-CR
Trial Court Case No. 03-185426

THE STATE OF TEXAS	§	TENTH COURT OF APPEALS
	§	
VS.	§	MCLENNAN COUNTY COURTHOUSE
	§	
Ronald Edwin Duncan, Sui Juris	§	WACO, TEXAS

Judicial Notice

Pursuant under 201(d) & (g) of the Texas

and Federal Rules of Evidence

Writ of Error, Advancing Fourth Error; Trial Court Failed To Uphold Provisions of Article 1 Sec. 2-3-3a & 9 of The Texas Constitution (1876)

Appellant advances a fourth point of error, that being, a blatant violation of Article 1 Section 2-3-3a and 9 of the "Bill of Rights" within The Texas Constitution.

Section 2 states, "All political power is inherent in the people, and all free governments are founded on **"their authority"**, and instituted for **"their benefit"**.

Section 3 states, "All free men, when they form a social compact, **have equal rights,** and **no man**, or **set of men**, is entitled to exclusive separate public emoluments, **or privileges**, but in consideration of public service".

Section 3a states, "Equality under the law shall not be denied or abridged because of sex, race, color, creed, or national origin. This amendment is self-operative."

Section 9 states, "The people shall be secure in their persons, houses, papers and possessions, from all unreasonable seizures and searches, and no warrant to search any place, or to seize any person or thing, shall issue without describing them as near as may be, nor without probable cause, supported by oath or affirmation.

Trooper Caryn McAnarney, violated the above listed sections of the "Bill of Rights" and numerous due process mandates, when, on April 18th, 2003A.D., she initiated an unwarranted custodial arrest on me, and my traveling companion.

She acted on her own volition, and with conscious intent, even though she had no probable cause, witnessed no felonious act, witnessed no breach of the peace, and no exigent circumstances existed. She gave false testimony, concerning events at the scene, to responding officers, when she testified that neither detainee identified himself. The video clearly reveals that I relinquished an expired Texas "DRIVERS" license, for identification purposes, to Trooper McAnarney, and she can be heard reciting the numbers to the dispatcher, she was informed of my identity, and afterwards, spoke my full name, when the dispatcher revealed such.

She also ignored the testimony of responding Officer Valenzuela, when he informed her of my identity, address, and gave her a synopsis of similar behavior, he had observed, when he detained me, approximately two months earlier.

Yet, in the face of all evidence, of my true identity, and the testimony of responding Officer Valenzuela, she, Trooper McAnarney, on her own volition, with willful and malicious intent, lied to responding officers, then, conspired with them, to determine an alleged offense. She then, initiated a custodial arrest, and charged me with "Interfering With the Duties of a Public Servant and Failure To Identify", even though I had not interfered with her duties, and she clearly had knowledge of my identity. Being that her commands were usurping by nature and our Constitution forbids slavery or involuntary servitude, and all unreasonable seizures and searches, she usurped her lawful authority.

Further, within the text of the cited code 38.15 (d); "It is a defense to prosecution under this section that the interruption, disruption, impediment, or interference alleged consisted of speech only. It is clear by the video and audio of the scene that my response was a vocal claim of my Constitutional right to travel, and to inform her that I did not consent to this procedure, therefore, a dismissal is in order.

Trooper McAnarney, attempted to communicate with the Seargent on Duty, which thereby establishes, that no exigent circumstances existed. She was never advised by her Sergeant, yet, she initiated an arrest without probable cause or warrant.

262

Trooper McAnarney usurped her authority, when she ordered the arrest of my travelling companion, Mikell Erwin, for "Failure To Identify". Trooper McAnarny never requested identification from Mr. Erwin. She, in fact, never spoke one word to Mr. Erwin, yet, that fact did not stop her from initiating a custodial arrest and charging him with, failing a request, he had never been given.

The people have the right to be secure in their person. Trooper Caryn McAnarney blatantly violated that inherent and inalienable right. By conspiring, and initiating an unjustifiable custodial arrest, Caryn McAnarney usurped her lawful authority.

I asked Trooper McAnarney, why was she arresting me? Her response was; "Because you disobeyed a direct order" End Quote! Being that, there is no slavery or involuntary servitude allowed in this country, and she was usurping, of her lawful authority, my response was; "You don't have authority to order me around!" End Quote! She then responded, Quote; I have all the authority in the world!" End Quote!

That claim reflects her misguided frame of mind, and thus, her willingness to engage in a blatant usurpation of authority. Because, no public servant has ever been bestowed, "all the authority in the world"!

Being that I, Eddie Duncan, Sui Juris have given "Constructive Legal Notice", on public record # 027-10-0438 on February 25th, 2002A.D., and have claimed all God given rights, and all constitutional rights, on the trial court record.

Further, I never relinquished any right to the trial court, and as a matter of record, my unchallenged "Constructive Legal Notice" stands as fact.

Therefore, I hereby petition the Tenth Court of Appeals to dismiss Trial Cause No. 03- 185426, on grounds that Trooper McAnarney blatantly violated the above cited sections of the Bill of Rights within the Texas Constitution (1876).

Petitioner further asserts harm, when Trooper Caryn McAnarney assaulted me, denied me of my God given liberty, and caused extreme mental anguish by her unauthorized and unjustifiable actions on April 18th, 2003A.D,.

Therefore, petitioner seeks relief, to which I am rightfully entitled.

UNITED STATES DISTRICT COURT SOUTHERN DISTRICT OF TEXAS HOUSTON DIVISION

Ronald-Edwin…Duncan, Sui Juris Plaintiff VS. Trooper Caryn Mosier McAnarney, Emp: ORA04-0905, Ind. And in her Official Capacity, and Montgomery County Sheriffs' Officer Jack Valenzuela #8211 Ind. and in his Official Capacity, and Officer Mike Shraub #0172 and All Responding Officers reflected in video, yet not Listed in February 24th, 2005A.D. Request for Information and the Montgomery County Sheriffs' Department and The Texas Department of Public Safety	§ § § § § § § § § § § § § § § § § § §	Civil Action No. H- 05-1698

PLAINTIFFS' AFFIDAVIT OF FACT AND TREATISE ON ARREST AND FALSE IMPRISONMENT

Comes Now, Ronald-Edwin…Duncan, Sui Juris, an emancipated sovereign man, a natural born American adult. As a free and lawful inhabitant of the state of Texas, I have the right, and hereby respectfully petition this court for relief of injuries suffered at the hands of usurping government agents, acting under color of law.

To further establish my status as an emancipated sovereign American, I enter into evidence, public record # 027-10-0438 through # 027-10-0443 and my Common Law Vehicular Judicial Notice – Constitutional Drivers License.

The Defendant claims that her arrest of the Plaintiff without warrant for the alleged violation of "traffic laws" was lawful.

Defendant has assumed that she is authorized "by statute" to make arrests for any violation of the laws of the state, whether they are a misdemeanor or a felony when committed in her presence.

The facts of this case lead to the conclusion of law that the defendant did not have any lawful authority to arrest the Plaintiff. The Defendant had no warrant for the arrest of the Plaintiff, and she alleged that she only witnessed Plaintiff commit a misdemeanor, i.e., a traffic violation. There was no claim of a felony committed or of a breach of peace committed. At common law, and under the provisions of Due Process of Law, such an arrest without a warrant can not lawfully be made.

Since the arrest deprived the Plaintiff of his liberty by an act not pursuant to due process of law, the arrest is unlawful. Due Process is not determined by the legislature. Therefore Plaintiff hereby requests the court to take Judicial Notice of my discovery level petition being "Non-Assumpsit" which therefore brings into question all aspects of any alleged contract, that would mandate my compliance.

*It is manifest it was not left to the legislative power to exact any process, which might be devised. The [due process] article is a restraint on the legislative as well as on the executive and judicial powers of government, and cannot be so construed as to leave congress free to make any process "due process of law" by its' mere will. Murray's Lessee v. Hoboken Imp. Co., 18 How. (59 U.S.) 272, 276 (1855).

- The expressions "due process of law" and "law of the land" have the same meaning. The "law" intended by the Constitution is the common law, that had come down to us from our forefathers, as it existed and was understood and administered when that instrument was framed and adopted.
State v. Doherty, 60 Maine 504, 509 (1872).
- In interpreting what due process of law is, it has been held that "none of our liberties are to be taken away except in accordance with established principles". Ekern v. McGovern, 154 Wis. 157, 142 N.W. 595, 620 (1913).

Thus, the mode of arrest by which one can be deprived of his liberty is to be determined by the pre-existing common law principles and modes of procedure. A properly constituted warrant of arrest is a process at common law by which people could be deprived of their liberty.

The common law on arrest without warrant recognized only certain specific and well defined cases whereby a citizen could be deprived of his liberty. These provisions cannot be abrogated or changed by the legislature.

- It must not be forgotten, <u>there can be no arrest without due process of law</u>. An arrest without warrant has never been lawful, except in those cases where the public security requires it: and this has only been recognized in <u>felony</u>, and in <u>breaches of the peace</u> committed in the presence of the officer. Ex parte Rhodes, 202 Ala. 68, 79 So. 462, 465;citing, Sarah Way's Case, 41 Mich. 304, 1 N.W. 1023 (1879), et al. Also cited and affirmed in Pinkerton v. Verberg, 78 Mich. 573, 44 N.W. 579, 583 (1889); State v. Williams, 45 Ore. 314, 77 Pac. 965, 969, (1904); Adair v. Williams, 24 Ariz. 422, 210 Pac. 853, 856 (1922).

The Alabama Supreme Court in the Rhodes case went on to say that, "the phrase 'due process' must be determined by what it meant at the common law, and when the Constitution was adopted". (p. 469). The Court then cites the case of Tillman Beard, 121 Mich. 475, 80 N.W. 248 (1899), by stating:

- Officers are justified in arresting without warrant, only in cases of felony and breaches of the peace. This is elementary. It is needless to cite authorities.
- The fundamental constitutional guaranties of personal liberty protect private individuals in the right of enjoyment of personal freedom, without unlawful restraint, and it is universally recognized that no one may be arrested except by due process of law. (2 R.C.L. 463, ~~ 21).

In Tiedeman's "Treatise on the Limitations of Police Power" (1886) ~~33, is found the requirements for a lawful arrest and the exceptions to a warrantless arrest:

33. What constitutes a lawful arrest? – As a general proposition, no one can make a lawful arrest for a crime, except an officer who has a warrant issued by a court or magistrate having the competent authority.

33a. Arrests without a warrant! – Although, it is the general rule of law that there can be no arrest without a warrant of the nature just described, yet there are cases in which the requirement of a warrant would so obstruct the effectual enforcement of the laws, that the ends of justice would be defeated.

For public reasons, therefore, in a few cases, the personal security of the citizen is subjected to the further liability of being arrested by a police officer or private individual without a warrant. But the right thus, to arrest without a warrant must be confined to the cases of strict public necessity. The cases are few in number, and may be stated as follows:

1. When a felony is being committed, an arrest may be made without warrant to prevent any further violation of the law.
2. When a felony has been committed, and the officer or private individual is justified, by the facts within his knowledge, in believing that the person arrested has committed a crime.
3. All breaches of the peace, in assaults and batteries, affrays, riots, etc., for the purpose of restoring order immediately.

The rule of the common law, that a peace officer or private citizen may arrest a felon without a warrant, or on view of a breach of the peace, has never been extended to any and all misdemeanors. Therefore, arrests are not lawful where only a misdemeanor occurs, unless it is in the nature of a "breach of the peace".

Here again, we find that this principle of arrest, only by due process of law was once universally recognized. Yet, the Defendant has ignored such process in her arrest of the Plaintiff.

The philosophy and/or practice of enforcing any statute, whereby any "public" servant, might/can abrogate constitutionally protected rights, is hypocritical in its' application, by allowing an unjustifiable abrogation of constitutionally protected rights, and due process of Law.

Therefore, such practices are a clear and obvious violation of their oath of office, and the precedent set in Murray's Lessee v. Hoboken Imp. Co., 18 How. (59 U.S.) 272, 276 (1855).

I hereby petition the court to take Judicial Notice of Shapiro vs. Thompson 394 U.S. 618 and Murdock vs. Pennsyvania 319 U.S. 105 and Schuttlesworth vs. BIRMINGHAM, ALABAMA, 373 U.S. 262 and

MARBURY vs. MADISON, 5 U.S. 137 (1803) which has never been overturned in over 194 years, see Shephards' Citations.

Please see U.S. vs. Bishop 412 U.s. 346 and Article 3, Section 2, Paragraph (1) and (2) of the U.S. Constitution. Please see Zobel vs. Williams, 457 U.S. 55 and Miller vs. UNITED STATES 230 F2d 486. (will supplement)

To further establish my right to travel, and my right to Common Law, I refer to the following definitions;

a. Thesaurus – 1. A storehouse or repository, as of words or knowledge: a dictionary, encyclopedia, or the like. 2. A treasury.

b. Treatise – 1. A book or writing treating of some particular subject. 2. One containing a formal or methodical exposition of the principals of the subject.

c. Ordain – 1. Ecles: to invest with ministerial or sacerdotal functions; confer holy orders upon. 2. To appoint authoritatively. 3. To select or appoint to an office. 4. To decree, give orders for. 5. (Of God, fate, etc.) to destine or predestine.
6. Lat. Arrange.

d. Affidavit – A written declaration upon oath. Esp. one made before an authorized official. [Lat. He has made oath]

e. Emancipate – 1. To free from restraint of any kind. 2. Roman and Civil Law (a) to free a slave (b) to terminate parental control over.

f. Sovereign – 1. One who has sovereign power or authority. 2. Having supreme rank, power or authority 3. Supreme, as power, authority etc. 4. Self-governing.

g. Person – Blacks Law Dictionary, Revised Fourth Edition and Bouviers 3rd Revision Vol. 3 P to Z, Page 2575, 1st Paragraph, under the heading of "person". Quote; A "county" is a "person" in a legal sense. Lancaster Co. v. Trimble, 34 Neb. 752, 52 N.W. 711; "but a sovereign is not"! End Quote!

h. Sui Juris – 1. Law – One capable of managing his affairs and assuming legal responsibility for his acts, as distinguished from others, as lunatics and infants, whose legal capacity is limited.

i. Name – Blacks' Law Dictionary, 5th Edition declares on page 2287; The omission of the Christian name by either plaintiff or defendant in legal process, prevents the court from acquiring jurisdiction, there being no other description or identification and no appearance of waiver of process. Whitney v. Masemore, 75 Kan. 522, 89 Pac. 914, 11 L.R.A. (N.S.) 676, 121 Am. St. Rep. 442

j. Abrogate – 1. To abolish summarily; annul by an authoritative act; repeal : To abrogate a law.

k. Non-Assumpsit – Bouviers 3rd Revision Vol. 3, P to Z, Page 2354 right column, 7th paragraph, (Latin – He did not undertake) Under this plea, almost every matter may be given into evidence, on the ground, it is said, that as the action is founded on the contract, and the injury is the non-performance of it, evidence which disaffirms the obligation of the contract, at the time when the action was commenced, goes to the gist of the action. 1 B. & P. 481. See 12 Viner, abr. 189; Com Dig. Pleader (2G1).

l. Driver – Blacks' Law 5th Edition defines "driver" as one whom "is employed" to operate a motor vehicle. (will supplement)

m. Color of Law – Defined under United States Code, Title 18 – Crimes and Criminal Procedure > Part 1 – Crimes > Chapter 13 – Civil Rights > Section 242

Whereas, in view of public record, the cases cited above, and the mandates established within the Texas Administrative Code, and the Texas and National Constitutions, Trooper Caryn McAnarneys actions were clearly without lawful authority.

And further, Trooper Caryn McAnarney actions were in association with Trooper Mike Schraub, whom, has admitted on public record, within the 221st Judicial District, that he acted under color of state law.

Within Defendant Mike Schraub's Original Answer, Affirmative Defenses and Demand For Jury, and labeled exhibit E, under III. Defendant's Original Answer, #10 of page number three, the Defendant admits; Quote! Defendant admits that he acted under color of state law at all times during the incident in question. End Quote! Therefore, should a "public" servant, (whom, has admitted to acting under color of law) be entitled to "immunity"? Why would someone claim (to have) constitutional rights, if "public" servants can abrogate those rights, at will, and with immunity? How could a free society truly exist, wherein "public" servants may, on impulse, usurp the limits of their authority, with immunity?

Trooper McAnarney further criminally incriminated herself by lying to responding officers at the scene. She declared to a responding officer, when questioned; "Did both suspects refuse to identify?" She responded, yes. Her (that) affirmative response was a lie.

The true facts pertaining to the question of identification, posed by a responding officer at the scene, and referring to Mike Erwin and myself, are as follows.

I am not a licensee, nor am I required to be, as I am/was not employed to drive at the time of the arrest. And further, at the initial contact, I informed Trooper McAnarney that I had claimed my constitutional right to travel, and that I was in my private conveyance, and that I did not consent to the procedure.

Upon her request, I relinquished to Trooper McAnarney, an expired license, "for identification purposes only". She "never" spoke to Mr. Erwin, and therefore, "she did not request to see his identification".

She proceeded to contact her dispatcher and professed the numbers on my identification to her. The dispatcher responded by stating my name and address to Trooper McAnarney, and she herself, professed my name aloud.

Further, Officer Jack Valenzuela arrived, and recognized my automobile, and stated to Trooper McAnarney; Quote- That's Duncan, he's just going to hand you a license out of the window, he lives down there on Peach Creek. End Quote!

Therefore, she was fully informed of my identity, by dispatchers' response, and by the testimony of Officer Jack Valenzuela. Yet, she ignored the testimony of officer Valenzuela, when he identified me, and described similar behavior by me, that he had encountered, when he had detained me a few weeks earlier.

Therefore, she should have realized that my claim of rights was/is reasonable, and my behavior was not out of the ordinary, and that, I am a free and lawful Citizen, entitled to liberty and the protection of "public" servants.

Instead, she lied to other responding officers at the scene, when she declared to them that each of us had failed to identify. She further proceeded to violate the rights of Mike Erwin and myself, by charging each of us with "Failure to Identify", even though, she had personal knowledge of my identity, and "<u>she never requested identification from Mr. Erwin</u>".

Further, as specified in Texas Penal Code Sec. 38.02 (a) one is only required to produce credible ID, "after" one has been placed under lawful arrest. Any law, that would require people to produce credible ID, simply upon the discretion of a "public" servant, would be an invasion of privacy, and would give unwarranted discretion and certainly unwarranted arresting powers to "public" servants.

Further, she violated the Thirteenth Amendment to the Constitution; Section 1 Quote; Neither slavery nor involuntary servitude, except as a punishment for crime, whereof the party shall have been duly convicted, shall exist within the United States, or any place subject to their jurisdiction. End Quote!

Therefore, her unauthorized usurpation of power, while attempting to order me from my private property, (when not under lawful arrest) to do anything, is a clear violation of the constitutional provision cited above.

Plaintiff hereby petitions the Court to take Judicial Notice of the trial transcripts from trial case number 03-185425. The trial court transcript will reveal that Trooper Caryn McAnarney admitted under oath and on the stand that she had never seen the book known as, "The Texas Administrative Code".

That book defines, and is the basis upon which, the procedures and duties of DPS officers are to be administered. Yet, Trooper McAnarney admitted in open court, that she had no knowledge of its' content.

Therefore, she had no knowledge of lawful administrative procedures, or her actual duties. Therefore, her charge that I interfered with the duties of a "public" servant is groundless, in view of the fact that she willfully abrogated numerous constitutional rights, usurped her authority, and "in fact" had no knowledge of her prescribed duties, or the associated administrative provisions.

Therefore, she was acting under "color of law" and not in accordance with her duties, as defined in the Texas Administrative Code.

Further, the video of the events reveals that she conspired with responding officers, who eventually suggested to her, that she could charge me with "interfering with the duties of a public servant". She responded; Quote! "I can"! He's going down! Who wants to break the windows? End Quote!

That fabricated accusation, derived only from, and after, conspiring with responding officers, that she had intentionally misled, is a clear violation of the [Due Process of Law], her oath of office and the "Texas Administrative Code".

Further, the conspired charge, created and alleged, "only", after conversing with responding officers, is completely unjustifiable, not only in light of its' conception, but, the fact that the alleged offense consisted of speech only, confirms that the charge is groundless.

I refer to the Texas Penal Code, Sec 38.15 (5) (d) Quote; "It is a defense to prosecution under this section that the interruption, disruption, impediment, or interference alleged consisted of speech only". End Quote! Therefore, in view of the methodical and lawfully questionable steps taken. By which, Trooper McAnarney eventually concluded that she could lodge this accusation, and in view of section (5) (d) of Sec. 38.15, and in view of the fact, that my alleged interference consisted of speech only, the charge is groundless.

Further, the charge was conceived and only brought, "after" she and the responding officers began to consider and to conspire, to determine, what accusation (charge) would allow her to make a custodial arrest. Trooper McAnarney had no probable cause and no conception of the charge that she might lodge, until, the responding officers, (whom she had intentionally misled) suggested an option that "statutorily" gave her an excuse, to initiate a custodial arrest.

Therefore, whereas she had no probable cause, no concept of proper procedure, and no concept of her actual authority, she acted under color of law. Further, her assertion that; Quote; "I have all the authority in the world" End Quote!), must be construed as usurping, by its' nature, in view of Article 1 Sec. 3 of the Texas Bill of Rights, which establishes equal rights for all men and women.

Therefore, she was not acting within the provisions defining her actual duties, and Due Process. Further, she did not initiate the custodial arrest, until after lying to, questioning, and conversing with responding officers. That willful procedure clearly constitutes conspiracy and false arrest.

To further assert my lawful constitutional claims, I hereby enter into evidence, specific and relevant sections of the Bill of Rights, within the Constitution of the state of Texas 1876.

PREAMBLE

Humbly invoking the blessings of Almighty God, the people of the state of Texas, do "ordain" and establish this Constitution.

Article 1
Bill of Rights

That the general, great and "<u>essential principles of liberty</u>" and free government may be recognized and established, we declare:

Sec. 1. Freedom and sovereignty of state. Texas is a free and independent state, subject only to the Constitution for the united States, and the maintenance of our free institutions and the perpetuity of the Union depend upon the preservation of the right of local self-government, unimpaired to all the states.

Sec. 2. Inherent Political Power; Republican Form of Government. All political power is inherent in the people, and all free governments are founded on their authority, and instituted for their benefit. The faith of the people of Texas stands pledged to the preservation of a republican form of government, and, subject to this limitation only, they have at all times the inalienable right to alter, reform or abolish their government in such manner as they may think expedient.

Sec. 3. Equal Rights. All free men, when they form a social compact, have equal rights, and no man, or set of men, is entitled to exclusive separate public emoluments, or privileges, but in consideration of "public" services.

Sec. 3a. Equality Under the Law. Equality under the law shall not be denied or abridged because of sex, race, color, creed, or national origin. This amendment is self-operative. (Added Nov. 7, 1972.)

Sec. 8. Freedom of Speech and Press; Libel. Every person shall be at liberty to speak, write or publish his opinions on any subject, being responsible for the abuse of that privilege: and no law shall ever be passed curtailing the liberty of speech or of the press. In prosecutions for the publication of papers, investigating the conduct of officers, or men in public capacity, or, "when the matter published is proper for public information, the truth thereof may be given in evidence". And in all indictments for libel, the jury shall have the right to determine the law and the facts, under the direction of the court, as in other cases.

Sec. 9. Searches and Seizures. The people shall be secure in their persons, houses, papers and possessions, from all unreasonable seizures or searches, and no warrant to search any place, or to seize any person or thing, shall issue without describing them as near as may be, nor without probable cause, supported by oath or affirmation.

Sec. 10. Rights of Accused in Criminal Prosecutions. In all criminal prosecutions the accused shall have a speedy public trial by an impartial jury. He shall have the right to demand the nature and cause of the accusations against him, and to have a copy thereof. He shall not be compelled to give evidence against himself, and shall have the right of being heard by himself or counsel, or both, shall be confronted by the witnesses against him and shall have compulsory process for obtaining witnesses in his favor, except that when the witness resides out of the state and the offense charged is a violation of any of the anti-trust laws of this state, the defendant and the state shall have the right to produce and have the evidence admitted by deposition, under such rules and laws as the Legislature may hereafter provide; and no person shall be held to answer for a criminal offense, unless on indictment of a grand jury, except in cases in which the punishment is by fine or imprisonment, otherwise than in the penitentiary, in cases of impeachment, and in cases arising in the army or navy, or in the malitia, when in actual service in time of war or public danger.   (Amended Nov. 5, 1918.)

(Will Supplement)

UNITED STATES DISTRICT COURT SOUTHERN DISTRICT OF TEXAS HOUSTON DIVISION

Ronald-Edwin...Duncan, Sui Juris Plaintiff VS. Trooper Caryn Mosier McAnarney, Emp: ORA04-0905, Ind. And in her Official Capacity, and Montgomery County Sheriffs' Officer Jack Valenzuela #8211 Ind. and in his Official Capacity, and Officer Mike Shraub #0172 and All Responding Officers reflected in video, yet not Listed in February 24th, 2005A.D. Request for Information and the Montgomery County Sheriffs' Department and The Texas Department of Public Safety	§ § § § § § § § § § § § § § § § §	Civil Action No. H- 05-1698

PETITION TO DISMISS TRIAL COURT JUDGEMENT, FOR FAILURE TO OBTAIN SUBJECT MATTER JURISDICTION

Plaintiff hereby petitions the Court to take Judicial Notice of the fact that the Trial Court failed in its' duty to complete the Court, by failing to appoint counsel for the Defendant, and thereby lost jurisdiction to proceed. As evidence, I submit "WAIVER OF RIGHT TO COUNSEL", presented to me by Brett Peabody on July 12th, 2004 A.D. (the day of trial) and was refused.

Since the Sixth Amendment constitutionally entitles one charged with a crime to the assistance of counsel, compliance with this constitutional mandate is an essential jurisdictional prerequisite of a court's authority to deprive an accused of his life or liberty.

In Patton v. United States, 281 U.S. 276, 50 S.Ct. 253, 70 A.L.R. 263, the court noted approvingly, a state court decision pointing out that the humane policy of modern criminal law has altered conditions, which had existed, 'in the days when the accused could not testify in his own behalf, (and) was not furnished counsel', was without ability to summon witnesses, and not permitted to tell his own story...'

[304 U.S. 458, 465] The constitutional right of an accused to be represented by counsel invokes of itself, the protection of a trial court, in which the accused- whose life or liberty is at state – and he, is without counsel. The protecting duty imposes the serious and weighty responsibility upon the trial judge, of determining whether, there is an intelligent and competent waiver by the CAUSE NO. 05-04-03361-CV

When this [304 U.S. 458, 468] right is properly waived, the assistance of counsel is no longer a necessary element of the courts' jurisdiction to proceed to conviction and sentence.

If the accused, however, is not represented by counsel and has not competently and intelligently waived his constitutional right, the Sixth Amendment stands as a jurisdictional bar to a valid conviction and sentence depriving him of his life and liberty. A courts' jurisdiction at the hearing of trial may be lost in the course of the proceedings due to failure to complete the court as the Sixth Amendment requires by providing counsel for an accused who is unable to obtain counsel, who has not intelligently waived this constitutional guaranty, and whose life or liberty is at stake. 22 If this requirement of the Sixth Amendment is not complied with, the court no longer has jurisdiction to proceed. The judgement of conviction pronounced by a court without jurisdiction is void, and one imprisoned thereunder may obtain release by habeas corpus. 23 A judge of the United States to whom a petition for habeas corpus is addressed should be alert to examine the facts for himself, when, if true as alleged, they make the trial absolutely void. (Johnson v. Zerbst, supra)

Therefore, Plaintiff requests the court to take Judicial Notice of Plaintiffs' Petition to Arrest Trial Court Judgement, For Failure to Obtain Subject Matter Jurisdiction. And further, to rule on any motions or defenses, citing that dysfunctional conviction, (brought in Trial Court Cause # 03-185426 on July 14th, 2004A.D.) as groundless, and without merit. It is irrelevant to cite a trial court verdict, wherein the court lacked jurisdiction, and its' verdict is thereby clearly, a null and "void judgement".

For the record, I am entering a copy of the Waiver of Right To Counsel, presented to me by Brett Peabody on July 12th, 2004A.D. Whereas, it was refused, I clearly remained entitled to competent counsel. And further, failure to fulfill that constitutional right, shall (without question) deny the court, jurisdiction to proceed.

Therefore, the trial court clearly violated the Sixth Amendment, and therefore failed a necessary element of a lawful trial, and therefore, acted without jurisdiction.

Therefore, any verdict delivered, where jurisdiction to proceed is lacking, is null and void, and rightfully, to be viewed as such.

Therefore, in view of trial courts' failures of Due Process, and its' clear lack of jurisdiction, Plaintiff petitions all parties associated with Cause 05-04-03361-CV to hereby be informed of the clear lack of jurisdiction, by the trial court to proceed. Further, the judgement of conviction pronounced by a court without jurisdiction is void, and one imprisoned thereunder may obtain release by habeas corpus.

Therefore, Plaintiff petitions the Court to take Judicial Notice of the trial courts' failure to obtain subject matter jurisdiction, and therefore, to dismiss the conviction, associated with Cause No. 03-185426 & 301000, as null and void.

And further, Trooper Caryn McAnarney actions were in association with Trooper Mike Schraub, whom, has admitted on public record, within the 221st Judicial District, that he acted under color of state law. Within Defendant Mike Schraub's Original Answer, Affirmative Defenses and Demand For Jury, and labeled exhibit E, under III. Defendant's Original Answer, #10 of page number three, the Defendant admits; Quote! Defendant admits that he acted under color of state law at all times during the incident in question. End Quote! Therefore, should a "public" servant, (whom, has admitted to acting under color of law) be entitled to "immunity"? Why would someone claim (to have) constitutional rights, if "public" servants can abrogate those rights, at will, and with immunity?

How could a free society truly exist, wherein "public" servants may, on impulse, usurp the limits of their authority, with immunity?

Eternally,
A Brother In Christ
"All God Given
Rights Reserved"

Thanks and Recognition

The following article was obtained from the Internet, from public domain files, because of its' inherent nature, and the value of its' subject matter. Because of the mandates of the Constitution, securing the self-governing rights of the People, this historic information, is a matter of "Public Record", and available on demand.

1. Congressman McFadden on the Federal Reserve Corporation at http://user.icx.net/~drherb/mcfaddenfrd.html

Eternally,
A Brother in Christ
Eddie Duncan

On May 23, 1933, Congressman, Louis T. McFadden, brought formal charges against the Board of Governors of the Federal Reserve Bank system, The Comptroller of the Currency and the Secretary of United States Treasury for numerous criminal acts, including but not limited to, CONSPIRACY, FRAUD, UNLAWFUL CONVERSION, AND TREASON.

The petition for Articles of Impeachment was thereafter referred to the Judiciary Committee and has YET TO BE ACTED ON. So, this ELECTRONIC BOOKLET should be reprinted, reposted, set up on web pages and circulated far and wide.

Congressman McFadden on the Federal Reserve Corporation Remarks in Congress, 1934 AN ASTOUNDING EXPOSURE

Congressman McFadden's Speech On the Federal Reserve Corporation

Quotations from several speeches made on the Floor of the House of Representatives by the Honorable Louis T. McFadden of Pennsylvania. Mr. McFadden, due to his having served as Chairman of the Banking and Currency Committee for more than 10 years, was the best posted man on these matters in America and was in a position to speak with authority of the vast ramifications of this gigantic private credit monopoly. As Representative of a State which was among the first to declare its freedom from foreign money tyrants it is fitting that Pennsylvania, the cradle of liberty, be again given the credit for producing a son that was not afraid to hurl defiance in the face of the money-bund. Whereas Mr. McFadden was elected to the high office on both the Democratic and Republican tickets, there can be no accusation of partisanship lodged against him. Because these speeches are set out in full in the Congressional Record, they carry weight that no amount of condemnation on the part of private individuals could hope to carry.

The Federal Reserve-A Corrupt Institution

"Mr. Chairman, we have in this Country one of the most corrupt institutions the world has ever known. I refer to the Federal Reserve Board and the Federal Reserve Banks, hereinafter called the Fed. The Fed has cheated the Government of these United States and the people of the United States out of enough money to pay the Nation's debt. The depredations and iniquities of the Fed has cost enough money to pay the National debt several times over.

"This evil institution has impoverished and ruined the people of these United States, has bankrupted itself, and has practically bankrupted our Government. It has done this through the defects of the law under which it operates, through the maladministration of that law by the Fed and through the corrupt practices of the moneyed vultures who control it.

"Some people who think that the Federal Reserve Banks United States Government institutions. They are private monopolies which prey upon the people of these United States for the benefit of themselves and their foreign customers; foreign and domestic speculators and swindlers; and rich and predatory money lender. In that dark crew of financial pirates there are those who would cut a man's throat to get a dollar out of his pocket; there are those who send money into states to buy votes to control our legislatures; there are those who maintain International propaganda for the purpose of deceiving us into granting of new concessions which will permit them to cover up their past misdeeds and set again in motion their gigantic train of crime.

"These twelve private credit monopolies were deceitfully and disloyally foisted upon this Country by the bankers who came here from Europe and repaid us our hospitality by undermining our American institutions. Those bankers took money out of this Country to finance Japan in a war against Russia. They created a reign of terror in Russia with our money in order to help that war along. They instigated the separate peace between Germany and Russia, and thus drove a wedge between the allies in World War. They financed Trotsky's passage from New York to Russia so that he might assist in the destruction of the Russian Empire. They fomented and instigated the Russian Revolution, and placed a large fund of American dollars at Trotsky's disposal in one of their branch banks in Sweden so that through him Russian homes might be thoroughly broken up and Russian children flung far and wide from their natural protectors. They have since begun breaking up of American homes and the dispersal of American children. "Mr. Chairman, there should be no partisanship in matters concerning banking and currency affairs in this Country, and I do not speak with any.

"In 1912 the National Monetary Association, under the chairmanship of the late Senator Nelson W. Aldrich, made a report and presented a vicious bill called the National Reserve Association bill. This bill is usually spoken of as the Aldrich bill. Senator Aldrich did not write the Aldrich bill. He was the tool, if not the accomplice, of the European bankers who for nearly twenty years had been scheming to set up a central bank in this Country and who in 1912 has spent and were continuing to spend vast sums of money to accomplish their purpose.

"We were opposed to the Aldrich plan for a central bank. The men who rule the Democratic Party then promised the people that if they were returned to power there would be no central bank established here while they held the reigns of government. Thirteen months later that promise was broken, and the Wilson administration, under the tutelage of those sinister Wall Street figures who stood behind Colonel House, established here in our free Country the worm-eaten monarchical institution of the "King's Bank" to control us from the top downward, and from the cradle to the grave.

"The Federal Reserve Bank destroyed our old and characteristic way of doing business. It discriminated against our 1-name commercial paper, the finest in the world, and it set up the antiquated 2-name paper, which is the present curse of this Country and which wrecked every country which has ever given it scope; it fastened down upon the Country the very tyranny from which the framers of the Constitution sough to save us.

IN PRESIDENT JACKSON'S TIME

"One of the greatest battles for the preservation of this Republic was fought out here in Jackson's time; when the second Bank of the United States, founded on the same false principles of those which are here exemplified in the Fed was hurled out of existence. After that, in 1837, the Country was warned against the dangers that might ensue if the predatory interests after being cast out should come back in disguise and unite themselves to the Executive and through him acquire control of the Government. That is what the predatory interests did when they came back in the livery of hypocrisy and under false pretenses obtained the passage of the Fed.

"The danger that the Country was warned against came upon us and is shown in the long train of horrors attendant upon the affairs of the traitorous and dishonest Fed. Look around you when you leave this Chamber and you will see evidences of it in all sides. This is an era of misery and for the conditions that caused that misery, the Fed are fully liable. This is an era of financed crime and in the financing of crime the Fed does not play the part of a disinterested spectator.

"It has been said that the draughtsman who was employed to write the text of the Aldrich bill because that had been drawn up by lawyers, by acceptance bankers of European origin in New York. It was a copy, in general a translation of the statues of the Reichsbank and other European central banks. One-half million dollars was spent on the part of the propaganda organized by these bankers for the purpose of misleading public opinion and giving Congress the impression that there was an overwhelming popular demand for it and the kind of currency that goes with it, namely, an asset currency based on human debts and obligations. Dr. H. Parker Willis had been employed by Wall Street and propagandists, and when the Aldrich measure failed- he obtained employment with Carter Glass, to assist in drawing the banking bill for the Wilson administration. He appropriated the text of the Aldrich bill. There is no secret about it. The test of the Federal Reserve Act was tainted from the first.

"A few days before the bill came to a vote, Senator Henry Cabot Lodge, of Massachusetts, wrote to Senator John W. Weeks as follows:

New York City, December 17, 1913

"'My Dear Senator Weeks:

"'Throughout my public life I have supported all measures designed to take the Government out of the banking business. This bill puts the Government into the banking business as never before in our history. "'The powers vested in the Federal Reserve Board seen to me highly dangerous especially where there is political control of the Board. I should be sorry to hold stock in a bank subject to such dominations. The bill as it stands seems to me to open the way to a vast inflation of the currency. "I had hoped to support this bill, but I cannot vote for it cause it seems to me to contain features and to rest upon principles in the highest degree menacing to our prosperity, to stability in business, and to the general welfare of the people of the United States.

Very Truly Yours,
Henry Cabot Lodge.'"

"In eighteen years that have passed since Senator Lodge wrote that letter of warning all of his predictions have come true. The Government is in the banking business as never before. Against its will it has been made the backer of horse thieves and card sharps, bootlegger's smugglers, speculators, and swindlers in all parts of the world. Through the Fed the riffraff of every country is operating on the public credit of the United States Government.

THE GREAT DEPRESSION

"Meanwhile and on account of it, we ourselves are in the midst of the greatest depression we have ever known. From the Atlantic to the Pacific, our Country has been ravaged and laid waste by the evil practices of the Fed and the interests which control them. At no time in our history, has the general welfare of the people been at a lower level or the minds of the people so full of despair.

"Recently in one of our States, 60,000 dwelling houses and farms were brought under the hammer in a single day. 71,000 houses and farms in Oakland County, Michigan, were sold and their erstwhile owners dispossessed. The people who have thus been driven out are the wastage of the Fed. They are the victims of the Fed. Their children are the new slaves of the auction blocks in the revival of the institution of human slavery.

"In 1913, before the Senate Banking and Currency Committee, Mr. Alexander Lassen made the following statement: "The whole scheme of the Fed with its commercial paper is an impractical, cumbersome machinery- is simply a cover to secure the privilege of issuing money, and to evade payment of as much tax upon circulation as possible and then control the issue and maintain, instead of reducing interest rates. It will prove to the advantage of the few and the detriment of the people. It will mean continued shortage of actual money and further extension of credits, for when there is a shortage of money people have to borrow to their cost.' "A few days before the Fed passed, Senator Root denounced the Fed as an outrage on our liberties. He predicted: 'Long before we wake up from our dream of prosperity through an inflated currency, our gold- which alone could have kept us from catastrophe- will have vanished and no rate of interest will tempt it to return.'

"If ever a prophecy came true, that one did.

"The Fed became law the day before Christmas Eve, in the year 1913, and shortly afterwards, the German International bankers, Kuhn, Loeb and Co. sent one of their partners here to run it.

"The Fed Note is essentially unsound. It is the worst currency and the most dangerous that this Country has ever known. When the proponents of the act saw that the Democratic doctrine would not permit them to let the proposed banks issue the new currency as bank notes, they should have stopped at that. They should not have foisted that kind of currency, namely, an asset currency, on the United States Government. They should not have made the Government [liable on the private] debts of individuals and corporations, and, least of all, on the private debts of foreigners. "As Kemerer says: 'The Fed Notes, therefore, in form, have some of the qualities of Government paper money, but in substance, are almost a pure asset currency possessing a Government guarantee against which contingency the Government has made no provision whatever.'

"Hon. L.J.Hill, a former member of the House, said, and truly: "They are obligations of the Government for which the United States received nothing and for the payment of which at any time, it assumes the responsibility: looking to the Fed to recoup itself.'

"If this United States is to redeem the Fed Notes, when the General Public finds it costs to deliver this paper to the Fed, and if the Government has made no provisions for redeeming them, the first element of unsoundness is not far to seek.

"Before the Banking and Currency Committee, when the bill was under discussion Mr. Crozier of Cincinnati said: 'The imperial power of elasticity of the public currency is wielded exclusively by the central corporations owned by the banks. This is a life and death power over all local banks and all business. It can be used to create or destroy prosperity, to ward off or cause stringencies and panics. By making money artificially scarce, interest rates throughout the Country can be arbitrarily raised and the bank tax on all business and cost of living increased for the profit of the banks owning these regional central banks, and without the slightest benefit to the people. The 12 Corporations together cover y and monopolize and use for private gain- every dollar of the public currency and all public revenue of the United States. Not a dollar can be put into circulation among the people by their Government, without the consent of and on terms fixed by these 12 private money trusts.'

"In defiance of this and all other warnings, the proponents of the Fed created the 12 private credit corporations and gave them an absolute monopoly of the currency of these United States- not of the Fed Notes alone- but of all other currency! The Fed Act providing ways and means by which the gold and general currency in the hands of the American people could be obtained by the Fed in exchange for Fed Notes- which are not money- but mere promises to pay.

"Since the evil day when this was done, the initial monopoly has been extended by vicious amendments to the Fed and by the unlawful and treasonable practices of the Fed.

"Mr. Chairman, if a Scottish distiller wishes to send a cargo of Scotch whiskey to these United States, he can draw his bill against the purchasing bootlegger in dollars and after the bootlegger has accepted it by writing his name across the face of it, the Scotch distiller can send that bill to the nefarious open discount market in New York City where the Fed will buy it and use it as collateral for a new issue of Fed Notes. Thus the Government of these United States pay the Scotch distiller for the whiskey before it is shipped, and if it is lost on the way, or if the Coast Guard seizes it and destroys it, the Fed simply write off the loss and the government never recovers the money that was paid to the Scotch distiller.

"While we are attempting to enforce prohibition here, the Fed are in the distillery business in Europe and paying bootlegger bills with public credit of these United States. "Mr. Chairman, by the same process, they compel our Government to pay the German brewer for his beer. Why should the Fed be permitted to finance the brewing industry in Germany either in this way or as they do by compelling small and fearful United States Banks to take stock in the Isenbeck Brewery and in the German Bank for brewing industries? "Mr. Chairman, if Dynamit Nobel of Germany, wishes to sell dynamite in Japan to use in Manchuria or elsewhere, it can drew its bill against the Japanese customers in dollars and send that bill to the nefarious open discount market in New York City where the Fed will buy it and use it as collateral for a new issue of Fed Notes- while at the same time the Fed will be helping Dynamit Nobel by stuffing its stock into the United States banking system.

"Why should we send our representatives to the disarmament conference at Geneva- while the Fed is making our Government pay Japanese debts to German Munitions makers?

"Mr. Chairman, if a German wishes to raise a crop of beans and sell them to a Japanese customer, he can draw a bill against his prospective Japanese customer in dollars and have it purchased by the Fed and get the money out of this Country at the expense of the American people before he has even planted the beans in the ground. "Mr. Chairman, if a German in Germany wishes to export goods to South America, or any other Country, he can draw his bill against his customers and send it to these United States and get the money out of this Country before he ships, or even manufactures the goods.

"Mr. Chairman, why should the currency of these United States be issued on the strength of German Beer? Why should it be issued on the crop of unplanted beans to be grown in Chili for Japanese consumption? Why should these United States be compelled to issue many billions of dollars every year to pay the debts of one foreigner to another foreigner? "Was it for this that our National Bank depositors had their money taken out of our banks and shipped abroad? Was it for this that they had to lose it? Why should the public credit of these United States and likewise money belonging to our National Bank depositors be used to support foreign brewers, narcotic drug vendors, whiskey distillers, wig makes, human hair merchants, Chilean bean growers, to finance the munition factories of Germany and Soviet Russia?

THE UNITED STATES HAS BEEN RANSACKED

"The United States has been ransacked and pillaged. Our structures have been gutted and only the walls are left standing. While being perpetrated, everything the world would rake up to sell us was brought in here at our expense by the Fed until our markets were swamped with unneeded and unwanted imported goods priced far above their value and make to equal the dollar volume of our honest exports, and to kill or reduce our favorite balance of trade. As Agents of the foreign central banks the Fed try by every means in their power to reduce our favorable balance of trade. They act for their foreign principal and they accept fees from foreigners for acting against the best interests of these United States. Naturally there has been great competition among among foreigners for the favors of the Fed.

"What we need to do is to send the reserves of our National Banks home to the people who earned and produced them and who still own them and to the banks which were compelled to surrender them to predatory interests.

"Mr. Chairman, there is nothing like the Fed pool of confiscated bank deposits in the world. It is a public trough of American wealth in which the foreigners claim rights, equal to or greater than Americans. The Fed are the agents of the foreign central banks. They use our bank depositors' money for the benefit of their foreign principals. They barter the public credit of the United States Government and hire it our to foreigners at a profit to themselves.

"All this is done at the expense of the United States Government, and at a sickening loss to the American people. Only our great wealth enabled us to stand the drain of it as long as we did.

"We need to destroy the Fed wherein our national reserves are impounded for the benefit of the foreigners. "We need to save America for Americans.

SPURIOUS SECURITIES

"Mr. Chairman, when you hold a $10.00 Fed Note in your hand, you are holding apiece of paper which sooner or later is going to cost the United States Government $10.00 in gold (unless the Government is obliged to go off the gold standard). It is based on limburger cheese (reported to be in foreign warehouses) or in cans purported to contain peas (but may contain salt water instead), or horse meat, illicit drugs, bootleggers fancies, rags and bones from Soviet Russia (of which these United States imported over a million dollars worth last year), on wines whiskey, natural gas, goat and dog fur, garlic on the string, and Bombay ducks.

"If you like to have paper money- which is secured by such commodities- you have it in Fed Note. If you desire to obtain the thing of value upon which this paper currency is based, that is, the limburger cheese, the whiskey, the illicit drugs, or any of the other staples- you will have a very hard time finding them.

"Many of these worshipful commodities are in foreign Countries. Are you going to Germany to inspect her warehouses to see if the specified things of value are there? I think more, I do not think that you would find them there if you did go.

"On April 27, 1932, the Fed outfit sent $750,000 belonging to American bank depositors in gold to Germany. A week later another $300,000 in gold was shipped to Germany. About the middle of May $12,000,000 in gold was shipped to Germany by the Fed. Almost every week there is a shipment of gold to Germany. These shipments are not made for profit on the exchange since the German marks are blow parity with the dollar.

"Mr. Chairman, I believe that the National Bank depositors of these United States have a right to know what the Fed are doing with their money. There are millions of National Bank depositors in the Country who do not know that a percentage of every dollar they deposit in a Member Bank of the Fed goes automatically to American Agents of the foreign banks and that all their deposits can be paid away to foreigners without their knowledge or consent by the crooked machinery of the Fed and the questionable practices of the Fed.

[Ed. Note- Problem with next paragraph in original] "Mr. Chairman, the American people should be told the truth by their servants in office. In 1930, we had over a half billion dollars outstanding daily to finance foreign goods stored in or shipped between several billion dollars. What goods are these on which the Fed yearly pledge several billions of dollars. In its yearly total, this item amounts to several billions of dollars of the public credit of these United States?

"What goods are those which are hidden in European and Asiatic stores have not been seen by any officer of our Government but which are being financed on the public credit of the United States Government? What goods are those upon which the 17 United States Government is being obligated by the Fed to issue Fed Notes to the extent of several billions of dollars a year?

The Bankers' Acceptance Racket

"The Fed have been International Banks from the beginning, with these United States as their enforced banker and supplier of currency. But it is none the less extraordinary to see these these twelve private credit monopolies, buying the debts of foreigners against foreigners, in all parts of the world and asking the Government of these United States for new issues of Fed notes in exchange for them. "The magnitude of the acceptance racket as it has been developed by the Fed, their foreign correspondents, and the predatory European born bankers, who set up the Fed here and taught your own, by and of pirates, how to loot the people: I say the magnitude of this racket is estimated to be in the neighborhood of 9,000,000,000 per year. In the past ten years it is said to have amounted to $90,000,000,000.00. In my opinion it has amounted to several times that much. coupled to this you have to the extent of billions of dollars, the gambling in the United States securities, which takes place in the same open discount market- a gambling on which the Fed is now spending $100,000,000.00 per week.

"Fed Notes are taken from the U.S. Government in unlimited quantities. Is is strange that the burden of supplying these immense sums of money to the gambling fraternity has at last proved too heavy for the American people to endure? Would it not be a national [calamity to] again bind down this burden on the backs of the American people and by means of a long rawhide whip of the credit masters, compel them to enter another seventeen years of slavery?

"They are trying to do that now. They are trying to take $100,000,000.00 of the public credit of the United States every week, in addition to all their other seizures and they are sending that money to the nefarious open market in a desperate gamble to reestablish their graft as a going concern.

"They are putting the United States Government in debt to the extent of $100,000,000 a week, and with the money they are buying our Government securities for themselves and their foreign principals. Our people are disgusted with the experiences of the Fed. The Fed is not producing a loaf of bread, a yard of cloth, a bushel of corn, or a pile of cordwood by its check-kiting operations in the money market.

"Mr. Speaker, on the 13th of January of this year I addressed the House on the subject of the Reconstruction Finance Corporation. In the course of my remarks I made the following statement: In 1928 the member banks of the Fed borrowed $60,598,690,000. from the Fed on their fifteen-day promissory notes. Think of it. Sixty billion dollars payable on demand in gold in the course of one single year. The actual amount of such obligations called for six times as much monetary gold as there is in the world. Such transactions represent a grant in the course of one single years of about $7,000,000 to every member of the Fed.

"Is it any wonder that American labor which ultimately pays the cost of all banking operations of this Country has at last proved unequal to the task of supplying this huge total of cash and credit for the benefit of the stock market manipulators and foreign swindlers? "In 1933 the Fed presented the staggering amount of $60,598,690,000 to its member banks at the expense of the wage earners and tax payers of these United States. In 1929, the year of the stock market crash, the Fed advanced $58,000,000,000 to member banks.

"In 1930 while the speculating banks were getting out of the stock market at the expense of the general public, the Fed advanced them $13,022,782,000. This shows that when the banks were gambling on the public credit of these United States as represented by the Fed currency they were subsidized to any amount they required by the Fed. When the swindle began to fall, the bankers knew it in advance and withdrew from the market. They got out with whole skins- and left the people of these United States to pay the piper. "My friend from Kansas, Mr. McGugin, has stated that he thought the Fed lent money on rediscounting. So they do, but they lend comparatively little that way. The real discounting that they do has been called a mere penny in the slot business. It is too slow for genuine high flyers. They discourage it. They prefer to subsidize their favorite banks by making them $60,000,000,000 advances and they prefer to acquire assistance in the notorious open discount market in New York, where they can use it to control the price of stocks and bonds on the exchanges.

"For every dollar they advanced on discounts in 1928, they lent $33.00 to their favorite banks for whom they do a business of several billion dollars income tax on their profits to these United States.

The John Law Swindle

"This is the John Law swindle over again. The theft of Teapot Dome was trifling compared to it. What King ever robbed his subject to such an extent as the Fed has robbed us? Is it any wonder that there have been lately ninety cases of starvation in one of the New York hospitals? Is there any wonder that the children are being abandoned?

"The government and the people of these United States have been swindled by swindlers deluxe to whom the acquisition of American or a parcel of Fed Notes presented no more difficulty than the drawing up of a worthless acceptance in a Country not subject to the laws of these United States, by sharpers not subject to the jurisdiction of these United States, sharpers with strong banking "fence" on this side of the water, a "fence" acting as a receiver of a worthless paper coming from abroad, endorsing it and getting the currency out of the Fed for it as quickly as possible exchanging that currency for gold and in turn transmitting the gold to its foreign confederates.

Ivar Krueger, the Match King

"Such were the exploits of Ivar Krueger, Mr. Hoover's friend, and his rotten Wall Street bakers. Every dollar of the billions Kreuger and his gang drew out of this Country on acceptances was drawn from the government and the people of the United States through the Fed. The credit of the United States Government was peddled to him by the Fed for their own private gain. That is what the Fed has been doing for many years.

"They have been peddling the credit of this Government and the [signature of this] Government to the swindlers and speculators of all nations. That is what happens when a Country forsakes its

292

Constitution and gives its sovereignty over the public currency to private interests. Give them the flag and they will sell it.

"The nature of Kreuger's organized swindle and the bankrupt condition of Kreuger's combine was known here last June when Hoover sought to exempt Krueger's loan to Germany of $125,000,000 from the operation of the Hoover Moratorium. The bankrupt condition of Krueger's swindle was known her last summer when $30,000,000 was taken from the American taxpayers by certain bankers in New York for the ostensible purpose of permitting Krueger to make a loan to Colombia. Colombia never saw that money.

"The nature of Krueger's swindle was known here in January when he visited his friend, Mr. Hoover, at the White House. It was known here in March before he went to Paris and committed suicide.

"Mr. Chairman, I think the people of the United States are entitled to know how many billions of dollars were placed at the disposal of Krueger and his gigantic combine by the Fed, and to know how much of our Government currency was issued and lost in the financing of that great swindle in the years during which the Fed took care of Krueger's requirements.

"A few days ago, the President of the United States with a white face and shaking hands, went before the Senate of behalf of the moneyed interests and asked the Senate to levy a tax on the people so that foreigners might know that these United States would pay its debt to them.

"Most Americans thought it was the other way around. What does these United States owe foreigners? When and by whom was the debt incurred? It was incurred by the Fed, when they peddled the signature of the Government to foreigners- for a Price. It is what the United States Government has to pay to redeem the obligations of the Fed.

Thieves Go Scot Free

"Are you going to let these thieves get off scot free? Is there one law for the looter who drives up to the door of the United States Treasury in his limousine and another for the United States Veterans who are sleeping on the floor of a dilapidated house on the outskirts of Washington?

"The Baltimore and Ohio Railroad is here asking for a large loan from the people, and the wage earners and the taxpayers of these United States. It is begging for a handout from the Government. It is standing, cap in hand, at the door of the R.F.C. where all the jackals have gathered to the feast. It is asking for money that was raised from the people by taxation and wants this money of the poor for the benefit of Kuhn, Loeb and Co., the German International Bankers.

"Is there one law for the Baltimore and Ohio Railroad and another for the hungry veterans it threw off its freight cars the other day? Is there one law for sleek and prosperous swindlers who call themselves bankers and another law for the soldiers who defended the flag? "The R.F.C. is taking over these worthless securities from the Investment Trusts with United States Treasury money at the expense of the American taxpayer and the wage earner.

"It will take twenty years to redeem our Government. Twenty years of penal servitude to pay off the gambling debts of the traitorous Fed and to vast flood of American wages and savings, bank deposits, and the United States Government credit which the Fed exported out of this country to their foreign principals.

"The Fed lately conducted an anti-hoarding campaign here. They they took that extra money which they had persuaded the American people to put into the banks- they sent it to Europe- along with the rest. In the last several months, they have sent $1,300,000,000 in gold to their foreign employers, their foreign masters, and every dollar of that gold belonged to the people of these United States and was unlawfully taken from them.

Fiat Money

"Mr. Chairman, within the limits of the time allowed me, I cannot enter into a particularized discussion of the Fed. I have singled out the Fed currency for a few remarks because there has lately been some talk here of "fiat money". What kind of money is being pumped into the open discount market and through it into foreign channels and stock exchanges? Mr. Mills of the Treasury has spoken here of his horror of the printing presses and his horror of dishonest money. He has no horror of dishonest money. If he had, he would be no party to the present gambling of the Fed in the nefarious open discount market of New York, a market in which the sellers are represented by 10 discount corporations owned and organized by the very banks which own and control the Fed.

"Fiat money, indeed?

"What Mr. Mills is fighting for is the preservation, whole and entire, of the banker's monopoly of all the currency of the United States Government.

"Mr. Chairman, last December, I introduced a resolution here asking for an examination and an audit of the Fed and all related matters. If the House sees fit to make such an investigation, the people of these United States will obtain information of great value. This is a Government of the people, by the people, for the people. Consequently, nothing should be concealed from the people. The man who deceives the people is a traitor to these United States.

"The man who knows or suspects that a crime has been committed and who conceals and covers up that crime is an accessory to it. Mr. Speaker, it is a monstrous thing for this great nation of people to have its destinies presided over by a traitorous government board acting in secret concert with international usurers.

"Every effort has been made by the Fed to conceal its powers- but the truth is- the Fed has usurped the Government. It controls everything here and it controls all of our foreign relations. It makes and breaks governments at will.

"No man and no body of men is more entrenched in power than the arrogant credit monopoly which operated the Fed. What National Government has permitted the Fed to steal from the people should now be restored to the people. The people have a valid claim against the Fed. If that claim is enforced the Americans will not need to stand in the bread line, or to suffer and die of starvation in the streets. Women will be saved, families will be kept together, and American children will not be dispersed and abandoned.

"Here is a Fed Note. Immense numbers of the notes are now held abroad. I am told that they amount to upwards of a billion dollars. They constitute a claim against our Government and likewise a claim against our peoples' money to the extent of $1,300,000,000 which has within the last few months been shipped abroad to redeem Fed Notes and to pay other gambling debts of the traitorous Fed. The greater part of our money stock has been shipped to other lands.

"Why should we promise to pay the debts of foreigners to foreigners? Why should the Fed be permitted to finance our competitors in all parts of the world? Do you know why the tariff was raised? It was raised to shut out the flood of Fed Goods pouring in here from every quarter of the globe- cheap goods, produced by cheaply paid foreign labor, on unlimited supplies of money and credit sent out of this Country by the dishonest and unscrupulous Fed.

"The Fed are spending $100,000,000 a week buying government securities in the open market and are making a great bid for foreign business. They are trying to make rates so attractive that the human hair merchants and the distillers and other business entities in foreign land will come her and hire more of the public credit of the United States Government to pay the Fed outfit for getting it for them.

World Enslavement Planned

"Mr. Chairman, when the Fed was passed, the people of these United States did not perceive that a world system was being set up here which would make the savings of the American school teacher available to a narcotic-drug vendor in Acapulco. They did not perceive that these United States was to be lowered to the position of a coolie country which has nothing but raw material and heart, that Russia was destined to supply the man power and that this country was to supply the financial power to an "international superstate". A superstate controlled by international bankers, and international industrialists acting together to enslave the world for their own pleasure?

"The people of these United States are being greatly wronged. They have been driven from their employments. They have been dispossessed from their homes. They have been evicted from their rented quarters. They have lost their children. They have been left to suffer and die for lack of shelter, food, clothing and medicine.

"The wealth of these United States and the working capital have been taken away from them and has either been locked in the vaults of certain banks and the great corporations or exported to foreign countries for the benefit of the foreign customers of these banks and corporations. So far as the people of the United States are concerned, the cupboard is bare.

"It is true that the warehouses and coal yards and grain elevators are full, but these are padlocked, and the great banks and corporations hold the keys.

"The sack of these United States by the Fed is the greatest crime in history.

"Mr. Chairman, a serious situation confronts the House of Representatives today. We are trustees of the people and the rights of the people are being taken away from them. Through the Fed the people are losing the rights guaranteed to them by the Constitution. Their property has been taken from them without due process of law. Mr. Chairman, common decency requires us to examine the public accounts of the Government and see what crimes against the public welfare have been committed.

"What is needed here is a return to the Constitution of these United States.

"The old struggle that was fought out here in Jackson's time must be fought our over again. The independent United States Treasury should be reestablished and the Government should keep its own money under lock and key in the building the people provided for that purpose.

"Asset currency, the devise of the swindler, should be done away with. The Fed should be abolished and the State boundaries should be respected. Bank reserves should be kept within the boundaries of the States whose people own them, and this reserve money of the people should be protected so that the International Bankers and acceptance bankers and discount dealers cannot draw it away from them.

"The Fed should be repealed, and the Fed Banks, having violated their charters, should be liquidated immediately. Faithless Government officials who have violated their oaths of office should be impeached and brought to trial.

"Unless this is done by us, I predict, that the American people, outraged, pillaged, insulted and betrayed as they are in their own land, will rise in their wrath, and will sweep the money changers out of the temple.

"Mr. Chairman, the United States is bankrupt: It has been bankrupted by the corrupt and dishonest Fed. It has repudiated its debts to its own citizens. Its chief foreign creditor is Great Britain, and a British bailiff has been at the White House and the British Agents are in the United States Treasury making inventory arranging terms of liquidations!

Great Britain, Partner in Blackmail

"Mr. Chairman, the Fed has offered to collect the British claims in full from the American public by trickery and corruption, if Great Britain will help to conceal its crimes. The British are shielding their agents, the Fed, because they do not wish that system of robbery to be destroyed here. They wish it to continue for their benefit! By means of it, Great Britain has become the financial mistress of the world. She has regained the position she occupied before the World War.

"For several years she has been a silent partner in the business of the Fed. Under threat of blackmail, or by their bribery, or by their native treachery to the people of the United States, the officials in charge of the Fed unwisely gave Great Britain immense gold loans running into hundreds of millions of dollars. They did this against the law! Those gold loans were not single transactions. They gave Great Britain a borrowing power in the United States of billions. She squeezed billions out of this Country by means of her control of the Fed.

"As soon as the Hoover Moratorium was announced, Great Britain moved to consolidate her gains. After the treacherous signing away of American rights at the 7-power conference at London in July, 1931, which put the Fed under the control of the Bank of International Settlements, Great Britain began to tighten the hangman's noose around the neck of the United States.

"She abandoned the gold standard and embarked on a campaign of buying up the claims of foreigners against the Fed in all parts of the world. She has now sent her bailiff, Ramsey MacDonald, here to get her war debt to this country canceled. But she has a club in her hands! She has title to the gambling debts which the corrupt and dishonest Fed incurred abroad.

"Ramsey MacDonald, the labor party deserter, has come here to compel the President to sign on the dotted line, and that is what Roosevelt is about to do! Roosevelt will endeavor to conceal the nature of his action from the American people. But he will obey the International Bankers and transfer the war debt that Great Britain should pay to the American people, to the shoulders of the American taxpayers.

"Mr. Chairman, the bank holiday in the several States was brought about by the corrupt and dishonest Fed. These institutions manipulated money and credit, and caused the States to order bank holidays.

"These holidays were frame-ups! "They were dress rehearsals for the national bank holiday which Franklin D. Roosevelt promised Sir Ramsey MacDonald that he would declare.

"There was no national emergency here when Franklin D. Roosevelt took office excepting the bankruptcy of the Fed- a bankruptcy which has been going on under cover for several years and which has been concealed from the people so that the people would continue to permit their bank deposits and their bank reserves and their gold and the funds of the United States Treasury to be impounded in these bankrupt institutions.

"Under cover, the predatory International Bankers have been stealthily transferring the burden of the Fed debts to the people's Treasury and to the people themselves. They the farms and the homes of the United States to pay for their thievery! That is the only national emergency that there has been here since the depression began.

"The week before the bank holiday ws declared in New York State, the deposits in the New York savings banks were greater than the withdrawals. There were no runs on New York Banks. There was no need of a bank holiday in New York, or of a national holiday.

Roosevelt and the International Bankers

"Roosevelt did what the International Bankers ordered him to do!

"Do not deceive yourself, Mr. Chairman, or permit yourself to be deceived by others into the belief that Roosevelt's dictatorship is in any way intended to benefit the people of the United States: he is preparing to sign on the dotted line! "He is preparing to cancel the war debts by fraud!

"He is preparing to internationalize this Country and to destroy our Constitution itself in order to keep the Fed intact as a money institution for foreigners. "Mr. Chairman, I see no reason why citizens of the United States should be terrorized into surrendering their property to the International Bankers who own and control the Fed. The statement that gold would be taken from its lawful owners if they did not voluntarily surrender it, to private interests, show that there is an anarchist in our Government.

"The statement that it is necessary for the people to give their gold- the only real money- to the banks in order to protect the currency, is a statement of calculated dishonesty!

"By his unlawful usurpation of power on the night of March 5, 1933, and by his proclamation, which in my opinion was in violation of the Constitution of the United States, Roosevelt divorced the currency of the United States from gold, and the United States currency is no longer protected by gold. It is therefore sheer dishonesty to say that the people's gold is needed to protect the currency.

"Roosevelt ordered the people to give their gold to private interests- that is, to banks, and he took control of the banks so that all the gold and gold values in them, or given into them, might be handed over to the predatory International Bankers who own and control the Fed.

"Roosevelt cast his lot with the usurers. "He agreed to save the corrupt and dishonest at the expense of the people of the United States.

"He took advantage of the people's confusion and weariness and spread the dragnet over the United States to capture everything of value that was left in it. He made a great haul for the International Bankers.

"The Prime Minister of England came here for money! He came here to collect cash!

"He came here with Fed Currency and other claims against the Fed which England had bought up in all parts of the world. And he has presented them for redemption in gold.

"Mr. Chairman, I am in favor of compelling the Fed to pay their own debts. I see no reason why the general public should be forced to pay the gambling debts of the International Bankers.

Roosevelt Seizes the Gold

"By his action in closing the banks of the United States, Roosevelt seized the gold value of forty billions or more of bank deposits in the United States banks. Those deposits were deposits of gold values. By his action he has rendered them payable to the depositors in paper only, if payable at all, and the paper money he proposes to pay out to bank depositors and to the people generally in lieu of their hard earned gold values in itself, and being based on nothing into which the people can convert it the said paper money is of negligible value altogether.

"It is the money of slaves, not of free men. If the people of the United States permit it to be imposed upon them at the will of their credit masters, the next step in their downward progress will be their acceptance of orders on company stores for what they eat and wear. Their case will be similar to that of starving coal miners. They, too, will be paid with orders on Company stores for food and clothing, both of indifferent quality and be forced to live in Company-owned houses from which they may be evicted at the drop of a hat. More of them will be forced into conscript labor camps under supervision.

"At noon on the 4th of March, 1933, FDR with his hand on the Bible, took an oath to preserve, protect and defend the Constitution of the U.S. At midnight on the 5th of March, 1933, he confiscated the property of American citizens. He took the currency of the United States standard of value. He repudiated the internal debt of the Government to its own citizens. He destroyed the value of the American dollar. He released, or endeavored to release, the Fed from their contractual liability to redeem Fed currency in gold or lawful money on a parity with gold. He depreciated the value of the national currency.

"The people of the U.S. are now using unredeemable paper slips for money. The Treasury cannot redeem that paper in gold or silver. The gold and silver of the Treasury has unlawfully been given to the corrupt and dishonest Fed. And the Administration has since had the effrontery to raid the country for more gold for the private interests by telling our patriotic citizens that their gold is needed to protect the currency.

"It is not being used to protect the currency! It is being used to protect the corrupt and dishonest Fed. "The directors of these institutions have committed criminal offense against the United States Government, including the offense of making false entries on their books, and the still more serious offense of unlawfully abstracting funds from the United States Treasury! "Roosevelt's gold raid is intended to help them out of the pit they dug for themselves when they gambled away the wealth and savings of the American people.

Dictatorship

"The International Bankers set up a dictatorship here because they wanted a dictator who would protect them. They wanted a dictator who would protect them. They wanted a dictator who would issue a proclamation giving the Fed an absolute and unconditional release from their special currency in gold, or lawful money of any Fed Bank.

"Has Roosevelt relieved any other class of debtors in this country from the necessity of paying their debts? Has he made a proclamation telling the farmers that they need not pay their mortgages? Has he made a proclamation to the effect that mothers of starving children need not pay their milk bills? Has he made a proclamation relieving householders from the necessity of paying rent?

Roosevelt's Two Kinds of Laws

"Not he! He has issued one kind of proclamation only, and that is a proclamation to relieve international bankers and the foreign debtors of the United States Government.

"Mr. Chairman, the gold in the banks of this country belongs to the American people who have paper money contracts for it in the form of national currency. If the Fed cannot keep their contracts with United States citizens to redeem their paper money in gold, or lawful money, then the Fed must be taken over by the United States Government and their officers must be put on trial.

"There must be a day of reckoning. If the Fed have looted the Treasury so that the Treasury cannot

http://user.icx.net/~drherb/mcfaddenfrb.html

7/29/02

300

redeem the United States currency for which it is liable in gold, then the Fed must be driven out of the Treasury.

"Mr. Chairman, a gold certificate is a warehouse receipt for gold in the Treasury, and the man who has a gold certificate is the actual owner of a corresponding amount of gold stacked in the Treasury subject to his order.

"Now comes Roosevelt who seeks to render the money of the United States worthless by unlawfully declaring that it may No Longer be converted into gold at the will of the holder.

"Roosevelt's next haul for the International Bankers was the reduction in the pay of all Federal employees.

"Next in order are the veterans of all wars, many of whom are aged and inform, and other sick and disabled. These men had their lives adjusted for them by acts of Congress determining the amounts of the pensions, and, while it is meant that every citizen should sacrifice himself for the good of the United States, I see no reason why those poor people, these aged Civil War Veterans and war widows and half-starved veterans of the World War, should be compelled to give up their pensions for the financial benefit of the International vultures who have looted the Treasury, bankrupted the country and traitorously delivered the United States to a foreign foe.

"There are many ways of raising revenue that are better than that barbaric act of injustice.

"Why not collect from the Fed the amount they owe the U.S. Treasury in interest on all the Fed currency they have taken from the Government? That would put billions of dollars into the U.S. Treasury.

"If FDR is as honest as he pretends to be, he will have that done immediately. And in addition, why not compel the Fed to disclose their profits and to pay the Government its share?

"Until this is done, it is rank dishonesty to talk of maintaining the credit of the U.S. Government. "My own salary as a member of Congress has been reduced, and while I am willing to give my part of it that has been taken away from me to the U.S. Government, I regret that the U.S. has suffered itself to be brought so low by the vultures and crooks who are operating the roulette wheels and faro tables in the Fed, that is now obliged to throw itself on the mercy of its legislators and charwomen, its clerks, and it poor pensioners and to take money out of our pockets to make good the defalcations of the International Bankers who were placed in control of the Treasury and given the monopoly of U.S. Currency by the misbegotten Fed. "I am well aware that the International Bankers who drive up to the door of the United States Treasury in their limousines, look down with scorn upon members of Congress because we work for so little, while they draw millions a year. The difference is that we earn, or try to earn, what we get- and they steal the greater part of their takings.

Enemies of the People They Rob

"I do not like to see vivisections performed on human beings. I do not like to see the American people used for experimental purposes by the credit masters of the United States. They predicted among themselves that they would be able to produce a condition here in which American citizens would be completely humbled and left starving and penniless in the streets.

"The fact that they made that assertion while they were fomenting their conspiracy against the United States that they like to see a human being, especially an American, stumbling from hunger when he walks. "Something should be done about it, they say. Five-cent meals, or something! "But FDR will not permit the House of Representatives to investigate the condition of the Fed. FDR will not do that. He has certain International Bankers to serve. They not look to him as the man Higher Up who will protect them from the just wrath of an outraged people.

"The International Bankers have always hated our pensioners. A man with a small pension is a ward of the Government. He is not dependent upon them for a salary or wages. They cannot control him. They do not like him. It gave them great pleasure, therefore, to slash the veterans.

"But FDR will never do anything to embarrass his financial supporters. He will cover up the crimes of the Fed.

"Before he was elected, Mr. Roosevelt advocated a return to the earlier practices of the Fed, thus admitting its corruptness. The Democratic platform advocated a change in the personnel of the Fed. These were campaign bait. As a prominent Democrat lately remarked to me; "There is no new deal. The same old crowd is in control."

"The claims of foreign creditors of the Fed have no validity in law. The foreign creditors were the receivers- and the willing receivers- of stolen goods! They have received through their banking fences immense amounts of currency, and that currency was unlawfully taken from the United States Treasury by the Fed.

"England discovered the irregularities of the Fed quite early in its operations and through fear, apparently, the Fed have for years suffered themselves to be blackmailed and dragooning England to share in the business of the Fed. "The Fed have unlawfully taken many millions of dollars of the public credit of the United States and have given it to foreign sellers on the security of the Debt paper of foreign buyers in purely foreign transactions, and when the foreign buyers refused to meet their obligations and the Fed saw no honest way of getting the stolen goods back into their possession, they decided by control of the executive to make the American people pay their losses!

Conspiracy of War Debts

302

"They likewise entered into a conspiracy to deprive the people of the U.S. of their title to the war debts and not being able to do that in the way they intended, they are now engaged in an effort to debase the American dollar so that foreign governments will have their debts to this country cut in two, and then by means of other vicious underhanded arrangements, they propose to remit the remainder.

"So far as the U.S. is concerned, the gambling counters have no legal standing. The U.S. Treasury cannot be compelled to make good the gambling ventures of the corrupt and dishonest Fed. Still less should the bank deposits of the U.S. be used for that purpose. Still less should the national currency have been made irredeemable in gold so that the gold which was massed and stored to redeem the currency for American citizens may be used to pay the gambling debts of the Fed for England's benefit. "The American people should have their gold in their own possession where it cannot be held under secret agreement for any foreign control bank, or world bank, or foreign nation. Our own citizens have the prior claim to it. The paper [money men] have in their possession deserves redemption far more than U.S. currency and credit which was stolen from the U.S. Treasury and bootlegged abroad.

"Why should the foreigners be made preferred creditors of the bankrupt U.S.? Why should the U.S. be treated as bankrupt at all? This Government has immense sums due it from the Fed. The directors of these institutions are men of great wealth. Why should the guilty escape the consequences of their misdeeds? Why should the people of these U.S. surrender the value of their gold bank deposits to pay off the gambling debts of these bankers? Why should Roosevelt promise foreigners that the U.S. will play the part of a good neighbor, 'meeting its obligations'?

"Let the Fed meet their own obligations.

"Every member of the Fed should be compelled to disgorge, and every acceptance banker and every discount corporation which has made illegal profits by means of public credit unlawfully bootlegged out of the U.S. Treasury and hired out by the crooks and vultures of the Fed should be compelled to disgorge.

Federal Reserve Pays No Taxes

"Gambling debts due to foreign receivers of stolen goods should not be paid by sacrificing our title to our war debts, the assets of the U.S. Treasury- which belong to all the people of the U.S. and which it is our duty to preserve inviolate in the people's treasury.

"The U.S. Treasury cannot be made liable for them. The Fed currency must be redeemed by the Fed banks or else these Fed banks must be liquidated.

"We know from assertions made here by the Hon. John N. Garner, Vice-President of the U.S. that there is a condition in the [United States such] would cause American citizens, if they knew what it was, to lose all confidence in their government.

"That is a condition that Roosevelt will not have investigated. He has brought with him from Wall Street, James Warburg, the son of Paul M. Warburg. Mr. Warburg, alien born, and the son of an alien who did not become naturalized here until several years after this Warburg's birth, is a son of a former partner of Kuhn, Loeb and Co., a grandson of another partner, a nephew of a former partner, and a nephew of a present partner.

"He holds no office in our Government, but I am told that he is in daily attendance at the Treasury, and that he has private quarters there! In other words, Mr. Chairman, Kuhn, Loeb and Company now has control and occupy the U.S. Treasury.

Preferred Treatment for Foreigners

"The text of the Executive order which seems to place an embargo on shipments of gold permits the Secretary of the Treasury, a former director of the corrupt, to issue licenses at his discretion for the export of gold coin, or bullion, earmarked or held in trust for a recognized foreign government or foreign central bank for international settlement. Now, Mr. Chairman, if gold held in trust for those foreign institutions may be sent to them, I see no reason why gold held in trust for American as evidenced by their gold certificates and other currency issued by the U.S. Government should not be paid to them. "I think that American citizens should be entitled to treatment at least as good as that which the person is extending to foreign governments, foreign central banks, and the bank of International Settlements. I think a veteran of the world war, with a $20.00 gold certificate, is at least as much entitled to receive his own gold for it, as any international banker in the city of New York or London.

"By the terms of this executive order, gold may be exported if it is actually required, for the fulfillment of any contract entered into prior to the date of this order by an applicant who, in obedience to the executive order of April 5, 1933, has delivered gold coin, gold bullion, or gold certificates. "This means that gold may be exported to pay the obligations abroad of the Fed which were incurred prior to the date of the order, namely, April 20, 1933.

"If a European Bank should send 100,000,000 dollars in Fed currency to a bank in this country for redemption, that bank could easily ship gold to Europe in exchange for that currency. Such Fed currency would represent "contracts" entered into prior to the date of the order. If the Bank of International Settlements or any other foreign bank holding any of the present gambling debt paper of the Fed should draw a draft for the settlement of such obligation, gold would be shopped to them because the debt contract would have been entered into prior to the date of order.

Crimes and Criminals

"Mr. Speaker, I rise to a question of constitutional privilege.

"Whereas, I charge. . .Eugene Meyer, Roy A. Young, Edmund Platt, Eugene B. Black, Adolph Casper Miller, Charles S. Hamlin, George R. James, Andrew W. Mellon, Ogden L. Mills, William H. Woo W. Poole, J.F.T. O'Connor, members of the Federal Reserve Board; F. H. Curtis, J.H. Chane, R.L. Austin, George De Camp, L.B. Williams, W.W. Hoxton, Oscar Newton, E.M. Stevens, J.S. Wood, J.N. Payton, M.L. McClure, C.C. Walsh, Isaac B. Newton, Federal Reserve Agents, jointly and severally, with violations of the Constitution and laws of the United States, and whereas I charge them with having taken funds from the U.S Treasury which were not appropriated by the Congress of the United States, and I charge them with having unlawfully taken over $80,000,000,000 from the U.S. Government in the year 1928, the said unlawful taking consisting of the unlawful creation of claims against the U.S. Treasury to the extent of over $80,000,000,000 in the year 1928; and I charge them with similar thefts committed in 1929, 1930, 1931, 1932 and 1933, and in years previous to 1928, amounting to billions of dollars; and

"Whereas I charge them, jointly and severally with having unlawfully created claims against the U.S. Treasury by unlawfully placing U.S. Government credit in specific amounts to the credit of foreign governments and foreign central banks of issue; private interests and commercial and private banks of the U.S. and foreign countries, and branches of foreign banks doing business in the U.S., to the extent of billions of dollars; and with having made unlawful contracts in the name of the U.S. Government and the U.S. Treasury; and with having made false entries on books of account; and

"Whereas I charge them jointly and severally, with having taken Fed Notes from the U.S. Treasury and with having put Fed Notes into circulation without obeying the mandatory provision of the Fed Act which requires the Fed Board to fix an interest rate on all issues of Fed Notes supplied to Fed Banks, the interest resulting therefrom to be paid by the Fed Banks to the government of the U.S. for the use of the Fed Notes, and I charge them of having defrauded the U.S. Government and the people of the U.S. of billions of dollars by the commission of this crime, and

"Whereas I charge them, jointly and severally, with having purchased U.S. Government securities with U.S. Government credit unlawfully taken and with having sold the said U.S. Government securities back to the people of the U.S. for gold or gold values and with having again purchased U.S. Government securities with U.S. Government credit unlawfully taken and with having again sold the said U.S. Government security for gold or gold values, and I charge them with having defrauded the U.S. Government and the people of the U.S. by this rotary process; and

"Whereas I charge them, jointly and severally, with having unlawfully negotiated U.S. Government securities, upon which the Government liability was extinguished, as collateral security for Fed Notes and with having substituted such securities for gold which was being held as collateral security for Fed Notes, and with having by the process defrauded the U.S. Government and the people of the U.S., and I charge them with the theft of all the gold and currency they obtained by this process; and

"Whereas I charge them, jointly and severally, with having unlawfully issued Fed currency on false, worthless and fictitious acceptances and other circulating evidence of debt, and with having made unlawful advances of Fed currency, and with having unlawfully permitted renewals of acceptances and renewals of other circulating evidences of debt, and with having permitted acceptance bankers and discount dealer corporations and other private bankers to violate the banking laws of the U.S.; and

"Whereas I charge them, jointly and severally, with having conspired to have evidences of debt to the extent of $1,000,000,000 artificially created at the end of February, 1933, and early in March 1933, and with having made unlawful issues and advances of Fed currency on the security of said artificially created evidences of debt for a sinister purpose, and with having assisted in the execution of said sinister purpose; and

"Whereas I charge them, jointly and severally, with having brought about the repudiation of the currency obligations of the Fed Banks to the people of the U.S. and with having conspired to obtain a release for the Fed Board and the Fed Banks from their contractual liability to redeem all Fed currency in gold or lawful money at the Fed Bank and with having defrauded the holders of Fed currency, and with having conspired to have the debts and losses of the Fed Board and the Fed Banks unlawfully transferred to the Government and the people of the U.S., and

"Whereas I charge them, jointly and severally, with having unlawfully substituted Fed currency and other irredeemable paper currency for gold in the hands of the people after the decision to repudiate the Fed currency and the national currency was made known to them, and with thus having obtained money under false pretenses; and

"Whereas I charge them, jointly and severally, with having brought about a repudiation of the notes of the U.S. in order that the gold value of the said currency might be given to private interests, foreign governments, foreign central banks of issues, and the Bank of International Settlements, and the people of the U.S. to be left without gold or lawful money and with no currency other that a paper currency irredeemable in gold, and I charge them with having done this for the benefit of private interests, foreign governments, foreign central banks of issue, and the bank of International Settlements; and

"Whereas I charge them, jointly and severally, with conniving with the Edge Law banks, and other Edge Law institutions, accepting banks, and discount corporations, foreign central banks of issue, foreign commercial banks, foreign corporations, and foreign individuals with funds unlawfully taken from the U.S. Treasury; and I charge them with having unlawfully permitted and made possible 'new financing' for foreigners at the expense of the U.S. Treasury to the extent of billions of dollars and with having unlawfully permitted and made possible the bringing into the United States of immense quantities of foreign securities, created in foreign countries for export to the U.S. and with having unlawfully permitted the said foreign securities to be imported into the U.S. instead of gold, which was lawfully due to the U.S. on trade balances and otherwise, and with having lawfully permitted and facilitated the sale of the said foreign securities in the U.S., and

"Whereas I charge them, jointly and severally, with having unlawfully exported U.S. coins and currency for a sinister purpose, and with having deprived the people of the U.S. of their lawful medium of exchange, and I charge them with having arbitrarily and unlawfully reduced the amount of money and currency in circulation in the U.S. to the lowest rate per capita in the history of the Government, so that the great mass of the people have been left without a sufficient medium of exchange, and I charge them with concealment and evasion in refusing to make known the amount of U.S. money in coins and paper currency exported and the amount remaining in the U.S. as a result of which refusal the Congress of the U.S. is unable to ascertain where the U.S. coins and issues of currency are at the present time, and what amount of U.S. currency is now held abroad; and

"Whereas I charge them, jointly and severally, with having arbitrarily and unlawfully raised and lowered the rates of money and with having arbitrarily increased and diminished the volume of currency in circulation for the benefit of private interests at the expense of the Government and the people of the U.S. and with having unlawfully manipulated money rates, wages, salaries and property values both real and personal, in the U.S. by unlawful operations in the open discount market and by resale and repurchase agreements unsanctioned by law, and

"Whereas I charge them jointly and severally, with having brought about the decline in prices on the New York Stock Exchange and other exchanges in October, 1929, by unlawful manipulation of money rates and the volume of U.S. money and currency in circulation: by theft of funds from the U.S. Treasury by gambling in acceptances and U.S. Government securities; by service rendered to foreign and domestic speculators and politicians, and by unlawful sale of U.S. gold reserves abroad, and

"Whereas the unconstitutional inflation law imbedded in the so-called Farm Relief Act by which the Fed Banks are given permission to buy U.S. Government securities to the extent of $3,000,000,000 and to drew forth currency from the people's Treasury to the extent of $3,000,000,000 is likely to result in connivance on the part of said accused with others in the purchase by the Fed of the U.S. Government securities to the extent of $3,000,000,000 with U.S. Government's own credit unlawfully taken, it being obvious that the Fed do no not intend to pay anything of value to the U.S. Government for the said U.S. Government securities no provision for payment in gold or lawful money appearing in the so-called Farm Relief bill- and the U.S. Government will thus be placed in a position of conferring a gift of $3,000,000,000 in the U.S. Government securities on the Fed to enable them to pay more on their bad debts to foreign governments, foreign central banks of issue, private interests, and private and commercial banks, both foreign and domestic, and the Bank of International Settlements, and

"Whereas the U.S. Government will thus go into debt to the extent of $3,000,000,000 and will then have an additional claim of $3,000,000,000 in currency unlawfully created against it and whereas no private interest should be permitted to buy U.S. Government securities with the Government's own credit unlawfully taken and whereas currency should not be issued for the benefit of said private interest or any interests on U.S. Government securities so acquired, and whereas it has been publicly stated and not denied that the inflation amendment of the Farm Relief Act is the matter of benefit which was secured by Ramsey MacDonald, the Prime Minister of Great Britain, upon the occasion of his latest visit to the U.S. Treasury, and whereas there is grave danger that the accused will employ the provision creating U.S. Government securities to the extent of $3,000,000,000 and three millions in currency to be issuable thereupon for the benefit of themselves and their foreign principals, and that they will convert the currency so obtained to the uses of Great Britain by secret arrangements with the Bank of England of which they are the agents, and for which they maintain an account and perform services at the expense of the U.S. Treasury, and that they will likewise confer benefits upon the Bank of International Settlements for which they maintain an account and perform services at the expense of the U.S. Treasury; and

"Whereas I charge them, jointly and severally, with having concealed the insolvency of the Fed and with having failed to report the insolvency of the Fed to the Congress and with having conspired to have the said insolvent institutions continue in operation, and with having permitted the said insolvent institutions to receive U.S. Government funds and other deposits, and with having permitted them to exercise control over the gold reserves of the U.S. and with having permitted them to transfer upward of $100,000,000,000 of their debts and losses to the general public and the Government of the U.S., and with having permitted foreign debts of the Fed to be paid with the property, the savings, the wages, and the salaries of the people of the U.S. and with the farms and the homes of the American people, and whereas I charge them with forcing the bad debts of the Fed upon the general public covertly and dishonestly and and with taking the general wealth and savings of the people of the U.S. under false pretenses, to pay the debts of the Fed to foreigners; and

"Whereas I charge them, jointly and severally, with violations of the Fed Act and other laws; with maladministration of the h evasions of the Fed Law and other laws; and with having unlawfully failed to report violations of law on the part of the Fed Banks which, if known, would have caused the Fed Banks to lose their charters, and

"Whereas I charge them, jointly and severally, with failure to protect and maintain the gold reserves and the gold stock and gold coinage of the U.S. and with having sold the gold reserves of the U.S to foreign Governments, foreign central banks of issue, foreign commercial and private banks, and other foreign institutions and individuals at a profit to themselves, and I charge them with having sold gold reserves of the U.S. so that between 1924 and 1928 the U.S. gained no gold on net account but suffered a decline in its percentage of central gold reserves from the 45.9 percent in 1924 to 37.5 percent in 1928 notwithstanding the fact that the U.S. had a favorable balance of trade throughout that period, and

"Whereas I charge them, jointly and severally, with having conspired to concentrate U.S. Government securities and thus the national debt of the U.S. in the hands of foreigners and international money lenders and with having conspired to transfer to foreigners and international money lenders title to and control of the financial resources of the U.S.; and

"Whereas I charge them, jointly and severally, with having fictitiously paid installments on the national debt with Government credit unlawfully taken; and

"Whereas I charge them, jointly and severally, with the loss of the U.S. Government funds entrusted to their care; and

"Whereas I charge them, jointly and severally, with having destroyed independent banks in the U.S. and with having thereby caused losses amounting to billions of dollars to the said banks, and to the general public of the U.S., and

"Whereas I charge them, jointly and severally, with the failure to furnish true reports of the business operations and the true conditions of the Fed to the Congress and the people, and having furnished false and misleading reports to the congress of the U.S., and

"Whereas I charge them, jointly and severally, with having published false and misleading propaganda intended to deceive the American people and to cause the U.S. to lose its independence; and

"Whereas I charge them, jointly and severally, with unlawfully allowing Great Britain to share in the profits of the Fed at the expense of the Government and the people of the U.S.; and

"Whereas I charge them, jointly and severally, with having entered into secret agreements and illegal transactions with Montague Norman, Governor of the Bank of England; and

"Whereas I charge them, jointly and severally, with swindling the U.S. Treasury and the people of the U.S. in pretending to have received payment from Great Britain of the amount due on the British ware debt to the U.S. in December, 1932; and

"Whereas I charge them, jointly and severally, with having conspired with their foreign principals and others to defraud the U.S. Government and to prevent the people of the U.S. from receiving payment of the war debts due to the U.S. from foreign nations; and

309

"Whereas I charge them, jointly and severally, with having robbed the U.S Government and the people of the U.S. by their theft and sale of the gold reserves of the U.S. and other unlawful transactions created a deficit in the U.S. Treasury, which has necessitated to a large extent the destruction of our national defense and the reduction of the U.S. Army and the U.S. Navy and other branches of the national defense; and

"Whereas I charge them, jointly and severally, of having reduced the U.S. from a first class power to one that is dependent, and with having reduced the U.S. from a rich and powerful nation to one that is internationally poor; and

"Whereas I charge them, jointly and severally, with the crime of having treasonable conspired and acted against the peace and security of the U.S. and with having treasonable conspired to destroy constitutional Government in the U.S.

"Resolve, That the Committee on the Judiciary is authorized and directed as a whole or by subcommittee, to investigate the official conduct of the Fed agents to determine whether, in the opinion of the said committee, they have been guilty of any high crime or misdemeanor which in the contemplation the Constitution requires the interposition of the Constitutional powers of the House. Such Committee shall report its finding to the House, together with such resolution or resolutions of impeachment or other recommendations as it deems proper.

"For the purpose of this resolution the Committee is authorized to sit and act during the present Congress at such times and places in the District of Columbia or elsewhere, whether or not the House is sitting, has recessed or has adjourned, to hold such clerical, stenographic, and other assistants, to require of such witnesses and the production of such books, papers, and documents, to take such testimony, to have such printing and binding done, and to make such expenditures as it deems necessary."

After some discussion and upon the motion of Mr. Byrns, the resolution and charge was referred to the Committee on the Judiciary.

"Attacks on McFadden's Life Reported"

Commenting on Former Congressman Louis T. McFaddens's "heart-failure sudden-death" on Oct. 3, 1936, after a "dose" of "intestinal flu," "Pelley's Weekly" of Oct. 14 said:

Now that this sterling American patriot has made the Passing, it can be revealed that not long after his public utterance against the encroaching powers of Judah, it became known among his intimates that he had suffered two attacks against his life. The first attack came in the form of two revolver shots fired at him from ambush as he was alighting from a cab in front of one of the Capital hotels.

Public Notice

Affidavit of Fact; Declaring Factual Communications!

Dear Patriot,

I hereby present and declare that the following faxes and manuscripts, are true and correct copies of authentic articles, created by my hand, and submitted by fax, to President Bill Clinton. The first communication, (concerning Bosnia) was among dozens of purposeful submissions, that were faxed to Mr. Clinton, beginning May, Twenty Ninth, Nineteen Ninety Three A.D., Contact, (on my part) continued until January, Sixth of Two Thousand and One.

The following, are copies of faxes, revealing proof of origin, its' precise destination, and subject matter content of numerous submissions, delivered over the last eight years, to the Clinton administration, at fax number 202 456-2461, during that time period.

As of the time of this submission, there has been only one encounter (1993) with secret service agents, yet no constructive response from the Clinton administration. Yet, in his defense, I must add. Mr. Clinton addressed the problem in Haiti, and freed the people of years of inhumanity under a ruthless dictator. Mr. Clinton freed Bosnia. Mr. Clinton quelled the hostilities in Northern Ireland. He also "did" consult with Mr. Arafat, (recognizing the fact that the Palestinian lands "are" under invasion) which is evidence of a forthright concern for a suffering humanity.

On the other hand, the Bush administration, (George Jr.) bombed Iraq on his second day in office. He next, backed Sharon, after he defiantly marched into a recognized Palestinian Holy Place, and he continues to espouse a hard-line approach, on a victimized Palestinian populace.

For your information George; Mr. Arafat has attended every peace summit that was convened over the last twenty-five years, which is "a lot" more than I can say for you! You desperately need a "Reality Check", George, Yasar Arafat won the Nobel Peace Prize. You, George Jr. did not attend, even on your first opportunity, the peace summit in Africa, or the environmental summit addressing the Kyoto Treaty. You have shunned, and/or ignored your obvious duty, as a third party verifier to insure that peaceful measures were followed, to quell the inhumanity upon an invaded Palestinian people.

Israel is an invading force. Why do "you" condone, encourage, and supply the military armaments, used to carry out this horrible aggression on a people with a rightful claim to their land?

This Thirteenth day of March, in the year of our Lord, Two thousand and Three A.D.

kinko's
the copy center
14443 N. Dale Mabry Hwy.
Tampa, Florida 33618

Phone: (813) 961-5223
Fax: (813) 961-8518

NOTE:

fax cover sheet

Ronald E. Duncan Witness

FAX #: 202-456-2461   DATE: 5-29-03
TO: PRES. BILL CLINTON
COMPANY: WHITE Joh   5:24 pm
TELEPHONE: 202-456-1414

FROM: Eddie Duncan
COMPANY: Goldsmith Tree Service
TELEPHONE: 813-962-7315

You should have received __3__ pages including cover sheet.
Please call (813) 961-5223 if you are having problems or if you are
missing any pages. or call 813-(962-7315)

TRANSMISSION REPORT

THIS DOCUMENT WAS CONFIRMED
(REDUCED SAMPLE ABOVE - SEE DETAILS BELOW)

** COUNT **
TOTAL PAGES SCANNED   :   4
TOTAL PAGES CONFIRMED :   4

*** SEND ***

No.	REMOTE STATION	START TIME	DURATION	#PAGES	MODE	RESULTS
1	E O P	5-29-93 5:35PM	6'48"	4/ 4	48	COMPLETED 4800
		TOTAL	0:06'48"	4		

NOTE:
No. :	OPERATION NUMBER	48 :	4800BPS SELECTED	EC :	ERROR CORRECT	G2 :	G2-COMMUNICATION
PD :	POLLED BY REMOTE	SF :	STORE & FORWARD	RI :	RELAY INITIATE	RS :	RELAY STATION
MB :	SEND TO MAILBOX	PG :	POLLING A REMOTE	MP :	MULTI-POLLING	RM :	RECEIVE TO MEMORY

Arabelle Manga
5:41 p.m.
5/29/93

Mr. Clinton,   5/22/93

I realize that you are a busy man so I will be brief. Obviously the situation in Bosnia is an either or situation. If faced with no option other than to commit help, I suggest air support only. The least amount of innocent souls subjected to violence, the better.

Warriors and conquerors have chosen bloodshed and despair, and therefore carry it in their hearts. It is not for you to know the hearts of men. But wars fought on an even field are short and complete. Do not try to win it or control it. Your best option is to make it as even a standoff as your influence will effect, without committal of innocent souls to war.

Dear Sir, That is only a suggestion. It is not the only reason for this writing. The main reason is to suggest a jobs' plan, to fulfill a true need, (Eliminating Hunger!!!) and a true purpose(Brotherhood).

If you are determined to enlist homosexuals in the military, I suggest that a corps be established for them. I believe that enlistment into the "Provider Corp" would symbolize their sexual orientation and give them a worthy cause and corp on which they, and people of all preferences, can draw incentive.

An Eternal Friend
Eddie Numan

TRANSMIT CONFIRMATION REPORT

```
NO.            :   003
RECEIVER       :            202 456 2461
TRANSMITTER    :
DATE           :      FEB 11 '95   17:05
DURATION       :   02'45
MODE           :        STD
PAGES          :   03
 RESULT        :   OK
```

Dear Mr. President,   2 / 3 / 95

      I am delighted to be able to take this time to convey to you my deepest thanks for your decisive, yet sensitive actions regarding Haiti, and the murders and abuses going on there. Even though the Republicans had chosen,(for years) to ignore these people and were choosing to do so again. Even, as innocent children were being killed, in each new night. How could someone in power choose to ignore such injustice?

      We are honored to have such a thoughtful, caring and decisive man coordinating our mission. Know that brotherhood does not end at our borders. Giving honor to humanity brings its own justification.

      Your sensitive concern and your meaningful actions, show a true depth of concern for the value of humanity. Picture the smiles on the millions of faces that were freed from the terror of nightfall, and found their childhood once again.

      All will know the rewards of their efforts.(your deeds are fulfilled) As referenced in the Bible; I shall give you the desires of your heart.

      Dear Mr. Clinton, we are a fortunate nation to have such a humanitarian and visionary in such a position of power. We know that you have faced issues as complex as Travelgate, haircut, and plain old hypocritical resistance from envious people not in power. (hold true)

      At this point in time, I would like to take this opportunity to suggest the return of the soup kitchen. A place where foods can be donated and our hungry can be fed. This would not only coordinate efforts in serving a true need in an efficient, effective and productive way.(by placing hot food in front of a hungry face). It would also effectively eliminate a list of bachelors from the food stamp program. Re-invent government! Replace food stamps with food.

PS- Al Capone became a hero of people, when He opened a few soup kitchens. Hunger "IS" and always will be, "a constant need".

An Eternal Friend,
Eddie Duncan

Dear Sir,   3-15-96

     The republicans do not realize that the survival of a superfluous government, should not be at the expense of its' neediest peoples. The purpose of a democratic government is to provide for the common defense, and to secure and maintain the health and prosperity of its' peoples. Not for sake, of a government, itself.

     Sacrifice, must be made by a superfluous, wasteful, "federal" government, not by the needy people, it is to serve. Beauraucrats have plundered the public coffers, and neglected the needy, much too long! Example in point;

     After the hurricane hit Homestead, Florida. There were many days that the republicans took no action whatsoever. It seems that they simply chose to ignore the disastrous aftermath of a deadly storm, which weather radar had tracked for weeks. It is bewildering, why it took so long for them to send help?

     Three or four days after the storm had made landfall, the (Bush Administration) federal government, had made no effort to help. The really appalling evidence of their lack of concern was made clear by the camera footage of a news helicopter flying over the devastated area days later. Below them (and their camera lens) was a rooftop where survivors had created the sign: SEND HELP!

     I remind you that the film was taken three to five days after landfall, and after the storm had been tracked for weeks. They ignored the problem! They simply chose to ignore the problem! Much in the same way that they ignored the murders and abuses in Haiti.

     Thank you sir, for your time and attention. I would also like to thank you for the many humanitarian efforts you've undertaken. (Hold True!)

PS- I hope that the hurricane aftermath footage gives our people a true perspective of the republican priorities and agenda.

Thank You Sir,
For All That You Have Done,
And All That You Will Do!
An Eternal Friend,
Quey Quay

```
*****************************************************************************
*                                                                P.01      *
*                      TRANSACTION REPORT                                   *
*                      _____          MAY- 7-97 WED  2:53 PM     *
*                                                                           *
*           FOR: POSTAL BOXES HOU          4675511                          *
*_____*
*   DATE    START  RECEIVER          TX TIME PAGES TYPE        NOTE         *
*_____*
*  MAY- 7  2:51 PM 12024562461         1'34"   2  SEND         OK           *
*                                                                           *
*****************************************************************************
```

5/5/97

Dear Mr. President,

   Your message of education, training, and volunteering, is a rational
approach to caring, not only for our young, also our homeless and unemployeed.
Yet, the inescapable question remains. Where shall our homelesss, hungry and
needy go? Where shall our volunteers and the promise of Americorp begin?
   I suggest that Americorp and other volunteer organizations coordinate
their efforts in the same manner used by a caring Brazilian couple, to protect,
feed, and educate, 102 desparate Brazilian street children. This loving family
reached out to those hungry, lonely, children. Why? Because their heart willed it.
Now,their love for their fellow man is very obvious, by the number of loving
children about them.
   Yet, there is another reason that this family was able to help so many
children. LOCATION!!! They live on a farm. We should build Americorp Farms
across the nation. A safe haven where those in need can be sheltered and taught,
and those who want to help will be in a position to do so. Farming is the way to
insure that this country reaches its full potential. History reveals that the greatest
of all civilizations grew from their mastery of farming. The Aztecs, the Egyptian,the
communal farms of the Soviet Union, even the nameless Brazilian farming family,
raising 102 adopted children, show us that it will work.
   The promise of a successful farming community is many things. First and
foremost is, more food for the worlds' hungry. Employment for our homeless and
unemployeed, and a demand for machinery and housing in new farming
communities. Where, I repeat, Where!!! the promise of a threatened youth can
grow into his or her, God given potential. Where planned diversity can grow and
flourish. The promise of Americorp is where You put it! Build it and they will come!
The needy, the workers,the volunteers, and the sponsors.
   Yet, the promise that I clearly see, is the promise of nature and the lovely
garden in which we have been placed. The Bible says; The duty of man is to live in
the garden and to keep it. Be a wise stuart of our precious earth.

                              Your Eternal Friend,

                              Eddie Duncan

PS- Please send any response to fax# (713)802-0489
PS- Please feel free to call.- hm# (713) 984-8213

PS- We will all be better off, when we're all better off!

Thank You, Mr. Clinton. Your Eternal Friend, Eddie Duncan

```
********************
***   TX REPORT   ***
********************

TRANSMISSION OK

TX/RX NO              3912
CONNECTION TEL                  12024562461
SUBADDRESS
CONNECTION ID        WHITE HOUSE MAIL
ST. TIME             11/03 19:09
USAGE T              02'29
PGS. SENT                5
RESULT               OK
```

kinko's
Express Yourself.

Fax Cover Sheet

479 Sawdust Rd. • Spring, Texas 77380 • 281-364-7898 Phone • 281-364-7991 Fax

Date: 11-03-00 - 6:57PM.   Number of Pages 4

TO:

Name: Al Gore

Company: U.S. Government

Telephone: listed

Fax: 202-456-2461

FROM:

Name: Eddie Duncan - Quey Quay

Company: True Savers + Assoc.

Telephone: 936-445-1164

Fax: 936-264-4502

Comments: E.MAIL - QuayQuay.HotLINE.COM

More than 900 locations worldwide. For the location nearest you, call 1-800-2-kinkos

Mr. Clinton, Mr. Gore,

I wholeheartedly suggest that you address the Middle East problem by referring to Isaiah. Read the book of Isaiah! Some other suggestions for Mr. Gore; point out the following:

1. Campaign financing is the number one problem in the American political process. It is the method that effectively eliminates public access of qualified candidates that can not afford established methods. The use of public access television for all political campaigns will solve the number one problem in American politics.

2. In the first debate you, (Mr. Gore) replied to the question of campaign finance reform by declaring your intentions to sign the McCain Feingold bill as your first act as president. Amen!

3. When Bush was asked about the campaign finance reform bills, he could not even pronounce it. He called it campaign fund reform, twice! He also, incorrectly called it a first amendment right. Is it, his right to be lobbied by billionaires? That could be why, it does not bother George Bush that Trent Lott and his small majority of Republicans, will not bring the issue of campaign finance reform to the floor of the Senate. They do not intend to debate or reform it. Quite the contrary, they will not even talk about it. The indebtedness of our legislators, "to financiers" prior to serving in our government, is yet to be addressed by the Republican majority, nor will it ever be!

4. Why do the Republicans not debate campaign finance reform? Because it works for them, yet hinders all public efforts. It is the policy and practice that gives the HMOS' so much pull with the Republicans, that when Mr. Clinton appealed for a National Healthcare Policy, the Republicans demonized it.

To me, the word national, in this case, meant inclusive, a health plan for all citizens. The Republicans insisted that a National Healthcare System would somehow be detrimental to public welfare. I cannot fathom how/why "establishing" a National Healthcare system would, somehow, be detrimental to public welfare? You have to be a repulsive con (Republican) to believe and endorse that logic. Eight years ago, Clinton called for a helping healthcare plan, but the Republicants propagandized it.

5. In the last eight years the Republicans have presented no plan, no suggestions, and no bill. Their majority have done nothing, concerning our nations' healthcare, yet are quite responsive in blaming the Clinton administration, for trying.

6. The policy they now endorse allows Canada, after fuel and shipping costs are incurred, to pay 30% of the cost, for the same pill, sold in America. Now, that is not illegal, what is illegal, is to return and sell the same pill to Americans, at Canadas' discounted rate. Now, that is illegal.

7. Big government is not a bad thing. Big government can help more people, if concerned, focused, and organized! Yet, in the name of eliminating "big government", the Republicans want to send public funds to their local constituents, with no strings attached! The Republicans demand accountability from our teachers and students, (after furnishing half the budget of the Democrats), but no accountability from their constituents, who now control the funds.

8. Speaking of school funds, the Republicans demand performance and accountability, even though they have allotted only half of the funding as the democratic proposal, and they intend to let their constituents decide the coarse of the other 45% of your school budget. Under Bushs' plan, we now have less, and his <u>constituents</u> now control it. They send you down the rosy path of local control, by the constituents of a man, who found the number one problem in America to be; his rich friends were not rich enough. So that was the problem, his budget addressed.

9. Your policy, Mr. Clinton, of releasing strategic oil reserves has proven to lower oil prices, and produced a strategic heating oil reserve, for the winter needs of our poor and elderly of the northern areas. The Republicans expounded a hypothetical threat, or breach of security, concerning military or national defense capabilities by using strategic oil reserves, yet, had no concern for the welfare of fellow citizens, subjected to freezing temperatures, and life threatening conditions.

10. To be a professional smear slinger, you must first understand the impact of certain words, attached to certain statements. The word "national" was attached to the healthcare bill, when the Republicans heard the word "national" they loaded their guns and shot it like a snake, then and now, eight years later, we still have no prescription drug benefit and no patients' bill of rights. Another word that a "professional smear slinger" might incorporate is "strategic"! Now, when that word is attached to "oil reserves", the Republicans can somehow ignore the fact that winter is only months away. They refused to find the compassion, or admit to, the logic of transferring the oil reserves, even after its diversion was proven to be beneficial for markets, and the distressed of the north. The Republicans called it a "Political Action". Political action is the applicable smear terminology, pertaining to a decision in which they disagreed, even though the decision proved to be beneficial to all consumers, and the elderly citizens in the north, needing heat for their homes. Mr. Clintons' act of compassion was deemed a "Political Action".

11. Mr. Gore, I suggest that we reduce our nuclear destruction capabilities, still funded at cold war levels. To what end? A Fried Planet! Lower the number of "hot" missile silos, until there are no more. Nuclear missiles are not needed to address tyrants, or terrorism. Redefine and re-invent military priorities! The money saved by lowering nuclear destruction capabilities could finance the many needs, concerning our homeless and ill, and also deliver peace of mind to the entire world.

The "Cold War-Overkill Policy", still in force, drains our economy, to what end?

"A dead end!" Instead, we must fund humanitarian efforts.

12. Four hundred thirty seven million dollars, spent to smear a president, by obsessed Republicans. What did they find? A bidding system for the travel services needed by the White House, which incidentally, saved taxpayer dollars. The Republicans called it "Travelgate". Next, they discovered "Haircutgate". Air Force One wasted fuel on the tarmac, while President Clinton got a haircut, and the Republicans find "Haircutgate". How many tax dollars did Republicans waste, investigating and airing the insignificant details of "Haircutgate".

13. The Whitewater issue proved to be a non-issue. But, according to the "Republican Smear Slinging Strategy Rule", insinuate as many evil insinuations as you can possibly imagine, and associate.

14. The Republican "Graft Core" struck next. A personal and private indiscretion became a treasonous act, and the Republicans proceeded with impeachment proceedings, "against public wishes". Clinton lied, yes, to protect the peace within his personal life. When the Repulsive cons drew blood, they began a feeding frenzy, as they rushed to disclose every derogatory detail, to each person and vulnerable child in front of a television set, in every home across America.

15. The four hundred thirty seven million dollars, spent to impeach a president over a personal matter, "against public wishes", could have been used to fight hunger and homeless problems. The same "graft core" neglected to detect, or advertise the fact, that their fearless leader, Nute, was charged with income tax evasion. Nute was charged with stealing public funds. Real graft, real missing funds. Yet, the Republican graft core, have yet to advertise that fact to the American public. Ask yourself, WHY! Why did "Nute" resign his majority leadership role in Congress?

16. What happens to the trillions of "social security" dollars, if the market loses fifty points? If, it is a security fund for our elderly, keep it secure! The simple proposal, by Mr. Gore, of matching social security funds, will deliver fiscal security for all elderly, for decades to come.

17. Big government interference, is a "Republican smear slogan", professed to justify, their district <u>cons</u>tituents, controlling local allotments.

18. Mr. Gore, I can produce a tax free, sovereign alluvial trust system that will fund a war on hunger, homelessness, and poverty. It will also fund an environmental trust, to secure lands for public domain and environmental protection. It is a trust fund, founded and based in public domain, (on the Internet). It links inspiration and technology, to create a proficient method of securing health and harmony. Inspiration is the key! While trying to encourage Mr. Clinton, concerning the Middle East, this remarkably simple technique was revealed to me.

    If you would care to discuss the specifics of a public domain trust, for hunger, homelessness, and environmental restoration, you may call me at 936-445-1164. If not, you will be made aware of this environmental trust, shortly.

19. Recently, at the Al Smith memorial dinner, George Bush Jr. had the gall to quote John Cardinal Oconnor saying " Poverty in a wealthy nation is a scandal". How dare that man quote a true humanitarian, as if he actually honored his policies? The Bush policies "promote" poverty, in a wealthy nation. The rich get richer and the poor are deceived.

20. Healthcare, schools, military and the deficit are not the major problem plaguing American justice and democracy. The enduring problem plaguing the proficient performance of the peoples' government is the contradicting interests of corporate campaign contributors. The HMOs' lobbyists have proven their effect, for the last eight years, have they not?

21. The second part of this dilemma is Trent Lotts' Senate, holding a majority of seven, which have held, and will continue to hold the McCain Feingold bill from the floor.

10-23-00

They (our legislators) are locked into the failing procedures and policies that have prevailed under our silly two party system since its' foundation. They did this! They did that! They do this! They do that! They blocked this! They neglected that! They, "on the other side of the isle"! On and on and on! Why do we continue to settle for silly excuses from grown men, that cannot get along with each other, because he's, "on the other side of the isle". He may as well be, "on the other side of the world", when one considers the differing priorities, (the communication gap), between those two litigating parties.

The Republicans have fought any and all efforts to improve the healthcare of Americas' citizens. Rights, patients deserve rights? Not in this HMOs' Congress! Should we continue to allow corrupting, special and corporate interest lobbyists, to run our government? I hereby revise and extend my remarks to declare a public challenge to any Republican legislator, or any such vocal hypocrites as Rush Limbaugh and Sean Hannity and any other confused voices, that would care to compare relevant issues and policies.

I have a simple suggestion for the American people. Forget all party affiliations, you're not a Democrat, you're not a Republican, you're a "sovereign" American. Join one party, one unified, concerned party. With no excuses, and no other party to blame, for the combined failure of each.

Why do we send the same intransigent, abstinent, unconcerned, unproductive, and greedy legislators back to Washington DC, to play "their" same silly game. Pointing the same accusing "fickle finger of fault" at his or her constituents on "the other side of the isle". Rather than acknowledging the divisive effects, of current campaign finance laws, the Republicans cling to its' methods, claiming "it" (legalized bribery) is a first amendment right. Right, our forefathers amended the constitution (1st Amendment) so our legislators could receive endless funds from their rich friends? Right, all of the money you might need to spend; right George?

The first amendment, protects the rights of Citizens, to have their petitions heard before Congress, it guarantees the People, the right to redress the government for a grievance. It is "not" a campaign fund right. The first amendment, (Free Speech) has nothing to do with (money) campaign financing. Duh!

Aside from stonewalling all campaign finance reform efforts, the Republicans continue to fight against a minimum wage hike, a prescription drug benefit, and a patients bill of rights. All, in the name of small government.

What do you expect from small-minded, self-centered, sanctimonious, silly Republicans that conveniently isolate themselves from the world, ignore tyranny, and seek to slander, rather than to suggest?

Proverbs 15;7 states; The lips of the wise disperse knowledge: but the heart of the foolish doeth not so.

Proverbs 16; 30 He shutteth his eyes to devise froward things: moving his lips to bringeth evil to pass.

Point to ponder! Had Dole and his constituents, passed the gun bill they wanted, oozies could have been used at Columbine!

10-24-00

Mr. George W. Bush Jr., at a recent campaign rally, appearing on C-Span Primetime Public Affairs professed to know; what is right for freedom! After General Schwartzcof rolled through Iraq, arresting all Iraqi forces in two days, and categorically dismantled the royal guard, the following day. What happened then? Was it right for freedom?

Was leaving the tyrannical maniac, responsible for thousands of innocent deaths, in power, right for freedom, even though he was powerless. Yet, today he is ordering the death of innocent Iraqi citizens, and his troops are firing air to ground missiles at our planes, enforcing a no fly zone. We had the maniac subdued to helplessness, now we are spending billions to keep him contained.

Speaking of billions; Mr. George Bush Sr., during your administration, the Savings and Loan Administration, went bankrupt, after your constituents changed the banking laws, correct? Could you please inform me, who was in charge of the Savings and Loan, and did you appoint him?

In a recent interview, questioning the possibility of passing "his" proposed tax break, George Jr, answered; Quote, " we are running our members through the system", End quote!

We must join ranks and move our troops through the system, to secure the silly priorities, we have established. When will the Republicans realize that they're not troops, fighting against public welfare? They're supposed to be public servants.

Note how our current "silly party" political system operates. Corporate and/or special interest lobbyists finance, and "instruct", "our" candidates, and what do "we" get? Thirty seconds of the latest graft, and campaign smear tactics, all placing blame, "on the other side of the isle", "with no constructive suggestions, or productive techniques revealed, and it cost that candidate only, thirty million dollars, to condemn his opponent.

C-Span answered caller questions and reviewed numerous multi-million dollar ads at will. They reviewed dozens of multi-million dollar campaign ads on C-Span, for free! Then, panelist, not the candidates involved, viewed them, and hypothesized there meaning. Side by side interviews would allow the candidates to cross-examine each other, effectively revealing their policies. Therefore, it is obvious that C-Span or any public channel is certainly capable of that format.

So, we must choose, do we continue with thirty second, thirty million dollar smear ads, or do we insist on side by side, informative interviews of the candidates, for pennies on the dollar? I have observed and noted that in general conversations the Republicans target an office. The basic philosophies revealed by the troops of the Republicans, marching over first amendment rights by withholding McCain Feingold from debate, shows that joining ranks, and maintaining authority, is their only priority. Should a seven man majority in the Senate, allow Trent Lott to do that?

10-26-00   *6:11 AM*

Under the Bush policies, concern is dispensed on a percentage basis. His concern for our ill and elderly relatives, is less, a lot less than his concern for Donald Trump. George does not deal with the issue of poverty. He does not pick and choose. It's not his decision, to focus tax dollars. That's not Georges' job. He turns it into a percentage of income, and calls it fair.

A percentage of their pittance is a smaller pittance. The actual effect of the percentage system, promoted by Bush, returns an additional fifty thousand dollars to each millionaire, for each million earned.

My Dad is on social security, Mr. Bush, does he get a tax break? Why don't you give me a break! Step down! "Resign your ill-gotten station"! Your policies are inapt and corrupt. You recently quoted Cardinal Oconnor, quote; "poverty in a wealthy nation is a scandal". Would Cardinal Oconnor approve of your percentage of concern for his poor? I think not! How can our poor, possibly benefit on a percentage of their, terribly lacking, minimal income. Should we continue to support a "silly two party system" based on, and continually operating in, a combative, partisan atmosphere, that only encourages conflict and opposition, while seeking to satisfy the demands of lobbyists and their corporate interests?

Note the hypocrisy of our political system. Candidates of the two parties, slander, insinuate and demonize the other, for months on end. Then, after the election of these particular candidates, they're gonna cooperate. "Hog Wash".

They're gonna join ranks within their particular party, update their smearing list, and fight all worthy efforts of a "Common Man" agenda. Remember, certain words, attached to certain statements, when applied purposely, and methodically, can often solicit the emotional response that was sought. For example, the word "strategic" would be used by the Republicans, and attached to the words, "oil reserve", to influence the people, and warn them of an irresponsible, "Political Act". The "act" began when the Republicans pretended to care about "our" freezing poor in the north.

History has revealed that moving the oil reserves, lowered oil prices, and secured home heating supplies, desperately needed in the north. Attention, Republican members, it is a "strategic oil reserve", and it is being properly used to address the current "strategic" problem of "winter"! How could the Republicans demand that the oil reserves were a "national security reserve", essential in maintaining our "national security"? Hog Wash! We were not at war. Our ships and carriers are not lacking for fuel. What we have, is the prospect of a long cold winter! How did the two parties differ in their approach to the prospect of a long cold winter? Clinton moved the "strategic" oil supply, to where it was needed, for the heating needs of our freezing in the "north"!

Republicans wanted to leave those "strategic oil reserves", in the "south"!

10-26-00

Should we continue to send "our" candidates to Washington, to divide our People, suppress our rights, and tax us out of house and home? The Republican Congress has stirred any and every cauldron that holds an evil brew! Give us those, sexually explicit, adult oriented, presidential editorials again.

Was Nute Gengrich convicted, or did he just decide to quit Congress? I also recall that Nute and his constituents shut down the American government, for what reason? Should we not stir the cauldron of true conviction, unto a worthy purpose? I rest my case, and wholeheartedly endorse Mr. Gore.

10-27-00

Mr. Gore, and all Concerned Citizens,

I hereby direct this editorial to the Texas populous, its' local governing bodies, State and Federal Authorities. Mr. Gore, please point out to the Texas populous, that there is NO public defenders office in the state. It is not listed in the phone book or available over the information services of the local phone service, because it is non-existent. What we have out here now, is still, a Judge "Roy Bean" mentality, and truculent Texas Rangers, enforcing the law west of the Pecos on a misinformed populous, without "lawful" representation.

10-28-00   *1:07 AM*

Considering current continuing resolution financing, I would submit to the floor, that there is little justification in honoring the minutes of the chair, while under continuing resolution policies, if/when all constituents are not present.

If we are not doing it, through foresight and correctly, why are we doing it at all? I would reflect that the controlling majority dictates roll call of bills, which the majority, chooses to address. The beauty of daily, continuing resolutions is, "believe it or not", it brings the Republicans into reality, through a daily requirement to appear. Continue to remain calm, clear, and succinct.

The Republicans claim to be fair and just, in all matters. A percentage of income tax return is not as fair, as it is funny, to Donald Trump. Did you get your fair tax break this year, Donnie? "A fitting tribute to American diligence"! Hog Wash! When will we give a helping hand, to Americas' suffering?

In my honest opinion, life in prison would be "a fitting tribute" for all men that are tempted, and do behave, in such a manner. Ploys of pompous, partisan, finger pointing, sanctimonious Republicans, that simply share the same standard smearing list, is shameful.

The differing budget agendas are phenomenal, and Republicans do not want you to realize that fact. They plan to give you everything back, on a fair percentage basis. Point of Order! A fair percentage basis, pertaining to income, is as far from fair, as any percentage, of any pittance of an income, could be.

You get the same exact percentage basis tax return as all millionaires and billionaires. Does that sound fair, for a needy populous? Add it up and see where the money goes.

The silly, sanctimonious Republicans claim to be pro-life. Were the Republicans truly concerned about sanctity of life, they surely, would have involved themselves in stopping the murderous activities of the ruthless dictator, Raul Sadres, only a hundred miles from our shore. Thank you, Mr. Clinton, Mr. Carter, and Mr. Powell.

10-29-00   *12:55 AM*

Recently at the University of Denver, John McCain quoted the Supreme Court ruling on campaign financing. "Money is not free speech, money is property, when money is; etc. I find it amazing that the Republicans do not know the Supreme Court ruling. The only thing that the Republicans know, know for sure, is "The Future of Finger Pointing in America". Authored by Matt Bai of Newsweek, and held for publishing, until after the election. Talk about a charter!

Attention; Mr. Nader, Dear Sir,

Consider the negative consequences to the environment, should George get in. Endorse Mr. Gore, and thereby help to establish efforts to protect our planet, then justifiably claim your candidacy in 2004. Help us now and win in 2004.

Mr. Clinton,

At present our government is under a continuing resolution format. Demand roll call and presence of all 535 members. I consider it to be a national tragedy that half of the congressional members are missing, during a continuing resolution roll call. Thereby, we have legislators, ignoring their duties, while insisting on returning to their precincts, to seek re-election. Summon our lawmakers to order, and to honor the daily resolutions. They are obviously being ignored. Call them to order!

How are we profited by daily continuing resolutions that are completely ignored by our congressmen? Are the Republicans behaving responsibly?

Call them to order! I suggest that you assert all powers over the chair, determine member whereabouts, and summon them to order, and proceed from the record, orderly!

Senator Dick Durbin, Dem. Ill.
Assistant Minority leader

Senator Edward Kennedy, Dem. Maas.
HEL&P comte. Ranking member

Mr. Kennedy, while addressing the Senate about their lack of concern during the final days of this session, pointed out the fact that the minimum wage in Texas is $3.35 per hour. Not only is the minimum wage so depriving in Texas, a wage hike was postponed for six months, by a closed door policy, that was explained as a "clerical error", by our elite legislators? Give me a break! They made no clerical errors, concerning their $14,000 per year raise!

11-08-00   *Fax#202-456-2461*   *11:57AM*

Mr. Gore,

The Electoral College is history revisited. A very embarrassing history! Consider the questionable ballot procedures in Florida, the inherent problematic design of the butterfly ballot, resulting in an additional three thousand inexplicable votes for Buchanon in a smaller neighboring county. Consider the fact that Republican ballots were taken home and completed, or, the exorbitant amount of "questionable votes", that were simply not counted. They were not votes! They were dangling chads! Because, the "dangling ballot machines" were pre-located in Democratic precincts! After all of the questionable and improper procedures in Florida, I must truly question the logic of using an Electoral College. Considering the popular vote majority, for Mr. Gore, leads me to deem the questionable Electoral vote as, " null and void". Why did this nation turn over the most critical station within its' government, to a candidate claiming questionable votes, which did not change the national vote victory of Mr. Gore? WHY? Why, are we so accepting of our legislators' archaic and unconstitutional procedures, finger pointing, and obvious lack of productivity?

Dear Mr. Gore, and Mr. Clinton,

Point of Order; The Supreme Court "<u>must</u>?" recognize and verify a national majority! Why should a small vote lead in Florida, enable the Republicans to ignore the national totals, and its' mandate? The national vote totals deem Mr. Gore the winner. Why should an "<u>alleged</u>" victory in a particular state, overrule the national will. The Electoral College is an outdated, undemocratic, unjust and embarrassing part of our history. Why do our legislators continue to subject the will of the people to an archaic form of balloting that is clearly capable of perverting the will of the people? The national will of the people has been jeopardized twice, by use of the Electoral College. We must add and honor the totals, of a nationwide vote.

Dear Mr. Gore,

Thank you, for making lower and middle-income families a priority of your policies. In stark contrast to the Bush tax policies. Certainly we can't call it a tax break. Do we really believe that the wealthiest 1% of our people, deserve, or need a break? Why do the worlds' wealthiest, deserve more than our homeless, hungry and ill?

The Republicans point to and insinuate that campaign contributions from a Buddist temple were illegal. Yet, the Republicans know that it was not illegal, under the current campaign finance laws. The same corrupt campaign finance laws that the Republicans, hold from the floor, thus insuring the corrupt policies will continue.

The most telling portion of the first debate, came when questioned about Campaign finance reform. George mumbled nervously, mispronounced it twice, and called it campaign fund reform. Campaign financing is the root problem. Make that, and your position clear, then watch Bush squirm!

The fact that Bush wanted Russia to intervene in the Bosnia war, even though Russia had sided with, "war criminal" Melosivic, shows no knowledge of, or concept of current events, thus no realistic prerogative of foreign policy.

Mr. President Bill Clinton and Mr. Al Gore,

This article, now in your hand, is among dozens of submissions, dating from 5-22-93 until 11-08-00, containing advice about Bosnia, safe havens, air support only, gays in the military, your success in Haiti, the Middle East, and the problematic ballots, "used" in Florida. Yet, within this submission, is the ANSWER! The answer to the most difficult question of all, how do we secure true brotherhood? HOW?

Answer; Isaiah 1-27, By listing the faithful and penitent. MtZion. ws and its' principals of developing a penitent brotherhood, and its' purposeful mission were revealed to me, during my efforts to encourage you about the Middle East problem. Jerusalem remains unsettled, yet to carry MtZion.ws to Jerusalem would show all, a heavenly homeland, a redeeming purpose, and their eternal heritage.

MtZion.ws will be online and available for public scrutiny and participation. Deliver this declaration of prosperity to the Middle East, where it, is written to return. We could place (seat) this environmental, "public trust" in its' biblical homeland, in hopes to quell our longest, ongoing current dispute, and to stand to quell all others.

This could be our greatest gift to all peoples. Help me to proclaim MtZion.ws and join in its' fruition.

Thank You Sir,
An Eternal Friend,
Quey Quay
Eddie Duncan

PS- You efforts are inspiring, and peacemaker your legacy!

*Jerusalem should be restored, holy and free!

A Visitor From The Past...

I had a dream the other night, I didn't understand. A figure walking through the mist, with a flintlock in his hand. His clothes were torn and dirty, as he stood there by my bed, He took off his three-cornered hat, and speaking low, he said:

"We fought a revolution, to secure our liberty. We wrote the Constitution, as a shield from tyranny. For, future generations, this legacy we gave, in this, the land of the free and the home of the brave."

"The freedom we secured for you, we hoped you would always keep. But tyrants labored endlessly, while your parents were asleep. Your freedom gone, your courage lost, you're no more than a slave, in this, the land of liberty, and the home of the brave."

"You buy a permit to travel, and a permit to own a gun, and a permit to start a business, or to build a home for one. On land, that you believe you own, you pay a yearly rent. Yet, you have no voice in choosing, how the money is spent."

"Your children MUST attend a school that doesn't educate. Your Christian values can not be taught, according to the STATE. You read about alleged current events, in a regulated press. You pay a tax, you do not owe, to please the I.R.S."

"Your money is no longer made of silver or gold. You trade your wealth for paper, so your life can be controlled. You pay for crimes that make our nation turn from God in shame. You've taken Satan's number, as you traded in your name."

"You've given control, to people who do you harm. They padlock churches, and steal the family farm. They keep the country deep in debt, and put men of God in jail, harassing lawful fellow countrymen, while corrupted courts prevail."

"Your public servants no longer uphold the solemn oath they've sworn. Your daughters visit doctors, so their children won't be born. Your leaders ship deadly weaponry to foreign shores, and send your sons to slaughter, fighting their wars."

"Can you regain the freedom, for which we fought and died? Do you have the faith, and courage to stand with pride? Are there no more values, for which you will fight to save? Or, do you wish your children to live in fear, as a slave.

"Sons of the Republic, arise and take a stand! Defend the Constitution, the supreme Law of the Land! We must preserve our great Republic, and each God-given right, and pray to God, to keep the torch of freedom burning bright!"

"As I awoke he vanished, into the mist from which he came. His words were true! We are not free! We have ourselves to blame! For even now, as tyrants trample every God-given right, we only watch, and tremble, too afraid to fight."

"If he stood by your bedside, in a dream, while you were asleep, and asked you, what remains of the rights I fought to keep? What would be your answer, if, he called out from the grave? Is this still the Land of the Free and Home of the Brave?

Authors' Epilogue

Know this, and find the essential foresight, find faith, and make it relevant to your life. God created all things, within the layers of all life, and within each moment since, He has given all, the opportunity to realize the purpose of their lives. The "eternal" life, within! Seek to acquire true awareness, a true knowledge. How? By acknowledging the source of your presence, our creator, our true and eternal God.

Therefore realizing, the actual source, and the eternal dimension of your life, as one within, His eternal creation, is the first step in realizing your true and destined purpose. Thankfully strive to wholeheartedly understand your destined purpose, and be diligent to find, and fulfill it!

Therefore, realize, in order to justify, and enable, His claim to a worthy people, a choice of worthiness, and/or a doubtful temptation, must be presented. All choices, are then chosen, witnessed, and justly fulfilled! Do not be blinded by the glory of His creation, or blind to the fact, that it is about you, and, " you are", a willful participant!

Therefore, honor only a worthy desire, and consciously embark on your eternal destiny, that of honoring our brotherhood, and seeking His eternal reward, awaiting us. Truth and relevance are all answers, and your sensitivity is, your greatest teacher, and your source unto, your destined reward.

Jesus, a man, was given to us, as our greatest gift, and greatest example, by God, for all mankind. Realize, that Jesus did walk upon this earth, performed the miracles He did perform, and willfully walked, into certain death, to symbolize, His love for all mankind! Therefore, have faith!

The greatest gift of our God, was a man! Therefore, we must honor the principal of brotherhood, delivered by Jesus Christ! We must learn, "choose", to live with and cherish, our fellowman. Or, our humanity shall surely perish, by its' own hand!

Isaiah 13; 12 says, I will make a man more precious than fine gold, even a man, than the golden wedge of Ophir. We people, in order to form a "true brotherhood", must first acknowledge, and honor, the presence of each living soul within that common humanity/brotherhood.

Truth and relevance are all answers! Jesus came for all that would seek "His" purpose! Make His purpose relevant! And, yours also! Acknowledge the steps of Jesus, and obtain a true understanding, appreciation, and loving concern for your fellow man, and the "eternal life", within each soul.

May each soul, obtain a keen awareness of their "eternal" presence! May you find true serenity, and happiness, within the glorious fulfillment of all choices, from within a thankful, sensitive and repented heart. May He grant to you, the wisdom to honor only a worthy desire, and none other! For, deceit is always betrayed, while a worthy desire, is endlessly rewarded!

Witness to your heart, the fulfillment of every choice that you ever made, for they have delivered you to your present station in life. Witness the glorious creation that is, "our humanity". Honor each presence, and, the glorious garden sustaining us. Go thankfully, pray knowingly, love eternally, and consciously remain aware, of Gods' justice, within all things, here, and there.

Eternally,
A Brother in Christ
Quey Quay

About the Author

I am the second of three sons of Charles and Betty Duncan, and was born on October 4th, 1951 in York, South Carolina. I grew up, under the watchful eye, of the most grand of Grandmas, clinging to her apron strings daily, and/or roaming the foothills surrounding the family farm. The farm was located about five miles west of Clover, South Carolina in a pristine hollow, amid a vocal and vibrant forest. My love for Grandma, and that exuberant life on the family farm is beyond compare. She was the guiding, gracious and sensitive woman that gave our family such structure, love and purpose. She raised twelve children, and was loved and cherished by all that knew her. I am deeply thankful to have had such a grand woman, as the first and most influential part of my life.

My family moved to Tampa, Florida when I was ten years old, and I lived there for almost thirty years. I graduated from Hillsborough High School in 1969, with "great expectations".

It was not until learning the fundamentals of my sovereign birthright that I realized the true genius of "our" self-government, and felt, there is reason, for great expectations for this country once again!

Eternally, A
Brother in Christ
Quey Quay
Eddie Duncan

Printed in Great Britain
by Amazon